SEPTEMBER SWOON

William C. Kashatus

foreword by Gerald Early

SEPTEMBER SWOON

Richie Allen, the '64 Phillies, and Racial Integration

A KEYSTONE BOOK
THE PENNSYLVANIA STATE UNIVERSITY PRESS
UNIVERSITY PARK, PENNSYLVANIA

A KEYSTONE BOOK

A Keystone Book is so designated to
distinguish it from the typical scholarly monograph
that a university press publishes. It is a book intended
to serve the citizens of Pennsylvania by educating them
and others, in an entertaining way, about aspects of the
history, culture, society, and environment of the state
as part of the Middle Atlantic region.

Library of Congress Cataloging-in-Publication Data

Kashatus, William C., 1959–
September swoon : Richie Allen, the '64 Phillies, and racial integration /
William C. Kashatus ; Foreword by Gerald Early.
p.   cm.
"A Keystone Book."
Includes bibliographical references and index.
ISBN 0-271-02333-3 (cloth : alk. paper)
1. Philadelphia Phillies (Baseball team).
2. Baseball—Pennsylvania—Philadelphia—History—20th century.
3. Allen, Dick.
4. Discrimination in sports—Pennsylvania—Philadelphia.
I. Title.

GV875.P45 K275 2003
796.357´64´0974811—dc22
2003016988

Copyright © 2004 The Pennsylvania State University
All rights reserved
Printed in the United States of America
Published by The Pennsylvania State University Press,
University Park, PA 16802-1003

Second printing, 2004

The Pennsylvania State University Press is a member of the
Association of American University Presses.

It is the policy of
The Pennsylvania State University Press
to use acid-free paper. Publications on uncoated
stock satisfy the minimum requirements of American
National Standard for Information Sciences—
Permanence of Paper for Printed Library Material,
ANSI Z39.48–1992.

FOR MY SON BEN,

who brought happiness after a devastating loss

CONTENTS

FOREWORD BY GERALD EARLY

To have grown up in Philadelphia in the 1950s and 1960s, as I did, was to experience the American city, American life itself, on the cusp of dramatic change. The rise of reformist liberals in Philadelphia's politics in the 1950s coupled with a growing black activism in the city in the 1960s, particularly under the leadership of local NAACP president Cecil B. Moore, were the manifestation of one sort of change. The arc of the career of legendary cop Frank Rizzo, who went from being the "Cisco Kid" of the streets to police commissioner and eventually, in 1971, to mayor, was change as well, or the change that change produced. Few people who lived in most big American cities at the time could say that they were not cursed with having to live in an interesting time. Ironically, one could hardly sense this change, in many respects, even as one was living through such strange seasons that would disconnect us all from the past while leaving us unable to discern the future.

I can remember distinctly reading passages from the Bible in my elementary school classes and hearing them read before our weekly "Assemblies" and can vividly recall that teachers could and did use corporal punishment to chastise children. When I tell my children this, they think I grew up in a more primitive and even quaint time. Actually, nothing could be further from the truth. Reading the Bible in school probably did me at least this level of good: that I got to read that book at all in a setting that was not related to church, so I could think about it differently while learning to absorb its mighty language. I do not recall corporal punishment with any fondness at all. I thought it brutal and, perhaps oddly, a rather sensational way to discipline a child. I did not think it was terribly effective. Nor did I think that my teachers cared more about me because they were willing to slap me around. But I do not think, on the other hand, that they cared about me any less. (At least, those of us who went to public school thought, we don't get knocked around as much as the kids in Catholic school do by the nuns and priests.) I never feared any teacher's threat of physical violence nearly as much as I feared some of my classmates. And since it was common in the world I grew up in for parents to smack their children around, why not the teachers? There was something that was stabilizing and reassuring about the exercise of this type of authority. But change was on the way and by the time I had finished junior high school, Bible reading and corporal punishment were things of the past.

I grew up in South Philadelphia, near the Italian Market on Ninth Street, in the very heart of an ethnic mosaic of working-class Italians (Mario Lanza had grown up two blocks from where I lived), Irish Catholics, Jews, and, of course, African Americans. What I loved about South Philadelphia, indeed about Philadelphia as a whole, was the fact that the city, and especially this particular section of it, was built for pedestrians, made to be walked in. What I did for hours and hours in my youth was simply walk around all parts of South Philadelphia, sometimes alone, sometimes with friends. Had it not been for the terror of street gangs, I would have walked even more in the city than I did. It was one of the few charms that the city held for me as a child, other than riding public transportation. A surprising number of adults in my neighborhood did not own cars; many women particularly, including my mother, did not even know how to drive.

I saw the first housing projects built in the neighborhood (the Southwark Plaza Projects), and even remember that when they first opened many whites lived there. Of course, they did not stay for long, but in the first year or two those projects were the most integrated community I had seen or have seen since. (I thought it would be like that forever, for I could not, in my childhood, understand the differences that defined the races.) A certain balance existed among the various racial and ethnic groups, and while there were eruptions of violence, the mere telling of which made me tremble with loathing and a sense of entrapment, by and large these groups respected each other's space and even managed to get along with each other in ways that were positively inspiring. In the summer day camps, at Nebinger School and at the House of Industry, I remember Italian children and black children playing together our various games of "Dead-Box," "Checkers," or "Uncle Wiggly" or riding on the swings or the maypole or playing volleyball, reading comic books together, eating slices of cold watermelon with sticky fingers, singing camp songs together with nary a word about how we were all different from each other or needed role models from our own group. We quite understood what made us different, but we were mostly glad about what made us alike: watching "American Bandstand," which was still being filmed in Philadelphia in the early 1960s (although we black kids thought that the few black kids on the show danced better), "The Lloyd Thaxton Show," "The Adventures of Rocky and Bullwinkle," "Spin and Marty" on "The Mickey Mouse Club," "The Adventures of Zorro" with Guy Williams, all the latest movies with Troy Donahue or Steve Reeves, and "The Beverly Hillbillies," and listening to WIBG (or WIBBAGE) spinning the Top 40 hits with deejays like Hy Lit. (We black kids also listened to the soul stations like WDAS, with Georgie Woods "the Guy with the Goods," and WHAT with Sonny Hopson "the Mighty Burner," and to a white disc jockey named Jerry Blavatt, "The Geeter with the Heater.") And we all read the *Daily News*, the second-rate tabloid paper, religiously because our parents did. I perfected my early reading skills reading the sports pages of that paper. Everyone read the daily comic strips, especially "Nancy," to get clues for which numbers to play in the illegal lottery. (People read the strips as if they were deciphering the codes of ancient runes.) And there were three passions that both the blacks and the Italians shared in that neighborhood: going to Atlantic City or Wildwood in the summer, playing the numbers, and playing bingo at the neighborhood Catholic churches. Getting flavorful water ices from John's Water Ice on Seventh Street, walking with my sisters to their piano lessons at the Settlement Music School on Queen Street, standing at the corner of Broad and South on New Year's Day to watch the Mummer's Parade, walking along downtown Market Street at Christmastime to all the department stores— Strawbridge and Clothier, Lit Brothers, Gimbel's, and Wanamaker's. What a charm and sweetness Philadelphia was. It was a life that now seems long ago and far away. I think the year that I began to sense real change, a disruption in my own sense of innocence, was in 1964.

The whole country changed following the shocking assassination of John F. Kennedy in 1963. Nothing was ever to be the same again. But even before Kennedy's death, change was in the air. Martin Luther King's bloody campaign in Birmingham in 1963, which so effectively dramatized the civil rights movement, and the visionary "March on Washington," for which Georgie Woods, the deejay, provided bus transportation for anyone who wanted to go, suggested something remarkable, a sea change, in black life, even if life seemed to go on pretty much as it had before. Everything felt different.

The summer of 1964 was even more startling: "freedom summer" in Mississippi, the deaths of Chaney, Schwerner, and Goodman that so riveted the nation, the Mississippi Freedom Democratic Party upsetting the Democratic National Convention, Martin Luther King's badly failing campaign in St. Augustine, Florida, and a race riot in Philadelphia that eventually helped to make Frank Rizzo the police commissioner and sent Howard Leary, the police commissioner Rizzo hated, to New York. It was not as big a race riot as what was to come the next summer in Watts or later in the decade in Detroit, but it was bad enough—three million dollars in damage in 1964 dollars, and the North Philadelphia neighborhood where the riot occurred would never recover economically, at least not during the rest of the time I lived in Philadelphia. (I left the city in 1977.) Police brutality was a huge topic in the black community of Philadelphia in those days. The black newspaper, the *Tribune*, wrote about it all the time, and it seemed that things just exploded on Friday, August 28, when rumors spread through the black community of North Philadelphia that a woman named Odessa Bradford, who was pregnant, had been killed by the police in a traffic stop. It turned out that Mrs. Bradford was stopped by the police, but she was not harmed. The two officers who stopped her in fact wound up going to the hospital when she resisted arrest. Mrs. Bradford was not pregnant, either.

The riot unfolded anyway and no important black leader at the time could stop it, not Raymond Pace Alexander, one of the city's prominent black lawyers and a former city councilman that many wrongly considered an Uncle Tom, not the popular Georgie Woods, who Frank Rizzo grabbed from the stage of the Uptown Theater during one of Woods's rock-and-roll shows on the night of the riot to try to talk people into going home, not the tough ex-marine and militant president of the local chapter of the NAACP, Cecil B. Moore, who was hit in the head with a brick by the rioters. Mass violence tends to lead a life of its own once the momentum gets it going and people take on the aspects of a mindless mob and principled insurrectionists.

It was this 1964 summer that the Philadelphia Phillies, who played in a stadium not far from the site of the riot, were contending for the pennant, after years of mediocrity. It was the year that Richie Allen, their muscular rookie third baseman, would become the team's first black superstar. It is the story of Philadelphia in the summer of 1964, of this particular Philadelphia team, of this particular player, Richie Allen, that William C. Kashatus tells so richly and compellingly in *September Swoon*. My only surprise is that no one told this story sooner.

Kashatus tells the story of that entire season almost day by day—how a Philadelphia team, an odd mix of veterans and youngsters, unexpectedly came from nowhere to nearly win the pennant, only to collapse in the last two weeks of the season and lose ten of its last twelve games, blowing a six-and-a-half game lead. Spiritually, I don't think Philadelphia ever recovered from that loss until the team won the World Series in 1980. Kashatus also tells the story of race relations in Philadelphia, how Allen's arrival affected not only the team but the city itself, a city that had worked out over many long decades its way of dealing with blacks only to find that the old way of doing business was coming to an end.

In my growing up, very few black people I knew rooted for the Phillies, most having long memories of how Philadelphia manager Ben Chapman mercilessly taunted Brooklyn Dodger Jackie Robinson with racial insults and invective when Robinson arrived in the Majors. As my mother said to me once, "I'll root for the Phillies when hell freezes over." In 1964, for my mother, hell definitely did not freeze over and she was in fact ecstatic when the team went into its free fall at the end of the season. I suppose I wanted the Phillies to win, but I was not very disappointed when they lost. I almost expected it. But the impact of that season has stayed with me all my life, in a way that no other baseball season has.

Allen himself was a curious man, moody and often incommunicative with the press, but possessed of tremendous power and athletic ability. Most black people felt that Allen was poorly covered by the white press, blamed for the team's collapse, and eventually run out of town, and Kashatus ably tells the story of how the press shaped and misshaped Allen's public persona. *September Swoon* is a wonderful book and an important one as well, not just for baseball fans, but for readers interested in race and sports, and sports and its impact on urban history. As a former Philadelphian who lived through the days he describes, I am very grateful to him for having written the book.

It is perhaps not a kindness, as a person who grew up in Philadelphia, that I wound up living in St. Louis. First, it was St. Louis that beat Philadelphia for the 1964 pennant and went on to beat the Yankees in the World Series. Second, Dick Allen (he never wanted to be called Richie, he said) was traded to the St. Louis Cardinals in 1969 for outfielder Curt Flood. (Other players were involved in the trade, but Allen and Flood were the principals.) Flood never played a game in Philadelphia, opting instead to sue baseball under the nation's antitrust laws, saying that the sport's reserve clause prevented him from exercising the same right as other American workers, the right to offer his services to whoever might want them. He didn't win the suit, but it did set things in motion that eventually led to free agency in 1975. At the time of Flood's suit, I thought to myself, "Geez, the guy would rather destroy his career and sue baseball than play in Philadelphia." That thought so depressed me that I stopped following baseball for several years. In recent years, I was not happy when J. D. Drew chose to come to St. Louis instead of signing with Philadelphia; nor was I happy when Scott Rolen came to St. Louis either, after rejecting the Phillies. I have no sentimental feelings for Philadelphia and I don't desire to live there again, but something about what Drew and Rolen did wounded me deeply. I enjoy St. Louis and feel lucky to live in a city with such a competitive baseball team. It nearly goes without saying, as I live in St. Louis, I root for the St. Louis Cardinals, a great franchise, as I have done for the last twenty years. Except when they play Philadelphia.

Washington University in St. Louis

ACKNOWLEDGMENTS

September Swoon could not have been written without the help of the 1964 Phillies themselves, especially: Dick Allen, Ruben Amaro Sr., Jack Baldschun, Dennis Bennett, Johnny Briggs, Johnny Callison, Clay Dalrymple, Tony Gonzalez, Dallas Green, John Herrnstein, Art Mahaffey, Cookie Rojas, Roy Sievers, Tony Taylor, and Rick Wise. I am extremely grateful to all these former players, who agreed to lengthy interviews and were generous with their time and memories.

Other members of the Phillies organization, past and present, were also helpful in the research process, including: Ruben Amaro Jr., the late Rich Ashburn, Howie Bedell, Robert R. M. "Ruly" Carpenter III, Rob Holliday, Grant Jackson, Frank Lucchesi, Tim McCarver, Ken Raffensberger, Robin Roberts, Mike Schmidt, Howie Schultz, Andy Seminick, Larry Shenk, Curt Simmons, and Harry Walker.

My interest in baseball and race relations was inspired by many of the Philadelphia Stars of the old Negro Leagues. The late Gene Benson, Lee Carter, Bill "Ready" Cash, Mahlon Duckett, Stanley "Doc" Glenn, Wilmer Harris, and Marvin Williams gave me their trust, unconditional support, and encouragement throughout the research and writing process. As I learned of their personal journeys, I came to admire these men for their perseverance, integrity, and dedication to a game that failed to give them a well-deserved opportunity to compete at the major league level during the prime of their careers. I shall always be grateful to them for their examples.

Because Philadelphia's sportswriters played an instrumental role in this story, I made an earnest effort to contact and interview those who covered the Phillies during the 1960s. Both Frank Dolson and Allen Lewis were generous with their time and insight. Lewis also reviewed an earlier draft of the manuscript and still agreed to write an endorsement for the book. Other writers failed to return my phone calls.

Special thanks is extended to those who assisted in the preparation of the book. Gerald Early of Washington University, V. P. Franklin of Drexel University, Bruce Kuklick of the University of Pennsylvania, and attorneys Peter Baumann and David Jordan all read initial drafts and provided helpful counsel, both scholarly and legal. I am also grateful to Gerald Early for writing the Foreword, and to David Jordan for his endorsement of the book. Tim Wiles and Bill Burdick of the National Baseball Hall of Fame, Michael Schefer of the *Philadelphia Daily News*, Brenda Wilson of Temple University's Urban Archives, and the Microfilm Department of The Free Library of Philadelphia provided important access to their collections. In addition, I had the good fortune to work with Peter Potter and the staff at Penn State Press, who navigated me through the editorial process.

Finally, I cannot adequately express my gratitude to my wife, Jackie, and our sons, Tim, Peter, and Ben. Without their love and unconditional support, this book would not have come to fruition.

INTRODUCTION

On Sunday, October 4, 1964, Richie Allen, the Phillies' rookie third base-man, walked into the visitor's clubhouse at Cincinnati's Crosley Field and readied himself for the most important game of a promising career. As he dressed in his gray-flannel uniform, Allen tried to make sense of what had happened to his team during the stretch. Up by six and a half games on September 20 with just twelve left to play, the "Fightin' Phils" appeared to have clinched their first pennant in more than a decade. But the following day they went into a tailspin, losing ten straight before beating the Cincinnati Reds on October 2. Now the Phils were one game behind the Reds and the St. Louis Cardinals, both of whom were locked in a first-place tie.

Allen realized that his team no longer controlled its destiny. Not only would the Phillies need to defeat the Reds again today, but the Cards would have to lose their third game in a row to the lowly New York Mets. Only then would there be a three-way tie for first, forcing a round-robin playoff. On this final day of the season, then, Richie Allen found himself rooting for the cellar-dwelling Mets.[1]

Out on the field, Frank Thomas, a power-hitting first baseman obtained from the Mets in early August as insurance, was taking batting practice. When Allen got to the cage, Thomas reminded his younger teammate, "It's our turn today. The Reds started us on our ten-game skid. It's our turn to get them back."[2]

Friday's victory provided some relief for the team. Suddenly, they were themselves again, confident that they would win a playoff for the pennant. Now, on Sunday, they were seeking vindication, and it looked as if they might very well get it. Jim Bunning, the staff ace and a veteran of postseason play, would get the start. If the Phils could give him a few runs, Bunning could deliver the victory.

The Phillies bats came alive in the third inning when Allen doubled off the center-field fence, driving in Tony Gonzalez for the team's first run. Reds manager Dick Sisler, had Johnny Callison intentionally walked, loading the bases. Wes Covington followed with a two-run single to right. Sisler lifted his starter, John Tsitouris, and called in left-hander Joe Nuxhall to face Tony Taylor, who promptly delivered a broken-bat single for a 3–0 Phillies lead.

On the bench, shortstop Ruben Amaro, who had already ordered $1,800 worth of World Series tickets, was praying. "Please, God, give us a shot," he whispered. "Give us one more game."[3]

Allen struck again in the fifth, when he crushed a homer to center and followed it with a three-run blast to right the next inning. When the game was over, Bunning had pitched a six-hit shutout, walking just one batter, as the Phillies went on to a 10–0 whitewashing of the Reds.

Afterward, Gene Mauch, the temperamental Phillies manager, sat in the visitors' clubhouse listening to the last few innings of the Cards' 11–5 victory over the Mets. It was over for the Phils. St. Louis had clinched the pennant. All that could be heard was the sound of the radio and the hissing spray of the showers as players sat near their lockers, stunned. The Phillies had just suffered the greatest collapse of any team in major league baseball history.

When the sportswriters entered, it was left to Mauch to explain the unexplainable.

"I just wore the pitching out," he admitted, taking a long drag on a cigarette.

"Would you have done anything differently?" asked a scribe, almost apologetically.

"If I knew how it was going to come out, I might've done a couple of things different," Mauch replied. "When you manage the way I want to manage, you don't miss something by a game or two."

Again there was silence. Over the course of the 162-game season, the sportswriters knew when to tread lightly, especially with the Little General, who had a short fuse.

"All I can say is that I wish I did as well as the players did," said Mauch, wanting to end the interview. "They did a great job. That's all I've got to say."

Before he could get away, though, another reporter tried to buttonhole him. "Are you implying you did something wrong?"

"No," snapped Mauch, "I'm implying nothing." And with that he walked away.[4]

Later that night, when the team's chartered plane arrived at Philadelphia International Airport, there were 2,000 fans waiting for them. As the plane stopped at the gate, Mauch, expecting a lynching, stood and faced his players. "I want to be the first one off," he told them. "You guys didn't lose it. I did."[5]

Instead, he and his young club were enthusiastically cheered. Philadelphia had fallen in love with the Phils in defeat.

There would be no "next year" for those Phillies. Despite a lineup of talented young players and two of the era's best pitchers, the team never did recover from the 1964 swoon, instead spiraling downward into mediocrity. In his elusive quest to capture the pennant, Mauch began to overmanage his young team. Frustrated with the results, he then traded away the Phillies' future for proven veterans from other teams, few of whom panned out. Richie Allen, 1964 Rookie of the Year, was the pivotal figure of those teams. He was the Phillies' first African American superstar but he was also his own worst enemy. Although he hit over .300 during the next three seasons and added another 177 home runs through 1969, his off-the-field behavior earned him a twenty-eight-day suspension, a $500-a-day fine, and ultimately a trade to the Cardinals.[6] Johnny Callison was the other half of the Phillies' slugging tandem, and the fan favorite. Voted runner-up to the National League's Most Valuable Player in 1964, Callison almost slugged the Phils into the World Series with his thirty-one homers and 104 RBIs. Once dubbed "the next Mickey Mantle," he finally seemed to realize his enormous potential. But after 1965 he never hit higher than .276 or more than 16 homers or 65 RBIs in a season.[7]

Jim Bunning and Chris Short were the workhorses of the pitching staff in 1964. On three separate occasions during the stretch, Mauch gave each man the ball with only two days' rest. Never did they refuse. Nor could they win, for they were exhausted by that point. Nevertheless, both pitchers continued to be productive after that fateful season. Bunning, who posted a 19–8 record in 1964, including a perfect no-hit game against the New York Mets, would go on to win another fifty-five games for the Phils and to see his earned-run average drop over the next three years before he was traded to Pittsburgh. Similarly, Short, 17–9 in 1964, would post another sixty-six victories over the next four seasons before his career was cut short by back surgery.[8] If the Phils had had an effective bullpen, both Bunning and Short would have enjoyed even greater success.

Allen, Callison, Bunning, and Short were the nucleus of the team. As they went, so went the Phillies. The supporting cast was solid, but not nearly as talented as the core. It was also Philadelphia's first truly integrated baseball team. Latin American players like Ruben Amaro, Tony Gonzalez, Cookie Rojas, and Tony Taylor provided speed on the base paths and a steady defense. African American players like Johnny Briggs, Wes Covington, and Alex Johnson added some power. Whites dominated the pitching staff as well as the catching. Dennis Bennett, Art Mahaffey, Ray Culp, and rookie Rick Wise were the other starters. Jack Baldschun, Ed Roebuck, and Bobby Shantz were in the bullpen. Clay Dalrymple and Gus Triandos split the catching duties.[9] In 1964 this was a *good* team having a *great* year through 150 games. But in the final two weeks of the season, they were unable to jell. Nor would they ever again come as close to capturing the pennant. From 1965 to 1969, injuries, poor trades, and personal conflict among the players prevented the Phillies from finishing any higher than fourth place. Thus, a team that had the potential to contend for the next five seasons became tail-enders for the balance of the decade.

Today, Connie Mack Stadium, where the team played, no longer exists. Most of the players are now in their sixties and live far from Philadelphia. Only one, Jim Bunning, made it into the National Baseball Hall of Fame at Cooperstown. Yet the 1964 Phillies still have a strong emotional hold on the City of Brotherly Love.

More than any other team in Philadelphia's sports history, the 1964 Phillies saddled the city with a reputation for being a "loser." Even when victory seemed certain, Philadelphia found a way to lose. Call it "bad luck" if you will, but the team's infamous reputation became so ingrained in the fabric of the city's sports culture that even when the Phillies managed to win their one and only world championship in 1980, the victory did not evoke as much emotion as the 1964 swoon. But beyond the fact that the

1964 Phillies managed to blow the pennant when it seemed to be theirs for the taking, there is another, more subtle, reason that the team evokes so much emotion among the fans. It was Richie Allen, whose remarkable talent and controversial behavior forced Philadelphians to confront the racism that existed in their city during the most tumultuous period of the civil rights era.

The Phillies' reputation as a racially segregated team in a racially segregated city is not without foundation. During Jackie Robinson's quest to break the color barrier in 1947, the Phillies treated the Dodgers' rookie worse than any National League team did. Pitchers threw at his head, infielders purposely spiked him on the base paths, and—in one of the lowest moments in baseball history—the Phils humiliated Robinson by standing on the steps of their dugout, pointing their bats at him, and making gunshot sounds.[10] The Phillies were also the last team in the National League to integrate. They did not field an African American player until 1957, when infielder John Kennedy appeared in five games for the Phils—a full decade after Robinson broke the color line. Even then the Phillies maintained segregated spring-training facilities, a practice that was finally abandoned in 1962.[11]

To their credit, however, the organization made an earnest effort to integrate during the 1960s. Talented African American and Hispanic players were added to the roster, and their white teammates quickly welcomed them. They were young players, most of them in their early twenties, and their youthfulness as well as their desire to win transcended the racism of the earlier generation. By 1964 the players had created, both on and off the field, a special team chemistry that allowed them to play exceptional baseball for 150 games. It looked to be a team of destiny, the first Phillies squad to capture a pennant since the Whiz Kids fourteen years earlier—until the last fateful weeks of the season.

For myself, those Phillies, the very first team I followed in any sport, provided me with an introduction to the national pastime itself. Like most other passionate fans, I fell in love with the Phillies as a youngster and continue to follow them today. Their successes and failures provide certain benchmarks in my own life. Predictably, some of the most vivid memories of my childhood come from September 1964: hiding under the bed covers at night listening to the games with a transistor radio to my ear; my bus driver delivering an animated play-by-play on the ride to school; and, after the season ended, seeing tears in the eyes of so many fans—including grown men—who had had such high hopes.

Forty years later, I still wonder what exactly it was about that season that made grown men cry. After all, it seems foolish to get wrapped up with anything so insignificant as other grown men playing a child's game. I guess I really did not know until I began writing this book. What I discovered is that while it's easy to glory in a team triumphant, some of us fall in love even with a team in defeat. There is something uniquely endearing about the 1964 Phillies because they lost the pennant after such great striving. But there is something *magical* about a franchise that has a shameful history of race relations going on to field an integrated team that almost won the first pennant in more than a decade.

What it all boils down to is the business of caring. In 1964 the Phillies got many, many people to care deeply and passionately about the game at a turbulent period in Philadelphia's—and the nation's—history. Just as the Vietnam War, the civil rights movement, the counterculture, and the violence in the streets were beginning to rock the city, so too did an extraordinarily gifted team of young African American, Hispanic, and white athletes. While they were hardly the Brooklyn Dodgers, the Phillies were, for many of us, our very own "Boys of Summer." They provided some stability in a period of great instability, something we could count on night after night, at least for 150 games. We reveled in their triumphs and cried in their defeat, probably because in them we saw a reflection of ourselves. In all these ways the 1964 Phillies won not only our loyalties but also our hearts.

Based on personal interviews, player biographies, and newspaper accounts, *September Swoon* details the careful cultivation, history, and eventual breakup of Philadelphia's first integrated baseball team as well as the bittersweet season of 1964. Chapter 1 addresses the shameful story of race relations in Philadelphia's baseball past and provides a useful context for understanding the challenges and rewards of integrating the Phillies during the late 1950s and early 1960s. Chapter 2 explores the process of integration itself for both African American and Hispanic players, how the club's white players responded to that process, and the Phillies' discovery and cultivation of Richie Allen, their first African American superstar.

The 1964 season is the focus of Chapters 3, 4, and 5. From the club's fast start in the spring through mid-September, readers will appreciate the summer-long soap opera of close games, influential trades, and key victories that propelled the Phillies into first place and kept them there until the last week of the season. The September swoon may be difficult for many of the more seasoned fans to revisit, but for those who want to understand the collapse there is a game-by-game summary as well as ample explanation for it. Chapters 6 and 7 trace individual and team highlights, as well as Allen's ongoing conflict with management, fans, and the sportswriters, a clash that ultimately led to the team's breakup in 1969. The book concludes with a brief statement about the significance of the 1964 Phillies and Allen's legacy to the history of race relations in Philadelphia baseball. In combination with the statistical material included in the appendixes, the Conclusion reveals the tragedy of unrealized potential for a team that should have been contenders throughout the period 1964 to 1969.

Still, 1964 will forever remain an enchanted summer for Phillies fans. For a team that had lost more games in the twentieth century than any other major league franchise, 1964 was a season to dream—of a pennant, of a perennial contender, and of a city of brotherly love.

1

A SHAMEFUL PAST

At the turn of the twentieth century, William Edward Burghardt Du Bois walked the cobblestone streets and trash-strewn alleys of Philadelphia's Seventh Ward, where the city's African American population was concentrated. The first black person to earn a doctorate from Harvard University, Du Bois looked woefully out of place in his homburg, spats, and Victorian suit.

But his refined manner and genteel demeanor also served to disprove the popular stereotype among whites of the African American community's social and intellectual inferiority. Hired by the University of Pennsylvania in 1896, the twenty-seven-year-old scholar was directed to investigate the deeply ingrained notion among Philadelphia's white middle class that their "great, rich, and famous city was going to the dogs because of the crime and venality of its Negro citizens."

Of course, Du Bois believed that his employers were "thinking wrong about race." Their self-described "Negro problem" was, he concluded, not the result of race at all, but the result of the environmental and social conditions that confronted Philadelphia's black community. What he found was a "city within a city"—40,000 African Americans living among more than one million whites but isolated by race prejudice, poor housing patterns, job discrimination, and the legacy of slavery. His findings were published as *The Philadelphia Negro*, a ground-breaking study of African American life that disproved the negative perceptions the white middle class had of the city's black community.

At the same time, Du Bois did not exonerate African Americans because of their poor living circumstances. Although he asked whites for greater understanding and tolerance for the "Negro problem," the black scholar faulted the city's more successful blacks for a lack of leadership. He called on this "talented tenth" to serve as leaders and role models for Philadelphia's black community, which was the largest of any northern city. Unless they assumed a leadership responsibility for the less advantaged members of their race, he warned, the black community would become "permanently separated from the mainstream of society."[1]

Du Bois's theory of social and economic uplift depicted Philadelphia's African Americans not merely as the victims of white racism but also as active agents in achieving material success and social acceptance. Indeed, the city's black community faced a difficult challenge because of the twin identity. More than three decades after the American Civil War, which was meant to establish freedom and fairness for former slaves, Philadelphia blacks had few opportunities to better themselves economically. Not only did the industrial revolution require skills they did not possess at that time, relegating them to the ranks of unskilled laborers, but they had to struggle against the strong racial prejudice that prevailed in the "City of Brotherly Love." Many whites refused to hire qualified blacks, or even to work alongside blacks as stevedores, street and sewer cleaners, trash collectors, porters, and waiters. They also refused to rent to blacks outside the Seventh Ward, where the worst slums in the city were located. Segregation became even more fixed as the twentieth century unfolded because of increased migration of African Americans from the South, lured by the promise of better employment opportunities.[2]

To cope with these circumstances, and in hopes of navigating the complicated process of assimilation, Philadelphia's African Americans created and joined fraternal organizations, mutual improvement societies, and churches. While these institutions enabled them to respond better to depressed working and living conditions, they also became places within which social and economic divisions emerged between native Philadelphians and the newcomers from the South. Differences in class and regional background thwarted attempts to create a unified black community in the face of racial oppression. Often, these institutions became sites of struggle for the status and power that could not be secured outside the black community.[3] The relationship that African Americans had with baseball also reflected this dual struggle against white racism, on one hand, and internal division on the other.

Since 1887, when the owners of the white-organized major leagues entered a tacit "gentleman's agreement" to exclude African Americans, Philadelphia was home to a divided baseball tradition.[4] Whites followed the National League's Phillies, established in 1883, and, later, Connie Mack's American League Athletics, established in 1901. Blacks went to see a number of different Negro League teams over the next half-century, including the Pythians, the Mutuals, the Orions, the Giants, the Hilldales, and, later, the Stars.[5] Whites cheered their teams on from the most up-to-date facilities, going to Baker Bowl and later Shibe Park, the nation's first concrete-and-steel stadium. Blacks rooted for their teams from the rickety old bleachers of wood-constructed, bandbox ballparks in Fairmount Park, or across the Delaware River in Camden, New Jersey.[6]

In the early days of the Negro Leagues, the Hilldales were the dominant African American team in the Philadelphia area. Originally an amateur boys' club from nearby Darby, the Hilldales were established by black businessman Ed Bolden in 1910. Shortly afterward, Bolden incorporated the club, purchased a field with the profits from stock sales, and built a 5,000-seat grandstand. By the 1920s his canny business sense and reputation for "fair dealing and clean playing" had catapulted his team to the top of black professional baseball. With such star performers as William "Judy" Johnson, Oscar Charleston, and Bill Yancey, the Hilldales won three Eastern Colored League championships during that decade.[7] Their talent, which paved the way to integrating baseball, was a threat to the white majors.

Occasionally, Connie Mack agreed to play the Hilldales in an exhibition game, taking the risk that the Negro Leaguers would beat his Athletics—which in fact happened a few times during the 1920s. One of the great personal highlights of Judy Johnson's career was a 6–1 drubbing of Lefty Grove. "He just hated us," recalled the Negro League Hall of Famer. "It was nigger this and nigger that. I never wanted a hit so bad in my life as the first time I came up against him." In fact, Johnson got two hits off the A's ace that day, a double and a single, which he hit right back up the middle, "taking the cap right off [Grove's] head."[8] In later years, Grove would

Figs. 1 & 2 During the 1920s, Ed Bolden, president of the Hilldale Negro League club, often scheduled exhibition games with local white semi-pro teams in order to disprove the myth of black inferiority. On those occasions, black and white players competed on equal terms, even when arguing an umpire's call. Fans both black and white came to watch these interracial contests. (Chester County Historical Society)

deny *ever* playing against the Hilldales, or any Negro League team for that matter.[9] Mack was different, though.

The legendary manager of the Philadelphia Athletics was ambivalent about integrating the majors. Years after the color barrier had been broken, Mack hired Judy Johnson as a scout for his Athletics, and the two men became good friends. "I asked him one day," recalled Johnson, "I said, 'Mr. Mack, why didn't you ever take any of the colored boys in the big leagues?' He said, 'Well, Judy, if you want to know the truth, there were just too many of you to go in.'"[10] While the remark seems to suggest that Mack did not want to take too many jobs away from the white players, some Negro Leaguers who played in the Philadelphia area seemed to feel that the A's manager genuinely wanted to sign African American ballplayers.

"I remember when the A's played the '29 World Series," said Napoleon Cummings, an infielder for the Hilldales. "They were short of ballplayers, and Connie Mack was trying to get our catcher, Biz Mackey, to help them

Fig. 2

Fig. 3 William "Judy" Johnson starred for the Negro League Hilldales during the 1920s. After the color barrier was broken, the future Hall of Famer was hired as a scout by Connie Mack, manager of the Philadelphia Athletics. (National Baseball Hall of Fame and Library)

out. But they wouldn't let Negroes on that ballclub. No soap."[11] Apparently, Mack buckled under the pressure of the gentleman's agreement as well as the racial prejudice of the players themselves, about a third of whom were Southerners and would not play with or against African Americans.[12] In fact, several of Mack's own players during the 1920s were exposed as members of the Ku Klux Klan.[13] It was not until 1953 that the Athletics signed their first black player, pitcher Bob Trice.[14] A year later the Mack family sold the team and the Athletics moved to Kansas City, where it would later sign its first black superstar, Reggie Jackson.[15]

While the national pastime afforded an important opportunity for Philadelphia's African American community to challenge whites' notions of racial inferiority, it also precipitated social divisions within the black community itself. Aside from the precarious financial state of the Negro Leagues, which resulted in teams disbanding after only a season or two, there were tensions within the black community over the operation of the leagues. For example, most teams in the Eastern Colored League, organized in 1923, were owned by white businessmen. The players in that league were often chastised by the more established—and black-controlled—Negro National League, founded by Rube Foster in 1920. An interleague war ensued when the Eastern Colored League began luring the Negro National League's star players with promises of higher wages if they jumped leagues.[16]

Hilldale was at the center of the controversy. Ed Bolden, the club's president, was initially condemned by the city's African American press for failing to secure an all-black umpiring staff. "Are we still slaves?" asked the editors of the *Philadelphia Tribune*. "Is it possible that colored baseball players are so dumb that they will resent one of their own race umpiring their game? Or is it that the management of Hilldale is so steeped in racial inferiority that it has no faith in Negroes? Aside from the economic unfairness of such a position, the hiring of white umpires for Negro ball games brands Negroes as inferior. It tells white people in a forceful manner that colored people are unable to even play a ball game without white leadership. It is a detestable, mean attitude, and there is no excuse for it when Hilldale depends on colored people for its existence."[17]

When Bolden scheduled games with local white teams, often ignoring Philadelphia's other African American clubs, or sought financial sponsorship from the white business community, he was called an "Uncle Tom."[18] In fact, however, Bolden considered himself a businessman first and "a race man" second. He realized that the financial success of the Hilldales, and in some years the very survival of the club, was inextricably linked to white involvement.[19] Black teams simply could not rely solely on the day-to-day support of their own fans. Without white support, both at the gate and in the wider business community, the Hilldales would not have been able to meet their payroll. "Close analysis will prove that only where the color line fades and cooperation is instituted are our business advances gratified," Bolden insisted. "Segregation in any form is not the solution."[20] But mounting criticism from the black press and the Negro National League, as well as Bolden's inability to retain his star players, resulted in the disbanding of the team after the 1928 season. Five years later, the Hilldales would return as the Philadelphia Stars of the Negro National League.

Fig. 4 The 1939 Philadelphia Stars of the Negro Leagues. Gene Benson (*first row, third from right*) was the team's flashy centerfielder. Ed Bolden (*standing in back row in civilian clothes*) was the owner of the club. (National Baseball Hall of Fame and Library)

It was the golden era of Negro League baseball. The majors were at a low ebb, with many of the greats like Ty Cobb, Babe Ruth, and Al Simmons either retired or in the twilight of their careers. White fans wanted to see more than the home run. They were ready for a more fast-paced, colorful style of play. Black baseball, with its emphasis on base-stealing, drag-bunting, and the hit-and-run, provided the kind of excitement they wanted. There were also exciting young players, like Gene Benson of the Stars, who captured the attention of African American and white fans alike.

Only 5 feet 8 inches tall and 180 pounds, Benson was a soft-spoken but flashy centerfielder with exceptional range and a rifle for an arm. He quickly established himself as one of the finest defensive outfielders in the Negro Leagues. Three times selected for the East-West All-Star Game, Benson pioneered the over-the-shoulder basket catch that was later copied and popularized by Willie Mays of the New York Giants.[21] "Negro baseball was more exciting than the kind of ball being played in the majors," recalled Benson. "We'd steal bases, dance down the third-base line to shake up the pitcher, lay down the bunt, play hit-and-run baseball. Even our defensive play was more exciting to watch. Outfielders played in near the infield and could make running, over-the-shoulder catches. The major leaguers didn't do those things. But white fans were impressed by that kind of play"[22]— so impressed that, by 1940, whites were turning out in droves to see the Stars play.

On Monday nights when the major leaguers were traveling between cities, Connie Mack allowed the Stars to play in Shibe Park, and the team drew as many as 30,000 spectators. Average attendance at their own park at Forty-Fourth and Parkside was between 20,000 and 25,000, and often there were more whites than blacks in the stands. The Phillies, by comparison, were lucky to draw 10,000 for a doubleheader.[23]

Mahlon Duckett, an impressionable seventeen-year-old who was the Negro National League Rookie of the Year in 1940, still remembers looking into those smoke-filled stands at Forty-Fourth and Parkside and being impressed by the sight. "At night, the smoke from the train engines at the Pennsylvania Railroad next to our field would leave soot on the fans' clothing, but we still got capacity crowds."[24]

"Women used to come to the ballpark dressed up—high-heeled shoes, silk stockings, fine dresses, and long-sleeved gloves," adds Stanley Glenn, who caught for the Stars. "Men came dressed in suits, shined shoes, and hats. It was almost as if people were going to a fashion show. You have to understand that black folk didn't have many things to do for entertainment.

There was, of course, church, and we went there in droves. Next there was jazz music. And for six months of the year there was Negro League baseball."[25]

Glenn, who graduated from Philadelphia's John Bartram High School in 1944, joined the Stars that June. Manager Oscar Charleston had scouted the young catcher and was impressed with his defensive skills, but some opposing players were not. In one of Glenn's first starts, Josh Gibson of the Homestead Grays purposely spiked him sliding into home plate. As the future Hall of Famer got to his feet, he reminded Glenn to learn the sweep tag, or "next time you'll really get hurt."[26] It was a classic example of Negro League behavior—play hard and aggressively, but be sure to mentor the younger generation so they will improve and, if they have the opportunity to crack the color barrier, do the race proud.

Within five years Glenn found himself calling pitches for one of the greatest—and most colorful—hurlers in the history of the game: Satchel Paige. "I caught Satchel when he pitched for the Stars in 1949," Glenn recalled. "As hard as he threw, his ball was like a feather it was so soft. The great thing about him was his accuracy, though. You'd just put the glove up there and he'd hit it. Once we were barnstorming together and Joe DiMaggio came to the plate. Satch said to him, 'They tell me you're a great fast-ball hitter. Well, get ready, cause here comes my number one and I'm going to throw it belt high on the inside.' He'd do just that and get him out."[27]

By the 1940s, the exhibition games between white major league teams and Negro League teams had ceased. Postseason barnstorming, however, enabled the Negro Leaguers to showcase their ability against individual big leaguers who agreed to play against them. For example, both Paige and Bob Feller of the Cleveland Indians had all-star teams, and they would barnstorm across the Midwest after the World Series had ended. "But you sure weren't going to play a major league team intact," insisted Benson. "Just think of the implications if one of our teams beat someone like the New York Yankees, especially when Baseball Commissioner Judge Kenesaw Mountain Landis—probably as big a racist as anyone in this world—was operating on the faulty assumption that blacks couldn't compete at the major league level."[28] Still, barnstorming served as important proof that African American ballplayers could compete against their white counterparts.

Benson remembers playing an exhibition game against Feller's all-stars at Pittsburgh's Forbes Field in 1940. Feller had won twenty-seven games during the regular season for the Cleveland Indians, a team that contended

Fig. 5 In one of his first games for the Philadelphia Stars, catcher Stanley "Doc" Glenn was purposely spiked by Josh Gibson of the Homestead Grays. As he got to his feet, Gibson, a future Hall of Famer, reminded the rookie: "Learn to use the sweep tag, or next time you'll really get hurt." (Stanley Glenn)

for the American League pennant. "I hit him all over that park," said Benson. "Got a single and two doubles off him. After the game, he told me, 'Nobody hits me that way. Am I signaling my pitches or something?' What I found out about Bob Feller was that while everyone was talking about how hard he threw, he had more confidence in his curveball when men were on base."

"Truth is that hitting major league pitching was a picnic," Benson added. "If I could have hit major league pitchers all year, every year, with no knock-downs or spitballs—which was fair game in the Negro Leagues—I'd have hit .400 lifetime."[29] Duckett agrees: "Most of us played just as good as the major leaguers. We had so many outstanding players that when we'd go barnstorming we'd often win."[30]

While Negro Leaguers did not play with the same kind of discipline as the major leaguers, and nostalgia for their youthful achievements may have resulted in an exaggerated assessment of their true skills, their entertain-ing style of play captured the imaginations of both black and white fans. Integration was just around the corner. Major league owners recognized the powerful appeal of black baseball, not only in terms of player talent but also in the droves of African Americans who would turn out to see games. Integrating the national pastime was a simple matter of dollars and cents. The first attempt came in 1943 when Bill Veeck, son of former Chicago Cub owner William Veeck Sr., arranged to purchase the hapless Phillies from then-owner Gerry Nugent. Veeck planned to stock the Phillies with top Negro League talent to bolster a roster that had been stripped of talent by the manpower shortage during World War II. "With Satchel Paige, Roy Campanella, Luke Easter, Monte Irvin, and countless others available from the Negro Leagues," said Veeck, "I had not the slightest doubt that in 1944—a war year—the Phils would have leaped from seventh place to the pennant."

Before he finalized the deal, Veeck notified baseball commissioner Judge Landis of his plans. Although he was aware of Landis's desire to keep African Americans out of baseball, he knew that the only way the commis-sioner could block the move was to rule officially that blacks were detri-mental to the game. But with black soldiers fighting and dying abroad, such a ruling was unthinkable. Instead, Landis ran interference by forcing Veeck to purchase the Phillies through National League President Ford Frick rather than Nugent. Frick acted immediately. Before Veeck could begin the negotiations, the National League president sold the Phillies to William Cox, a lumber dealer, for half the price offered by Veeck. He then proceeded to brag throughout the baseball world—off the record, of course—about how he had stopped Veeck from "contaminating the league."[31]

When questioned about the incident, Landis denied any part in a conspiracy, stating simply: "There is no rule, formal or informal, against the hiring of Negro players in organized baseball."[32] Not until his death in 1944, however, did baseball open the door for integration.

To the dismay of the club owners who appointed him, the new commissioner, Albert "Happy" Chandler, was adamant in defending the "freedom of blacks" to "make it in major league baseball," especially those who had served in World War II.[33] The owners had believed that Chandler, a U.S. Senator from Kentucky, would follow the "gentleman's agreement" of segregation condoned by Landis.[34] They were wrong.

When Branch Rickey, president of the Brooklyn Dodgers, signed Jackie Robinson of the Negro League's Kansas City Monarchs to a professional contract in 1945, Chandler's support for integration provoked the open hostility of fifteen of the sixteen club owners, including new Phillies owner Robert R. M. Carpenter Jr.

Carpenter, scion of the wealthy Du Pont family of Wilmington, Delaware, insisted he was not "opposed to Negro players" but said he wasn't "going to hire a player of any color or nationality just to have him on the team."[35] Ironically, Carpenter, who purchased the Phillies in 1943, would have greatly benefited by signing some of the available African American talent. His team was in shambles. Perennial losers who had not finished higher than fifth place since 1932, the Phillies had few players of any real substance, and a worthless farm system.

To address the unenviable task of rebuilding the franchise, Carpenter appointed longtime friend and former Yankee pitcher Herb Pennock as general manager. Between 1944 and 1948, Pennock spent his bosses' money freely, handing out $1,250,000 in bonuses to such future white stars as Robin Roberts, Richie Ashburn, Curt Simmons, Granny Hamner, and Willie Jones—all of whom would form the nucleus of the 1950 pennant-winning Whiz Kids. "We're interested in any ballplayers of any race, color, or creed who can help the club," Pennock insisted, echoing Carpenter's own feelings on integration.[36] Not a single dollar was invested in black talent, though. Nor was any serious consideration given to scouting the Negro Leagues, an implicit policy that was reinforced by Manager Ben Chapman, Pennock's best friend and former Yankee teammate.[37]

Chapman was an aggressive, volatile, and demanding skipper who battled frequently with umpires, cajoled his own players, and often sounded off in the press. Joining the Phillies in 1945, he rode his players almost constantly in order to get the most from them. His tactics paid off the following season when the team jumped from the cellar of the National League to a fifth-place finish. But Chapman, an Alabaman, was also known for his intense bigotry. As a player for the New York Yankees in the 1930s, he gained notoriety for launching anti-Semitic epithets at the team's Jewish fans. His remarks were so vicious that they prompted 15,000 fans to sign a petition urging the front office to banish him, which the Yankees did in 1936 to the Washington Senators.[38]

Essentially, the Phillies brain trust was racist on principle, and as such they hurt the quality of their teams. But their white fans did not seem to mind, for they too proved to be committed to the tacit segregation that prevailed in the city. Philadelphia's African American baseball community, on the other hand, realized the significance of Robinson's quest and ceased its internal bickering in order to support him.

To be sure, in terms of baseball talent there were better candidates than Robinson. Two of the most talented Negro Leaguers had Philadelphia roots. Roy Campanella, born and raised in the Nicetown section of the city, had also captured Rickey's attention. A catcher for the Baltimore Elite Giants, "Campy" was, by the early 1940s, a rising star in the Negro Leagues. Wanting to play in his hometown, he approached Phillies scout Jocko Collins in 1942 for a tryout. Duly impressed, Collins recommended that then-owner Gerry Nugent sign the twenty-two-year-old backstop. Nugent, of course, refused.[39] There was also Marvin Williams, an infielder for the Stars, who was a better hitter than Robinson. Along with Jackie and Sam Jethroe of the Cleveland Buckeyes, Williams had been invited to try out for the Boston Red Sox in April 1945.[40]

"Most people don't know that Jackie Robinson couldn't make the starting lineup of the Kansas City Monarchs," said Williams. "That's a fact. Their infield was so good there was no place for him to play. At the same time, I don't know of a fiercer competitor than Jackie. He was tough. So while he wasn't the best player in the Negro Leagues, he was certainly the best man for the job of integrating the majors, being a college-educated, military veteran."[41]

Williams revealed that the Red Sox tryout was more of a publicity campaign to promote Robinson and that he, realizing the importance of integration, had cooperated fully in that effort. Before the trio traveled to Boston, they met with Wendell Smith, a sportswriter for the African American weekly *Pittsburgh Courier.* Smith, who scheduled the tryout, told them he was "going to give Jackie more publicity because he had a degree from UCLA and he was a second lieutenant in the army." "If Jackie can fight alongside white soldiers," said Smith, "he certainly should be able to play with them."[42]

In April 1945, Williams, Jethroe, and Robinson joined a dozen other white prospects at Fenway Park. After shagging flies in the outfield and taking infield, they were called in to bat, and immediately all three demonstrated the ability to hit at the big league level. "We hit that Green Monster real hard—all of us," recalled Williams, referring to Fenway's legendary left-field wall. "We tried to tear it down. Jackie said, 'If we can't go over it, let's just knock it down!'"[43] But Williams, heeding Smith's advice, also made sure to allow Robinson's talent to shine.

The Negro Leaguers were not naive, though. "Not for one minute," Robinson later admitted, "did we believe that the tryout was sincere." While Red Sox Manager Joe Cronin and Coach Hugh Duffy praised their performances and had them fill out application blanks, the players were "certain that they wouldn't call us."[44] According to Williams, President Franklin D. Roosevelt's unexpected death and the national mourning that followed resulted in the "cancellation of another tryout with the Boston Braves." Soon afterward, Smith "launched a big publicity campaign to get Jackie into the majors."[45] As a result, Robinson caught the attention of Clyde Sukeforth, chief scout for the Brooklyn Dodgers, and on August 28, 1945, Rickey signed the Monarchs infielder.

Gene Benson, another Philadelphia Star, also played an instrumental role in breaking baseball's color barrier. To prepare Robinson for the challenges he would later face, Rickey arranged for him to join a group of Negro League all-stars on a barnstorming tour of Venezuela during the winter of 1945, and purposely selected Benson to room with and mentor the youngster.

At the age of thirty-four, Benson, in the twilight of his career, was never seriously considered as the player to break the color line. Because of his baseball talent, however, he was well respected in the black baseball world. His strong sense of humility, his exceptional ability to turn the other cheek in the face of discrimination, and his soft-spoken manner endeared him to the younger Negro Leaguers. All these qualities made Benson the perfect choice to become Robinson's mentor. Initially, Benson had reservations. "I had been told that Jackie was controversial and used to get involved in fisticuffs all the time," he recalled. "But I didn't see any of that when we started rooming together. I found out Jackie was a clean-living man. He

Fig. 6   Gene Benson, a flashy centerfielder for the Philadelphia Stars, prepared Jackie Robinson to break the color barrier by mentoring him on a barnstorming tour of Venezuela during the winter of 1945. (National Baseball Hall of Fame and Library)

didn't drink or smoke or hang out with the wrong crowd. If he got into a fight it was because of his strong sense of pride, and it was provoked. Never did he start anything."[46]

Over the course of the winter, Benson advised, assured, and encouraged the young Dodger, preparing him for the challenges he would face as the first African American in major league baseball. "We talked baseball all the time, sometimes staying up half the night," recalled Benson, years later. "A lot of it really had to do with confidence-building. Jackie would say, 'You're a better ballplayer than me. Why didn't they choose you?' I'd tell him, 'I'm too old. No one is going to give a thirty-four-year-old a chance. But you're young and you've got ability. You'll make it.' But I wouldn't tell him that I was better than he was. He didn't know how good he was because he hadn't proven himself. He hadn't had the opportunity." Benson convinced Robinson that Negro League pitchers were more difficult to hit than those in the majors because they were permitted to throw at the hitter and use the spitball. "Over our time together in Venezuela, I could see that Jackie had the determination and intelligence to make it to the majors," said Benson. "I saw that you needed to tell him something only once. He never forgot anything. He also carried himself like an athlete. Not only did he have great natural ability, but he respected that ability by the clean way he lived."[47]

Benson also taught Robinson how to hit the curveball, though he was too humble to accept the credit for it. To be sure, the two men were completely different in their approach to hitting. Benson sported one of the most unusual batting stances in the game. Turning his body almost a full 90 degrees so that he was facing the pitcher, he held the bat near his waist. This allowed him to keep his hands still as long as possible, waiting until the last second to drive pitches to the opposite field—something that enabled him to become a great curveball hitter. Despite his unorthodox style, available records indicate that Benson's lifetime batting average was over .300, with a peak mark of .370 in 1945.[48]

Robinson, on the other hand, held the bat over his right shoulder. Although he was more of a lunge hitter, Robinson also kept his hands back as long as possible—just as Benson had counseled. Because of that skill, he was one of the greatest curveball hitters of his generation.[49]

Benson's counsel helped to prepare Robinson for his historic role by giving him the confidence to succeed against opposing teams. But Robinson would need more than confidence to persevere against the Phillies, which of all the National League teams treated him the worst during his quest to break the major league color barrier.[50]

When the Phillies traveled to Brooklyn in April 1947 to play the Dodgers and Jackie Robinson, all hopes that integration would come peacefully were shattered. The Phillies, led by Manager Ben Chapman, launched a verbal assault on Robinson the likes of which had seldom, if ever, been heard in baseball. The abuse began during batting practice:

"Nigger, go back to the cotton fields where you belong," Chapman yelled.

By game time, many of the Phillies players had joined their manager in the insulting chorus:

"They're waiting for you in the jungles, black boy."

"Hey, coon, did you always smell so bad?"

"Hey, snowflake, which one of you white boys' wives are you shackin' up with tonight?"[51]

The fusillade of bigotry continued throughout the game. Harold Parrott, the Dodgers' traveling secretary, claimed it was the worst racial attack he had ever heard. "Chapman mentioned everything from thick lips to the supposedly extra-thick Negro skull, which he said restricted brain growth to almost animal level when compared with white folk," he contended. "He listed the repulsive sores and diseases he said Robbie's teammates would be infected with if they touched the towels or combs he used. He charged Jackie outright with breaking up his own Brooklyn team. The Dodger players had told him privately, he said, that they wished the black man would go back to the South where he belonged, picking cotton, swabbing out latrines, or worse."[52]

Robinson, standing at first base, was initially stunned by the abuse. But the longer it continued he became enraged, like a time bomb waiting to explode. Nothing—not even Rickey's role-playing, laced as it was with the anticipated racial epithets—had prepared him for the treatment he was experiencing. "For one wild and rage-crazed minute, I thought: 'To hell with Mr. Rickey's noble experiment,'" Robinson recalled many years later. "'It's clear it won't succeed. My best is not good enough for them.' I thought, What a glorious, cleansing thing it would be to let go. To hell with the image of the patient black freak I was supposed to create. I could throw down my bat, stride over to the Phillies dugout, grab one of those white sons-of-bitches, and smash his teeth in with my despised black fist."[53]

Robinson got his revenge in the eighth inning. With the teams dead-locked in a scoreless tie, he singled, stole second, advanced to third on a throwing error by the Phillies catcher, and scored the game's only run on Gene Hermanski's single. Going hitless in the final two games of the series, Robinson's slump only added to the Phillies' contention that he "didn't belong in the majors" and was "only there to draw those nigger bucks to the gate for Rickey."[54]

Bench jockeying was a tradition in baseball, and no topic was sacred. Personal problems, appearance, ethnicity, and race were all considered "fair game." But the Phillies' verbal abuse of Robinson exceeded even baseball's broadly defined sense of propriety. Fans seated near the team's dugout wrote letters of protest to Commissioner Chandler, who responded by contacting Phillies owner Bob Carpenter and demanding that the harassment cease immediately or he would be forced to invoke punitive measures against the organization.[55]

When he learned of Chandler's edict, Chapman defended his actions, insisting that the Phillies would "treat Robinson the same as we do any other man who is likely to step to the plate and beat us" and noting such players as Hank Greenberg of the Pirates and Joe Garagiola of the Cardinals, both of whom had been the targets of ethnic slurs. "There is not a man who has come to the big leagues who has not been ridden," said Chapman. "Besides," he added, "Robinson did not want to be patronized" and had been given nothing more than the "same test experienced by all rookies."[56]

Chapman's defense elicited the support of many Philadelphia fans and sportswriters who "commended him for his fair stand toward Robinson."[57] Robinson, himself, publicly downplayed the abusive treatment, stating that the Phillies' bench jockeys were "trying to get me upset" but that it "really didn't bother me." Nor did he "think Chapman was really shouting at me."[58] Just as he promised Rickey, Robinson turned the other cheek. His Dodger teammates, however, were not as forgiving.

Dixie Walker, a fellow Alabaman and a close friend of Chapman's, chastised the Phillies manager for his inappropriate behavior. Even Eddie Stanky, who had circulated a petition to prevent Robinson from joining the team, called Chapman a "coward" and challenged him to "pick on somebody who can fight back."[59] On another occasion, when Chapman began taunting Pee Wee Reese about "how it felt to be playing with an[expletive] nigger," the Dodger shortstop walked over to Robinson and, in a firm show of support, placed his arm around the first baseman's shoulders.[60] Inadvertently, Chapman had rallied the Dodgers around their black teammate and the cause of integration. They admired Robinson for his tremendous restraint in the face of discrimination. According to Rickey, Chapman's "string of unconscionable abuse unified thirty men, not one of whom was willing to sit by and see someone kick around a man who had his hands tied behind his back."[61]

Two weeks later, on May 9, the day before the Dodgers were to take a train to Philadelphia for the first extended road trip of the season, Rickey received a telephone call from Herb Pennock, the Phillies general manager.

"You just can't bring that nigger here with the rest of the team, Branch," Pennock allegedly said. "We're just not ready for that sort of thing yet. We won't be able to take the field if that Robinson boy is in uniform."

"Great!" Rickey exclaimed. "That means we win all three games by default," he added, calling the Phillies executive's bluff, "and the way things are going, we sure can use those victories." Infuriated by the response, Pennock hung up.[62]

Whether the conversation was fact or fiction remains a subject of controversy.[63] Originally quoted by Harold Parrott, the Dodgers' traveling secretary, in his 1976 book, *The Lords of Baseball*, the purported exchange was given greater legitimacy by Jules Tygiel's 1983 book, *Baseball's Great Experiment*, which historians widely consider to be the most accurate record of Robinson's quest to break the color line.[64] Neither Rickey nor Pennock is still alive to confirm the conversation, and Parrott's claim that the Dodger owner allowed him to eavesdrop on the exchange casts a shadow of doubt over the legitimacy of it.[65] In fact, Robinson himself attributed the telephone call to the Phillies owner, Bob Carpenter.[66] More recently, his widow, Rachel, admitted that she hadn't even heard of Pennock's alleged racial epithet and that because the conversation "is not sufficiently documented" she would "not take a position on it."[67]

Regardless of who made the telephone call to Rickey, one thing is clear: the Phillies front office had no intention of welcoming Robinson to Shibe Park. Just as clear was the team's intention to boycott the series. Of the Phillies who saw regular playing time in 1947, seven were from the south, including shortstop Lamar "Skeeter" Newsome, centerfielder Harry "The Hat" Walker, and third baseman Jim Tabor.[68] In spite of the strong southern sentiment on the club, level heads prevailed. According to catcher Andy Seminick, the Phillies had intended to boycott the Dodger series, until Newsome "called a meeting and convinced us not to do it." "Our manager, Ben Chapman, was adamant about not playing against Robinson," recalled Seminick. "Being from Alabama, he just couldn't understand why whites should have to play against blacks. So we were all set to boycott the Brooklyn series, until Newsome convinced us that a boycott would be morally wrong. He believed that Robinson, like any other man, should have the opportunity to play baseball. The fact that Newsome also came from Alabama, I think, carried a lot of weight with the other players."[69]

The Phillies relented, but Robinson still wasn't welcomed in the city. When the Dodgers tried to check in at the Benjamin Franklin Hotel, the bellhops stacked their luggage out on the sidewalk at Ninth and Chestnut streets. Harold Parrott, Brooklyn's traveling secretary, was told that no rooms were available and not to return "while you have any nigras with you." The response took him completely by surprise. While Parrott was aware that racist feelings ran high among the Phillies, he certainly did not antic- ipate any problems from the Ben Franklin, where the Dodgers regularly stayed, especially since he had included Robinson's name on the reservation list before the team's arrival and hotel officials had raised no objections. Now he was being told otherwise. Instead of forcing a confrontation, the Dodgers changed their accommodations to the more expensive Warwick Hotel, where the manager said he'd be delighted to have them.[70]

At Shibe Park the following day, a huge crowd came to see—and jeer— Robinson. Shortly before game time he made a much-publicized walk to the

Fig. 7 Phillies owner Bob Carpenter *(left)* hired close friend and Hall of Fame pitcher Herb Pennock as general manager shortly after purchasing the team in the early 1940s. Pennock tried to prevent Jackie Robinson from taking the field at Connie Mack Stadium during his historic quest to break baseball's color barrier in 1947. (National Baseball Hall of Fame and Library)

Phillies dugout for a conciliatory photograph with Chapman. In light of all the negative publicity of the first series between the two teams, both club owners requested the photo of the two men shaking hands. While Chapman agreed to pose for the photographers, he refused to shake Robinson's hand. The most he would do was share a bat with the Dodger first baseman. Rumors abounded that the Phils skipper agreed to pose for the picture only to save his job. But Chapman insisted that he agreed only because his good friend and general manager, Herb Pennock, asked him to do it for "the *New York Times*, which had requested the picture."[71] For Robinson, on the other hand, the photo shoot was a painful necessity. He later confessed that he had could "think of no occasion where I had more difficulty swallowing my pride than in agreeing to pose for a photograph with a man for whom I had the lowest regard."[72]

When the game started, the Phillies picked up where they left off in Brooklyn, harassing Robinson unmercifully. Chapman continued with his personal racial attacks with insulting remarks about thick lips and an extra-thick skull that restricted brain growth. "God himself could have come down and Ben would have been on him," said Phillies outfielder Harry "The Hat" Walker, who came to the Phillies on May 3 of that season in a trade with the St. Louis Cardinals. "Chapman just had a way of stirring up trouble, and when the color barrier was broken no one knew what to expect from him."[73] Ken Raffensberger, who pitched for the Phillies, admitted that Chapman issued "a standing order that whenever any pitcher had two strikes and no balls on Robinson he had to knock him down. If he didn't, the pitcher was fined $50." Raffensberger, who was considered a control pitcher, ignored the order, refusing to put himself in that situation. "I'd make sure to start Robinson off with a ball," he said, "then I might go to two strikes. But I wasn't going to bait Robinson, nor was I going to pay any $50 fine!"[74] Howie Schultz, the Phillies' regular first baseman, had similar feelings.

Ironically, Schultz had been traded to the Phils from the Dodgers before the opening of that series in order to make room at first base for Robinson. But he had no ill feelings toward his onetime teammate. In fact, Schultz developed a great deal of admiration for Robinson, having spent the entire season with him at Montreal in 1946 and seeing firsthand the admirable way he handled all the adversity. Now Schultz was playing for a man who, in his view, was "still fighting the Civil War." "There was a lot of verbal abuse from the Phillies dugout during that series," he recalled. "While I certainly wasn't proud of that behavior, I realized that I was the property of the Phillies and

Fig. 8 In 1947, Phillies Manager Ben Chapman led his team in a racist verbal attack against Jackie Robinson. When ordered to pose for a conciliatory photograph, Chapman grudgingly agreed, but he refused to shake Robinson's hand. (Temple University Urban Archives)

kept my mouth shut." When Robinson reached first base, Schultz, embarrassed, asked: "How can you stand this crap?" Robinson looked up at his former teammate and replied, "I'll have my day."[75] The Dodger first baseman had another bad game, which only led to more verbal abuse.

At the same time, however, Philadelphia's African American baseball fans turned out in record numbers to cheer for Robinson. "Never before had so many blacks come out to a Phillies game," recalled Stanley Glenn. "Blacks from as far as Baltimore, Harrisburg, and Wilmington, Delaware, chartered buses called 'Jackie Robinson Specials' and traveled all the way to Philadelphia just to see him play. We probably had close to 20,000 blacks at Shibe Park for that Dodgers series, and before Jackie broke the color barrier the Phils would be lucky to draw 10,000—white or black—for a doubleheader."[76] Complaints from the city's black fans also prompted the National League to order an immediate stop to the assault.[77] Silenced by the edict, the Phillies attempted to humiliate Robinson the following day by pointing their bats at him and making gunshot sounds in a mock display of the death threats that had been reported in the Philadelphia newspapers.[78]

When asked if he had instructed his players to ride Robinson, Chapman said: "Yes, I did. We not only did it to Robinson, but to all the other Brooklyn players. We're not treating him any better or worse than the other players. We didn't ride him because he is a Negro. We did it because we are trying to win."[79] But Chapman also insisted that the verbal abuse did not last long and was stopped on his orders, not those of National League President Ford Frick. "We found that every time we knocked Robinson down, verbally or physically, he would just get up and beat us," he said. "It was better not to get him mad, so after about the third time we played him I told our players to let him alone."[80]

Chapman was fired partway through the 1948 season. He would never again manage at the major league level, and instead spent the next five years coaching in the minors before retiring. For more than a quarter-century, the former Phillies manager refused to discuss his abusive treatment of Robinson. Then, in a 1973 *Sporting News* interview, he broke his silence, bluntly insisting that he had done "nothing wrong" and again dismissing the entire episode as little more than the heckling any young player would experience as a rookie. "Most of the things that people said that I and my players at Philadelphia said to Jackie were true," he admitted. "And I'm not ashamed of anything that happened. I wasn't then, and I'm not now. The fact of the matter is that we did nothing that we didn't do to any other rookie. Our purpose was to win, and if we could do that by getting a rookie rattled, we would. I guess that's happened to any rookie that ever put on a major league uniform. It happened to me, and they pick out the thing they think will get under your skin the most. The first thing I heard from the fans when I stepped onto the field in a Yankee uniform was 'Go back where you belong you Southern S.O.B.,' and the first thing I heard from the opposing dugout was, 'Stick it in the Southern S.O.B.'s ear and see how he looks sitting down!'"[81]

When Eddie Sawyer, a professor from Ithaca College, became the new manager at the end of the 1948 campaign, the Phillies' treatment of Robinson improved dramatically. Sawyer presided over a rebuilding process. Few veterans would remain. By 1950 the oldest regulars on the team were first baseman Eddie Waitkus and second baseman Mike Goliat, both of whom were thirty years of age. Younger stars dominated the team, the average age being twenty-four. These "Whiz Kids" left their mark on baseball history for being the youngest team ever to capture a pennant, which they did on the last day of the 1950 season in a hard-fought race against the Brooklyn Dodgers.

Among the brightest of the stars was pitching ace Robin Roberts, who had nothing but great respect for Robinson. "Certainly there was a lot of prejudice toward Jackie in 1947, his first year in the majors," said Roberts. "But by 1948 when I came up to the Phillies, there was no doubt as to his talent. From the first time I faced him, it was clear that he was not only an exceptional base runner but also a solid hitter and an all-around ballplayer. I was so nervous just being in the big leagues that I concentrated on getting him out. That was quite enough to worry about. I had no time to get involved in the racial thing or even listen to it."[82] Roberts attributed the Phillies' improved attitude toward Robinson to the change in managers. "Chapman was a good man," he said, "but also one who had grown up with racial prejudice and rode Jackie pretty hard. Eddie Sawyer was very different. He was a quiet man who judged a player solely on his abilities and didn't get involved in bench jockeying. It was immediately clear that Sawyer respected Robinson's abilities."[83]

Phillies centerfielder Richie Ashburn, who also was promoted to the majors in 1948, agreed that Chapman gave his respect to Robinson only begrudgingly, but he downplayed the racial overtones of his bench-jockeying. Instead, Ashburn insisted that Chapman "was not in an exclusive group" and that "everyone got on Jackie," including himself, and that being from Nebraska he "didn't have any racial feelings one way or the other."[84] But in a 1973 column he wrote for the *Philadelphia Bulletin*, Ashburn publicly apologized for his role in Phillies Robinson-bashing during the spring of

1948. He admitted that his purposeful spiking of the Dodger second base-man on the base paths was done more out of peer pressure and to follow Chapman's orders than to think clearly for himself. "Major league baseball is tough enough under ideal conditions," he confessed, "but Jackie had to battle the fans and the press as well as our club, which was exceptionally tough on him."[85]

If the Phillies had a problem with Robinson by the 1950s, then, it had little to do with the color of his skin and everything to do with his uncanny ability to beat them in the batter's box or on the base paths. "If a base hit was needed to win a game," said Ashburn, "Jackie always seemed to be the one to get it. And you have to remember that he played on a Dodger ball club with many great hitters. I just think the history between our two clubs gave him that extra incentive to excel against us."[86]

While the Phillies' infamous treatment of Robinson saddled the organization with a racist reputation, they were not the only club that resented his quest to break the color line. The St. Louis Cardinals, led by outfielder Enos Slaughter, had every intention of conducting an anti-Robinson boycott, until National League President Ford Frick threatened the team with a long-term suspension.[87] Cincinnati was another city where racial epithets spewed from the dugout and Robinson received death threats from the hometown fans.[88]

On the other hand, Robinson's example inspired the African American community by jolting the national conscience in a profound way. Until 1947 all baseball's heroes had been white men. Suddenly there was a black baseball star who could hit, bunt, steal, and field with the best of them. His style of play was nothing new in the Negro Leagues, but in the white majors it was innovative and exciting. Robinson revolutionized the game by introducing the black style of play. It was fast-paced, utilizing the bunt-and-run, the hit-and-run, base-stealing, and the suicide squeeze. "Jackie made things happen on the base paths," said Stanley Glenn. "If he got on first, he stole second. If he couldn't steal third, he'd rattle the pitcher by dancing off second so he could advance. Then he would try to steal home. The name of the game was to score runs without a hit, something that was very different from the power-hitting strategy of the major leagues."[89]

By the end of his celebrated ten-year career, Jackie Robinson had compiled a lifetime batting average of .311, some 1,518 hits, and 197 stolen bases. He was voted Rookie of the Year in 1947 and the National League's Most Valuable Player in 1949, and he was named to four All-Star teams as the league's second baseman. Leading the Dodgers to six pennants as well as to the 1955 World Championship, Robinson retired from baseball at the end of the 1956 season at the age of thirty-eight. Six years later, in 1962, he was inducted into the National Baseball Hall of Fame, the first African American to be so honored.[90]

Robinson's success, however, came at a price. "Jackie was high-strung by nature," remembers Gene Benson. "So high-strung that he paid with his life to go through with breaking the color barrier. He tried real hard not to make waves in the field so he could open doors for black ballplayers. It caused him an early death, too, because he just blew up inside. But then, Jackie was a man who would do anything to help one of his own. That was his way. He went out and gave his life for black athletes."[91]

Indeed, Robinson's success paved the way for other African American stars, such as Roy Campanella, Willie Mays, and Hank Aaron. By 1956 every National League club's roster was integrated, with the exception of Philadelphia's. Owner Bob Carpenter had good reason to believe that he did not have to integrate. In 1950 his Phillies had captured the pennant with a very young team. Affectionately known as the "Whiz Kids," the Fightin' Phils boasted an average age of twenty-six and promised to contend for years to come.[92] But instead, they turned out to be "one-year wonders."

Enamored with his young stars, Carpenter, who also assumed the role of general manager after Pennock's death, preferred to sign bonus babies and rush them to the majors instead of allowing them to gain the experience they needed in the minors. Not until 1954 did the Phillies give any serious consideration to scouting African American players. In that year, Carpenter hired Roy Hamey as general manager. Hamey, a veteran baseball executive who had worked in the New York Yankees and Pittsburgh Pirates organizations, realized the necessity of scouting the game's most recent pool of talent. He immediately ordered an extensive scouting of the Negro Leagues and hired Bill Yancey, a former Hilldale player, to conduct it. Still, none of the black prospects signed by the Phillies reached the majors until 1957, when shortstop John Kennedy of the Kansas City Monarchs became the first black player in the history of the organization.[93]

Invited to spring training at Clearwater, Florida, that year, Kennedy hit .333, convincing management that they had "hit the jackpot."[94] "Up at the plate, he meets the ball well," said Manager Mayo Smith. "He has confidence and poise wherever he is and his reflexes are excellent."[95] Hamey was so impressed with Kennedy that he slated him as the club's starting shortstop, saying: "If we do get somebody else in a trade, they'll have to win the job from Kennedy."[96] But when Hamey acquired Chico Fernandez from the Brooklyn Dodgers just before the team headed north to begin the regular

Fig. 9 Signed by the Phillies in 1957, infielder John Kennedy was the first black player in the history of the franchise. (Philadelphia Phillies)

season, there wasn't much of a competition at shortstop.[97] The twenty-four-year-old Cuban was immediately inserted as the team's regular.[98]

Claude Harrison of the *Philadelphia Tribune*, Philadelphia's African American newspaper, noted the inconsistency. "What does John Kennedy have to do in order to prove he's major league material?" he asked. "At the beginning of the season word came out of Clearwater that he couldn't hit. Yet John's batting average of .333 is the second highest on the team. We were told that he couldn't field either. Yet he has made only one blunder. While the other shortstop [Fernandez], who they paid $75,000 for, makes two in one game!"[99]

Nevertheless, Fernandez would become the regular Phillies shortstop for the next two seasons.[100] Kennedy's departure was only a matter of time. After going hitless in five regular season games, he was sent down to the minors, never to be heard from again.[101] Dallas Green, a young Phillies pitching prospect in 1957, dismisses any racial bias in management's handling of Kennedy, though. "It was early in the Phillies' scouting of black players," he recalled. "I think John was a young player who was forced into the majors too soon and he couldn't adjust as quickly as the Phillies needed him to. Fernandez had a little more playing experience at the major league level. He was also a Latino player, so I don't think you can say that the decision to take him over John was based on racism."[102]

At the same time, the Phillies' refusal to make a stronger attempt at integration had negative implications for the club's future. Curt Simmons, who pitched for the Phils from 1947 to 1960, believes the team hurt itself by ignoring the black talent that did exist in professional baseball during the 1950s. "The Phillies missed out on a lot of great players," he admitted. "Just look at the St. Louis Cardinals of the 1960s, with Curt Flood, Bill White, Lou Brock, and Bob Gibson. I played with those guys after I left Philadelphia, and I'll tell you, they made the Cards a regular contender."[103]

By 1960 it was clear that the 1950 pennant-winning Whiz Kids' best days were behind them. Carpenter's strong devotion to them had crippled the organization. Robin Roberts, the ace of that team, and Richie Ashburn, the sparkplug, were nearing the end of their brilliant careers. Age had also caught up with standout infielders Granny Hamner and Willie Jones, who were hampered by injuries. Other players had become lackadaisical, and it showed in their performance. The team had not finished higher than fourth since 1953.[104] Carpenter was forced to admit that it was time to rebuild and that he would have to rely on the ever-growing pool of African American talent in order to be successful in the future. Integration would be fraught with hope as well as turbulence, much like the 1960s itself.

2

INTEGRATING THE PHILLIES

In the spring of 1963, Richard Anthony Allen, the most highly rated prospect in the Phillies farm system, joined the team at their spring-training complex in Clearwater. The youngest of three boys raised by a single mother in Wampum, Pennsylvania, Allen was confident he had the talent to play in the big leagues. The Phillies, intrigued by his promise as a power-hitting shortstop, signed him three years earlier for $70,000, the highest bonus ever paid to an African American ballplayer at the time.[1] Allen's performance in the low minors demonstrated that he was worth the money.

The young infielder had an impressive debut at Elmira of the New York–Pennsylvania League in 1960, hitting .281 in eighty-eight games. The following season, he played at Magic Valley, Utah, in the Pioneer League and hit .317 with 21 homers and 94 RBIs. When he was promoted to Double A at Williamsport in 1962, Allen continued his prodigious power-hitting, despite being moved to a new position. He hit Eastern League pitching at a .332 clip with 20 home runs and 109 RBIs while learning to play center field.[2] The majors appeared to be on the horizon, especially after he led the Phils with 9 homers at the end of spring training in 1963.

Fig. 10   Richard Anthony Allen signed with the Phillies in 1960 for $70,000, the highest bonus ever paid to an African American player at the time. (National Baseball Hall of Fame and Library)

But there was no room for Allen in the Phillies outfield. Wes Covington, Tony Gonzalez, and Johnny Callison were proven veterans who gave the club an exceptional blend of speed, defense, and power-hitting. Allen, on the other hand, was only twenty years old, and management believed he needed more seasoning in the minors, this time at their Triple A club in Little Rock, Arkansas. If any possibility existed for being promoted, Allen himself had dashed that hope when he asked for a $50 raise as a symbolic reward for his season at Double A. John Quinn, the Phils' general manager, interpreted the request as a *demand* by an ungrateful prospect who had been given the opportunity of a professional career.[3]

When he learned of the Phillies' plans to send him to Little Rock—a segregated city with a team that had never fielded an African American player—Allen pleaded with Quinn to reconsider, but Quinn refused to listen.[4] Allen would become the first black ballplayer in Arkansas history, something the Phillies would later regret.

Richie Allen was the cornerstone of the team's rebuilding process and a player who would become the Phillies' first black superstar. Owner Bob Carpenter had planned it that way. By 1960, Carpenter, who had valuable family connections to the mammoth Du Pont Company, had had his fill of losing seasons. His unfulfilled expectations in an aging group of Whiz Kids and younger playboy athletes convinced him it was time to rebuild.[5] Manager Eddie Sawyer confirmed that belief when, after losing the first game of the 1960 campaign, he resigned. Frustrated at the prospect of another tail-ender, Sawyer explained his decision to Quinn, saying: "I'm forty-nine years old, and I'd love to live to be fifty."[6] The Phillies general manager seized the opportunity to overhaul the club. He started at the top, immediately hiring Gene Mauch as skipper. While neither man could be mistaken for a progressive thinker when it came to race relations, both understood that integrating the Phillies was the only way to ensure future success on the playing field and at the gate.[7]

Quinn, whose father was president of the Boston Red Sox and, later, the Boston Braves, was the architect of the 1957 World Champion Milwaukee Braves. It was an integrated team that contended throughout the 1950s and included such stars as Eddie Mathews, Hank Aaron, Red Schoendienst, Wes Covington, and Lew Burdette. What's more, Quinn's dealing came at bargain-basement prices. He excelled at negotiating minimum salary contracts and extracting top dollar from other clubs for stars in the twilight of their careers. He would perfect the strategy in Philadelphia.[8] Mauch,

manager of the Minneapolis Millers of the American Association, comple-
mented the general manager's tough-minded ways.

At thirty-four years of age, Mauch was a young disciplinarian who had
come up through the Brooklyn Dodgers organization in the late 1940s.
Having played for Branch Rickey, he experienced firsthand the process of
integration and learned to respect the abilities of his black teammates. At
the same time, his career batting average of .239 underscored that the game
had not come easy to him.[9] He was a better tactician than player, and one
who studied the game with exceptional attention to detail, a trait that
would later earn him the moniker "Little General." On good days, Mauch
was able to "steal a victory by manipulating his roster one step ahead of the
opposing manager." On bad days, he would overmanage, costing his team a
victory that had been within reach. No one could deny, however, that Mauch
had the temperament to manage. He was surly, sharp-witted, and refused to
back down from anyone, regardless of size or authority. The sportswriters
loved him for the ease with which he conducted a postgame interview, serving up some of the most colorful—if not unprintable—quotes imaginable.[10]

When he assumed the Phillies post in the spring of 1960, Mauch immediately set a new tone. In a closed-door clubhouse meeting, he criticized the
players' off-the-field behavior and set a strict curfew. "I want my players
to realize that baseball is their livelihood—not a way to have fun," he stated.
"My ultimate goal is to get this ball club to a point where it won't need
rules. But now they take privileges that good players on other clubs have
to ask for. I think if a player doesn't have respect for himself, he'll have a
hard time getting respect from someone else."[11]

Mauch, who was known to use racially inflammatory language, may not
have been color-blind, but he, like Quinn, certainly seemed to be "color
neutral" when it came to judging a player's abilities. Scouting reports indicate that the number of minority players in the Phillies farm system, which
consisted of approximately 200 players on ten teams, jumped from three
in 1958 to thirty-eight in 1961 and steadily increased through the mid-
1960s.[12] Among the more talented African American players in addition to
Richie Allen were outfielders Johnny Briggs, Richard and Robert Haines,
Alex Johnson, Larry Hisle, and Ted Savage, and pitchers Grant Jackson and
Ferguson Jenkins. The Phillies did not spare much expense in signing that
talent. With the exception of Jackson, who signed for a $1,500 bonus, the
others received bonuses of $8,000 or more. Briggs and Jenkins received
$8,000 each; Savage signed for $17,500; Johnson, for $18,000; the Haines

Fig. 11   Gene Mauch *(far right)* managed the first integrated team in Philadelphia's baseball history, with such star performers as *(left to right)* infielder Cookie Rojas, outfielder Johnny Callison, and third baseman Richie Allen. (*Philadelphia Daily News*)

brothers, for $40,000 each; Hisle, for $50,000; and Allen for the unprecedented sum of $70,000.[13] Similar white talent signed during the 1960s often received lower bonuses. Outfielder Joe Lis, for example, signed for $15,000 in 1964. Rick Wise, who would become the most consistent Phillies pitcher in the late 1960s, signed for $12,000 in 1963. And shortstop Larry Bowa, who would serve as the sparkplug for the pennant-contending Phillies of the late 1970s, received only $2,000 for signing in 1965.[14] If there was a racial bias in the Phillies' signing of prospects, it certainly seemed to favor the African American players. Indeed, integration was a conscious process.

Player records from the early to mid-1960s emphasize the race of African American prospects. The scouting report on outfielders Richard and Robert Haines, for example, refer to them as "broad-shouldered Negroes." Ted Savage is listed as a "Negro athlete with good outfield potential because of his speed." In addition, a separate roster of "Negro Players in Philadelphia National League Organization" was kept during the 1960s and listed both African American and Hispanic players. Of the thirty-four minority players identified on the 1960 roster, twenty four were African American, though none played on the major league club. Of the ten Latino players six were on the big league roster: Ruben Amaro, Ruben Gomez, Tony Gonzalez, Francisco Herrera, Humberto Robinson, and Tony Taylor.[15]

Although the Phillies were not the only major league organization to blur the identities of these two groups of players, the misconception that Hispanics were "Negroes" indicates a racial stereotyping by the team. The term *Hispanic* is an ethnic label, not a racial one. Hispanics are a racially mixed group, which includes combinations of European White, African Black, and indigenous American Indian. Just as in the African American community, there can be wide color variations in the same family.[16] The Phillies' careful recording and purposeful obfuscation of minority players was consistent with major league baseball's self-congratulatory attitude toward integration during the 1960s. It also made a liar out of Baseball Commissioner Ford Frick, who in 1963 extolled the virtues of integration before the Senate Commerce Committee.

Responding to an inquiry from Senator Warren Magnuson of Washington about the number of blacks in major league baseball, Frick replied: "We keep batting averages, pitching records, fielding, and other statistics, but no records on whether players are African American, white, or yellow because they are selected on the basis of whether they can pitch, hit, and field."[17] Shortly afterward, *The Sporting News* praised Frick's testimony, calling integration in baseball a "fait accompli." What's more, the publication boasted that Little Rock, Arkansas, "welcomed Richie Allen, the first Negro player to wear a Travelers' uniform," showing that "Negroes and whites could work together in perfect harmony and understanding."[18] But Allen certainly didn't see it that way.

At Little Rock, Allen was immersed in a racist environment that operated on stereotypes of African Americans as "troublemakers," "criminals," and "ignorant laborers." His emotional response was anger, confusion, and alienation. On opening night a capacity crowd of 7,000 fans packed Little Rock's Ray Winder Stadium to see history in the making. Outside, signs that read "DON'T NEGRO-IZE BASEBALL" and "NIGGER GO HOME" greeted Allen at the park. Inside sat Governor Orval Faubus, best known for his unsuccessful attempt to bar black students from Little Rock's Central High School just six years earlier. Faubus was waiting to throw out the ceremonial first pitch. Allen was scared.

Starting in left field for the Travelers that night, he botched the very first ball hit out to him. "It was a lazy fly," he recalled. "I just froze, then I took a few steps in and the ball flew over my head. I missed that ball because I was scared, and I don't mind saying it."[19] Later in the game, he made up for his miscue by hitting two doubles. The second one set up the Travelers' game-winning rally.

After the game, Allen purposely waited until the clubhouse cleared before walking out to the parking lot. "When I got to my car," he said, "I found a note on the windshield. It said. 'DON'T COME BACK AGAIN, NIGGER.' I felt scared and alone, and, what's worse, my car was the last one in the parking lot. There might be something more terrifying than being black and holding a note that says 'NIGGER' in an empty parking lot in Little Rock, Arkansas, in 1963, but if there is, it certainly hasn't crossed my path yet."[20]

Things only seemed to get worse as the season unfolded. Allen was forced to live with a family on the African American side of town and could not be served in a restaurant unless accompanied by a white player. He was stopped routinely by local police for no apparent reason, he received threatening telephone calls, and he was forced to endure the epithets of racist fans. Through it all, there was little support from the Phillies organization. With the exceptions of teammates Lee Elia and Pat Corrales, who encouraged the young prospect, Allen was a loner. Manager Frank Lucchesi, who had also been promoted from Williamsport in 1963, treated Allen just like any other ballplayer. "I had a lot of confidence in Richie," said Lucchesi in a recent interview. "Sure, he was treated poorly when he first came to Little Rock. But by the end of the season, Richie had won over the fans.

They voted him Most Valuable Player of the team that year. Do fans who hate a player vote him MVP and give him a new suit?"[21] To be sure, Lucchesi respected Allen's abilities, but he certainly could not relate to the young player's circumstances. In fact, no one could really understand Allen's situation.

Born on March 8, 1942, in the small town of Wampum, Pennsylvania, thirty miles northwest of Pittsburgh, Allen was raised with a deep respect for religion by his mother, Era. Her God-fearing ways underscored both the compassion and the hard-line discipline she employed to nurture a close-knit family in this predominantly white but integrated community.[22] With a population of only 1,000 residents, Wampum was in economic decline, its once-thriving steel and cement industries having been closed.[23] Race meant little in a community where everyone was poor.

As a child, Allen was accepted by the town's white youngsters as "one of their own" because of his athletic prowess. When an injury to Allen's right eye left the eyelid slightly contorted, they gave him the nickname "Sleepy" as a term of endearment.[24] By the time he was a senior at Wampum High School, Allen had established himself as an all-around athlete. One of only five African Americans in a class of 146 students, he excelled at sports because it gave him an identity that allowed him to be accepted by his white classmates. Following in the footsteps of his older brothers, Allen became the star of the basketball team. As captain and starting guard, he led Wampum to the Class B state championship.[25] But it was his baseball talent that in 1960 captured the attention of John Ogden, a gruff, no-nonsense sixty-six-year-old scout for the Phillies.

Ogden was rare among major league scouts. A member of the Religious Society of Friends and a graduate of Swarthmore College, his intellect was surpassed only by his ability to earn the trust of a young prospect. Whether it was his Quaker faith or his genuine humanity, the veteran scout refused to judge a prospect by skin color. Talent and personal character were the defining measures of the athletes he pursued. For Ogden, ability was less difficult to judge than character, which could be determined only by how the prospect handled himself off the playing field. It is not surprising that Ogden courted both his prospects and their families. He visited their homes, sat down to supper with them, and listened to their concerns.[26] Allen, a broad-shouldered high school athlete, was a "can't miss" prospect in terms of both talent and character. Ogden was just as impressed with the deference and respect he showed toward his mother as he was with Allen's ability to hit a baseball. Endearing himself to Era Allen, the veteran scout courted the entire family and agreed to sign all three of her sons to Phillies contracts. A personal visit by former Negro League great William "Judy" Johnson, who had recently joined the Phillies scouting ranks, sealed the deal.[27] "I don't think there was a greater scout in the game at that time," Allen said of Ogden, years later. "The thing that appealed to me most about him was his honesty. Everything he promised to me or to my mother he delivered. Nothing had to be written. His handshake was as good as his word."[28]

But in 1963 Allen believed that the Phillies were using him to break the color barrier in Arkansas: that the front office viewed him as Philadelphia's own "Jackie Robinson," and that his presence in Little Rock would be the club's first step toward dismantling its infamous reputation as a racist organization. What is worse, the Phillies neglected Allen, forcing him to fend for himself in an overtly racist environment.

"Sixty-three was the first season for Triple-A ball down there," Allen recalled. "It was the first season with the Phillies as parent club—and no blacks. They had no choice but to bust it. I didn't know anything about the race issue in Arkansas and didn't really care. Maybe if the Phillies had called me in, man to man, like the Dodgers had done with Jackie Robinson, and said, 'Dick, this is what we have in mind. It's going to be very difficult but we're with you'—at least I would have been prepared. I'm not saying I would have liked it. But I would have known what to expect. Instead I was on my own. Frank Lucchesi didn't understand me as a person. What did he know about abuse? While I was in bed listening to gunshots, he was eating at the best restaurants in Little Rock. Frank had only one thing in mind that year: managing in the majors. Richie Allen had only one thing in mind: playing in the majors. Lucchesi may not have liked the fact that I was going to get there before him."[29]

Allen was only twenty years old when he arrived in Little Rock. He was not familiar with southern culture or the manner in which the town's African Americans navigated the racial discrimination they experienced on a daily basis. He was an angry young man, left on his own without any support from an organization that refused to protect him. "There were fans in Little Rock who truly loved the game," admitted Allen. "For some of them, color didn't matter. I gathered my strength from them. But there were others who got off on racial intimidation. Between innings, coming in from the outfield to the dugout, I would hear the voices—'Hey, Chocolate Drop' or 'Watch your back, nigger.' I would look up, but I could never find the guy who made the remark. Racist fans have a way of hissing and mumbling under their breath that makes them hard to locate. Black players know this, and after a while learn not to look up. I would have loved to go a round with any one of them. I think a one-on-one slugfest with one of those racist cowards would have given me the release I needed."[30]

Robert "Ruly" Carpenter III, son of the Phils' owner and an administrator in the low minors, believes it wasn't that the Phillies *refused* to protect Allen as much as that they *didn't know how.* "Little Rock was a hotbed of racial unrest in the early 1960s," he said. "It wasn't a great place to be for a black ballplayer, and it was unfortunate that the Phillies had the Triple A club down there. But we did, and we were under contract to be there. It didn't make sense to keep Richie at [Double A] Williamsport. He wouldn't have gotten the kind of playing experience he needed there. We had no choice."[31]

Somehow, Allen managed to do more than survive. He compiled a .289 average, leading the International League in home runs (33), RBIs (97), and triples (12). The Phillies called him up in September, and he proceeded to hit major league pitching at a .292 clip. After the season was over, Allen declared that he was "ready for the majors," explaining that he "started out the season by pressing because I was the first colored player Little Rock ever had." But the September call-up and the experience he had that month showed him that "baseball is baseball, regardless of the level of competition" and that he "had the ability to move up."[32] Even though the Traveler fans voted Allen the team's Most Valuable Player, the discrimination he experienced at Little Rock left him bitter and distrustful of the Phillies organization.[33] It also made the organization's other African American prospects wary of playing for Little Rock.

"When I signed to play for the Phillies in 1963, my father insisted that I not play minor league ball in the South," said Johnny Briggs. "The Phillies were clear on that, and they sent me to Class A in Bakersfield, California. The very next year they promoted me to the big club and kept me there. If they didn't do that they knew they'd lose me to the draft because back then any player receiving a signing bonus of $8,000 or more had to be protected. I was lucky because that rule kept me from having the same experience as Richie."[34] Grant Jackson, who came from the poor black neighborhoods of Fostoria, Ohio, was not as fortunate. Signed by the Phillies in 1961 for the bargain sum of $1,500, Jackson didn't enjoy the luxury of being rushed to the majors. Instead, he climbed his way up the ladder, finding himself at Triple A Little Rock in 1964. "I didn't have a choice," he said years later. "If I wanted to make it to the majors, I had to go through Little Rock.

I experienced a lot of the same stuff as Richie, but I learned not to let it bother me. If anything, he paved the way for me. Besides, I knew going in there that a black ballplayer would have to fight harder than a white one to be promoted."[35] After the 1965 season, the Phillies moved their Triple A club to San Diego.[36] Perhaps they had finally learned from their mistake.

Ruly Carpenter discounts the theory that his father consciously integrated the team. "There's no question that the object of the organization was to put the best athletes you could find on the field, whether they were white, African American, or Hispanic," he said. "By the early 1960s everyone in baseball realized that there was a tremendous talent pool in the black community. The Phillies needed to draw from that pool because we certainly didn't have much in the way of talent in the system, at least in the low minors. So, we beefed up the full- and part-time scouting to find that talent in the United States. We also increased our presence in the Latin American countries and hired black scouts like [Negro League Hall of Famer] Judy Johnson, who was a father figure to many of the black and Latino players we were bringing into the organization at that time."[37]

To be sure, Philadelphia's rebuilding process was not limited to African American talent. The elimination of the color barrier in 1947 opened the door for Hispanic players as well. Although light-complexioned Latinos, easily mistaken for white players, had been in major league baseball since 1911, darker-skinned talent from Cuba, Venezuela, Panama, Mexico, and Puerto Rico was now being recruited by many American teams. Most of the players came from poor households and played baseball year-round. Scouts knew they could sign them cheaply. Predictably, the Caribbean was becoming a vital source of new—and inexpensive—talent for the major leagues.[38]

The Phillies tapped this small but highly talented pool of Hispanic players in 1957 when they acquired Chico Fernandez from the Brooklyn Dodgers and made him their regular shortstop. During the next two years they would sign or trade for a host of other Latinos, including Francisco "Pancho" Herrera, a twenty-four-year-old Cuban-born first baseman; and Ruben Amaro, a twenty-three-year-old Mexican-born shortstop who had played in the Cardinals organization. Quinn continued to recruit and sign Hispanic talent. In 1960 he acquired Tony Taylor, a twenty-five-year-old Cuban-born infielder, from the Chicago Cubs, along with catcher Cal Neeman, for veterans Ed Bouchee and Don Cardwell.[39] He dealt outfield veterans Wally Post and Harry Anderson to Cincinnati for twenty-three-year-old Tony Gonzalez, another Cuban-born player who would become the team's regular centerfielder.[40]

Herrera, Amaro, Taylor, and Gonzalez all had an immediate impact. During the 1960 season, the young quartet helped the club both at the plate and in the field. Taylor hit .287 and became a fan favorite at second base. Before each at-bat, the Cuban infielder said a prayer, asking for the Lord's help, blessed himself, and stepped into the batter's box to hit. Together with his upbeat personality and hustling style of play, the humble ritual endeared him to Phillies fans. Herrera, a 6-foot-3-inch 230-pound slugger, batted .281 with 17 homers and 71 RBIs. Gonzalez was called "Little Dynamite" by his teammates because of his explosive speed. The outfielder hit .299 with 33 RBIs while playing a near flawless center field. Amaro only hit .231, but he gave the Phils a solid defense at shortstop.[41] While all four of the players were initially disappointed when they learned that they were being traded, each quickly adapted to Philadelphia and discovered little difference from their original club in the way they were treated as persons of color.

"The United States, in general, was a very tough place to play for Latin American players," Taylor recalled. "Few Cuban ballplayers wanted to play in this country because of the discrimination. There was no distinction made between us and black players, especially dark-skinned Latin players. You had to room at a separate hotel. You couldn't eat with your white team-mates. But at least the Cubs had six or seven Latin American players. The Phillies had only one before 1960. I didn't want to play for a team like that."

"When I was given the news that I was traded to Philadelphia, I thought about quitting baseball and going back to Cuba," he admitted. "But my first game in with the Phillies, we played against the Cincinnati Reds. I got three hits and the fans made me feel wanted. From that day on, the Phillies were my team."[42]

Amaro thought he would play his entire career with the St. Louis Cardinals because of his fine defensive skills and the organization's need for a shortstop. Manager Fred Hutchinson thought so as well, routinely promoting Amaro through the farm system. But when Hutchinson resigned as the Cards manager at the end of the 1958 season, he was replaced by Solly Hemus, who had different plans. "Hemus always seemed to have reasons for trading or holding back certain players," said Amaro. "He didn't like Curt Flood because he was too small, and wanted to replace him in center field with Ken Boyer. He thought Bob Gibson would never be able to throw the ball over the plate. These were two of the best prospects in the Cardinals organization, one of whom went on to become a Hall of Famer. Apparently, Hemus didn't want too many dark-skinned players on his club."[43]

Fig. 12   When the Chicago Cubs traded Tony Taylor to the Phillies in 1960, the scrappy infielder considered quitting baseball and returning home to Cuba. Instead, he quickly won over the fans and enjoyed a fifteen-year playing career in Philadelphia. (Philadelphia Phillies)

The dark-skinned Amaro, whose paternal ancestors were African Moors, routinely experienced discrimination as a minor leaguer in the Texas League. Like Taylor, he gave serious consideration to quitting baseball and returning home to pursue a career in academia. But his father, who played professional ball in Mexico and Cuba, discouraged the idea. "We couldn't change the times," said Ruben. "Latinos, like the black players, had to live and eat in places that we didn't want to. It was that way in St. Louis and also in Philadelphia, at least in spring training at Clearwater. I remember the NAACP considering a boycott of the Phillies in 1960 because the team didn't have any black players. But there were Hispanic players—myself, Tony Gonzalez, Tony Taylor, and Pancho Herrera. We got along well with the white players like Art Mahaffey, Chris Short, Dallas Green. I came up in Buffalo with those players, and it really helped that all of us were young and starting out with the Phillies at the same time."

"If the Phillies had a race problem," he added, "it was the fault of the scouting system, and especially those scouts who came from the South who refused to sign black players."[44]

Gonzalez, who was originally signed by the Cincinnati Reds, agreed. "I don't think it was any different in Philadelphia than it was in any other major league city in those days," he said. "I remember going for a haircut in Cincinnati and the barber refused to cut my hair because I wasn't white. They also had segregation in spring training in Florida. So when I came to the Phillies it wasn't much of a problem. In fact, I thought the Phillies treated me better than the Reds. When I first came over, they made me an everyday player, and the fans treated me great from day one."[45]

Integrating the Phillies, however, was not a smooth process on or off the field. In 1960 the team finished last for the third straight year. The pitching staff was mediocre. The only starter to win more than eight games was aging veteran Robin Roberts, who posted a 12–16 record, and his days were numbered. Dick Farrell (10–6, 70 K, 2.71 ERA), Art Mahaffey (7–3, 56 K, 2.31 ERA), and Jack Meyer (3–1, 18 K, 4.32 ERA) posted winning records, but Mahaffey was the only one of the three who had any future.[46] Farrell and Meyer, along with pitcher Jim Owens, were better known for their wild-living ways off the field than for their on-field performances.

Dubbed the "Dalton Gang" by the sportswriters after outlaws from the Old West, the three hurlers, once thought to be "colorful," had fallen out of favor with both management and the writers by the end of the season. Meyer, the son of an affluent New Jersey family, was a graduate of Philadelphia's prestigious William Penn Charter School and attended Wake Forest and the University of Delaware. Blond-haired, handsome, and a stylish dresser, he suffered from an insatiable need to capture the limelight off the field. Once, the flame-throwing reliever tried to pick a fight with *Inquirer* sportswriter Allen Lewis outside a Pittsburgh night spot. The drunken Meyer was restrained by his roommate, Harry Anderson, who somehow managed to get him back to their hotel room. While laying waste to the room, Meyer injured his back. Mauch sent him back to Philadelphia the next day to get himself checked out. Quinn, upon learning of the pitcher's tirade, slapped him with a $1,200 fine, roughly 9 percent of Meyer's $14,000 salary. Meyer was furious.

"What does he think I am, a millionaire?" he complained to Carpenter. "I've got four kids to support."

Meyer not only threatened the Phillies owner with a lawyer to fight the fine, but also asked for his unconditional release so he could sign with another team.[47] The Phillies obliged the following year and, at the age of twenty-nine, Jack Meyer's major league career was over.[48]

Farrell, from a quiet middle-class Boston family, had overcome polio in his youth, but made up for his mild-mannered adolescence in the majors by initiating barroom brawls. Owens was worse. The product of a broken home, he started drinking at an early age. Quinn promised him a $500 bonus if he improved on the twelve wins he recorded in 1959 but also control his off-the-field behavior. Owens didn't even make it through spring training, getting involved in a barroom fight. He lost the bonus, and he was fined an additional $100. Both Farrell and Owens were also shown the door.[49]

Chris Short, a twenty-three-year-old southpaw who had been rushed to the majors the previous year, showed some promise in 1960, posting a 6–9 record with a 3.95 ERA. But Mahaffey was by far the brightest pitching prospect in the organization.[50] At 6 feet 1 inch and 185 pounds, he was big and strong and had a blazing fastball. Shortly after being brought up from Triple A Buffalo in late July, Mahaffey registered five straight victories. When the Phils returned from their road trip with a 6–18 record, Mahaffey felt justified in approaching Quinn for the additional $2,500 he was due as a major leaguer. Quinn refused the raise, insisting that the youngster could not make more than the $7,500 minor league rate until he had spent a full year in the majors. When Mahaffey threatened to telephone Warren Giles, president of the National League, Quinn relented and gave him the money.[51] It would be one of many confrontations the Phillies general manager would have with the members of the young team he was building.

Another bright spot for the Phillies in 1960 was Clay Dalrymple, a strong-armed catcher who was drafted from Sacramento in the Pacific Coast League for $25,000 the previous year. Initially assigned to veteran receiver Cal Neeman to learn how to improve his defensive skills, Dalrymple made himself useful as a pinch hitter. Going 12 for 42 in that role, Dalrymple batted a respectable .272 in eighty-two games for the Phillies that year while collecting 21 RBIs. Impressed with his pitch-calling, Phillies ace Robin Roberts went to Mauch and asked that the young backstop catch him on a regular basis, and, by August, Dalrymple was the team's regular catcher as well.[52]

Of all the acquisitions made by Quinn during his first year as general manager, Johnny Callison proved to be the most outstanding one. Callison, a strong-armed outfielder, had been dubbed "the next Mickey Mantle" by many baseball insiders who followed his climb through the Chicago White Sox farm system in the mid-1950s. But after the 1959 season when he hit only .173 with 3 home runs and 12 RBIs, Chicago, the American League pennant winners that year, gave up on him. In January 1960, while playing winter ball in Venezuela, Callison was traded to the Phillies for popular veteran third baseman Gene Freese. "I was very bitter about being traded," admitted Callison years later. "I was confused and couldn't understand what I had done wrong. I also became depressed. I didn't want to play for the Phillies. They were the worst team in baseball, and I had just come from the best in the American League."[53]

Realizing that he had been traded for a popular veteran player in Gene Freese, Callison tried too hard to be successful. The harder he tried, the worse he played. What made matters worse was that Mauch platooned the youngster, playing him only against right-handers. "I hated Gene Mauch at first," admitted Callison. "He was a real cocky type of guy, a very different personality than mine. Because he didn't play me regularly, I had trouble reading the hitters in the outfield and I couldn't get into any kind of a groove at the plate. The fans certainly didn't appreciate that. They tried to get rid of me by throwing pennies at me. I must have made at least $10 in one stretch of home games! Soon the money turned into beer cans and I was playing ball with one eye on the stands and the other on the hitter."[54] Despite the slow start, Callison completed the season with a .260 average, 9 home runs, and 30 RBIs.

Things didn't get much better for the Phillies in 1961. During spring training, the Jack Tar Hotel in Clearwater, where the Phillies lodged, refused to accommodate Mexican-born infielder Ruben Amaro. When Dallas

Green, the team's player representative, confronted the hotel manager, he was told that African American as well as Hispanic players were not given rooms as "a matter of policy." Green, with the permission of John Quinn, made arrangements for the team at another hotel, only to discover that although Amaro was permitted to room with his teammates there he would not be served in the cafeteria. The incident left the young team with a bad taste. Many of the white players had never witnessed racism. They accepted Amaro, not only as a teammate but also as a person. If there was not yet a "color-blind" policy in accepting teammates, it began on that day.[55]

While the Phillies might have struggled against racism off the field, their general manager made them a more competitive team on the field, at least on paper. Quinn improved the club through trades. Farrell was dealt to the Los Angeles Dodgers for Don Demeter, a soft-spoken slugger who contributed 20 home runs and 68 RBIs. Together with Gonzalez (.277, 12 HRs, 58 RBIs) and Callison (.247, 9 HRs, 47 RBIs), the Phils showed real promise in the outfield.[56] Quinn also brought Wes Covington, a power-hitting outfielder who led the Milwaukee Braves to a world championship in 1957, from the Kansas City Athletics. Called "The Lumberman" for being one of the best clutch hitters in the majors, Covington added another 7 home runs and 26 RBIs to the Phillies' offensive attack while hitting .303.[57] He also became the first African American with any substantial playing time on the Phillies. Ruben Amaro was made the regular shortstop, and Bobby Wine, a strong-armed prospect from nearby Norristown, filled in as a backup. Together with second baseman Tony Taylor, Amaro and Wine gave the Phils an excellent defense in the middle infield.

The pitching was not as solid. Hampered by a knee injury, Robin Roberts was at loggerheads with Mauch throughout the season. "He throws like Betsy Ross," said the Phillies skipper, disgusted with the future Hall-of-Famer's performance. Roberts, who completed the season with a dismal 1–10 record, was sold to the Yankees for a reported $25,000.[58] Art Mahaffey went 11–19, but also recorded 158 strikeouts and looked to be the future ace of the team. In an April 23 game, he fanned seventeen hitters en route to a four-hit shutout of the Chicago Cubs. At the time, the feat tied the National League record held by Dizzy Dean and was just one short of the major league record held by Bob Feller.[59]

Quinn bolstered the bullpen with Jack Baldschun, a castoff from the Cincinnati Reds. At the age of twenty-four, Baldschun was laboring in the minors when he discovered how to throw a screwball. "I was a .500 pitcher," admitted the future Phillie closer. "Didn't have an overpowering fastball.

Fig. 13 Jack Baldschun resurrected his pitching career by learning the screwball. Between 1962 and 1964 he won twenty-nine games and saved fifty others for the Phillies. (Philadelphia Phillies)

Didn't have a curve. I had a decent slider and a good sinker. But I was going nowhere after four years in the Reds organization. My wife wanted me to quit baseball. Then I came up with a screwball. I could make it go down and in, or down and away. That screwball kept me in the majors. No doubt about that."[60] Baldschun ended the 1961 campaign with a 3.87 ERA and the only winning record on the pitching staff (5–3), while leading the National League in appearances with sixty-five. His earned run average would continue to drop during the next two seasons.[61]

But 1961 is best remembered as the season in which the Phillies hit rock bottom. Not only did the team finish last for the fourth straight season, but the Phils suffered a twenty-three-game losing streak, a major league record that still stands today. It began on July 29 with a 4–3 loss to the San Francisco Giants at home. The Phils dropped the second game of that series the following day, 5–2, before heading out on a seven-game road trip to Cincinnati and St. Louis. With the exceptions of a 7–1 rout by the Reds and a 7–0 whitewashing by the Cards, all the losses were by only one or two runs. The Phils returned home on August 7 and extended their losing streak to thirteen games, dropping three more to Pittsburgh and another to Cincinnati. On August 17 the Phils lost their twentieth straight game, this one at Chicago, 9–2.[62] "It was a nightmare," said Tony Gonzalez. "You would walk onto the field feeling like you were never going to win again. Something always seemed to happen. We'd score two, but then the other team would come right back with three or four runs."[63] In fact, eight of the team's losses were by a single run. Nothing they seemed to do helped. "Gene did everything to put an end to the streak," said Baldschun. "He put a curfew on, made us work out before and after games. One time he even threatened to fine us if we were in our hotel room *before* 4:30 A.M. We didn't know where the hell to go after the bars closed. So we all crashed in the hotel lobby until 4:30 in the morning and then went to our rooms. It still didn't help. The next day we lost again."[64]

Even the newspapers in other cities were covering the losing streak with a macabre fascination. "To lose 20 straight ball games takes quite a bit of doing," reported the *New York Herald Tribune*. "And if the Phillies have not yet exhausted the possibilities of losing ball games, they certainly have explored them thoroughly. They have lost games in the first inning and in the ninth, on the mound, at the plate, and in the field. They have employed all the old methods and developed a few news ones. We make these observations with sympathy and even respect. There has been suspense in watching the Phillies lose. How long can they keep it up? When will their luck change? Can they go on like this forever? These are the questions being asked today—and probably tomorrow. And we hate to think of the answers."[65]

To add insult to injury, Callison's daughter, Cindy, came down with meningitis during the losing streak. Because the Phillies were on the road, he asked Mauch if he could go home, and the Phils' skipper granted him permission. Quinn was furious when he found out about it, and he demanded that Callison rejoin the team the very next day. The general manager responded in a similar fashion when Demeter asked to go home to be with his wife, who was in labor. "If you stay with your wife, I'll ship you back to the minors," Quinn threatened.[66]

John Buzhardt finally put an end to the Phils' misery on August 20 when he won the second game of a Sunday doubleheader at Milwaukee, 7–4. After the game, third baseman Lee Walls approached Mauch in the clubhouse and deadpanned: "Skip, we got you this far—now you're on your own!" Mauch grinned and said he was glad he was only thirty-five years old. "This kind of thing could kill an older manager." Then he shook his head and added, "I don't know why I'm trying to be funny with one victory in twenty-four games." Buzhardt, the winning pitcher, just sat in front of his locker angry that "nobody bothered to mention the double I hit."[67] That same night, about 150 fans waited at Philadelphia International Airport to greet the team. When he saw the crowd from the plane window, pitcher Frank Sullivan remarked to his teammates: "They're selling rocks at a dollar a pail. Get off in twos and threes so they can't get us all with one burst!"[68]

Despite all the losing, the Phillies still had a sense of humor, and maybe more. Mauch believed that the losing streak had actually molded his young players into a team. "We have a young team," he said. "We're building for the future. I think all the losing probably brought the team together and made them think of themselves as Phillies, instead of ex-Braves, or ex-Cubs or whatever. That's probably why they kept battling through all those losses. I never saw or heard of a team—winner or loser—which fought any harder than this one. It's something they should be proud of."[69]

To be sure, there was not a lot to be proud of in 1961 if you were a Phillies fan. The Phils were a bad team, and they played in an obsolete ballpark. Opened in 1909, Shibe Park was originally the home of the American League's Philadelphia Athletics, a team with a much more storied history than the Phillies, who moved into the park in 1938. Once compared to a French Renaissance castle in its appearance, the ballpark's name was changed to Connie Mack Stadium in 1953 and looked more like a run-down warehouse by the 1960s. Over the years, several patchwork additions for more seating and office space were made. If not for the two grandstand walls joined at Twenty-First and Lehigh where the domed tower of the entrance stood, it would be difficult to see any resemblance to the original ballpark.[70]

Inside, space was limited. The dugouts were smaller than those of many of the existing parks around the National League, and the clubhouse was just as crowded. The main locker area had a cold concrete floor and was bounded by a small manager's office at one end and an equipment room at the other. There were only five showers, so players were forced to take turns. The team's trainer worked in a small loft jammed with a whirlpool, a diathermy machine, two rubbing tables, and a supply cabinet.

Above the clubhouse were the offices of Owner Bob Carpenter, General Manager John Quinn, and Farm Director Paul Owens. Larry Shenk, public relations director, had his office above the employee entrance at Twenty-First and Lehigh. The traveling secretary and the sales and promotion staff also had their offices in this area. The Phillies finance department worked in a third set of offices in the domed tower at the corner of Twenty-First and Lehigh.[71] "None of the offices were connected," recalled Shenk. "If I wanted to see the general manager, I had to go down one flight of stairs, across the third-base side of the concourse, and up another flight of stairs. It was a tough place to communicate. You had to do it mostly by telephone because we were so spread out."[72] The press box, located at the top of the second level, seated about forty writers and presented a similar challenge. "You'd get there by taking an elevator to the press box level and then navigating a little catwalk from the landing," recalled Allen Lewis, who covered the Phillies for the *Inquirer*. "It wasn't the easiest place to get to. The press box was also pretty high, so you didn't see ground balls too well, though you did have a nice view of the entire playing field."[73]

At the same time, Connie Mack Stadium was fan-friendly. Admission prices had not increased much since the 1930s. A bleacher seat cost only 75 cents, general admission was $1.50, a reserved seat was $2.25, and a box seat was just a dollar more, $3.25. Fans could purchase a scorecard for 15 cents, and that included a pencil; a soda cost the same. Ortlieb's beer was only 40 cents a can, a hot dog just 50 cents, and Cracker Jack, 25 cents.[74] There was also a special intimacy to the old ballpark. The grandstands, which had a seating capacity of 33,000, hugged the infield, allowing the fans to see the expressions of the players and to feel part of the unfolding drama of the game. The players seemed to respond to the fans' approval or rejection. Adding to the excitement were the idiosyncratic dimensions of the ballpark:

334 feet from home plate down the left-field line; 447 feet to center field; and 329 feet down the right-field line. A 60-foot-long scoreboard in right center field towered above the 34-foot fence on either side. Batted balls hitting the scoreboard were still in play, as were balls hitting a 10-foot-high "Ballantine Beer" sign on top of it. If, however, a ball hit the Longines clock above the beer sign—75 feet above the playing field—it was ruled a home run.[75]

"That big old wall in right center killed me," said Johnny Callison. "It was only 329 to the fence, but the fence was 50 feet high to accommodate the scoreboard. Sure, I'd get a lot of triples off that scoreboard—but they didn't pay you for triples in those days. It was also 447 to center field with a 32-foot fence. Now what kind of a chance did you have to hit a ball out of there?"[76] Despite offensive challenges, shortstop Bobby Wine considered Connie Mack a "romantic ballpark." "It looked like a fortress on the outside, but inside it was a great place to play," he said. "It always gave me a warm feeling. The stands were close along the sidelines, though there was plenty of foul territory. Each spectator's wooden seat made them seem like they were sitting right across from you at the Thanksgiving table."[77]

Whether or not they liked playing at Connie Mack, the Phillies would have to learn to use the park to their own advantage, just as more experienced opponents were doing. If the Phils, for example, managed to get a runner on base and the next hitter drove the ball to right field, opposing outfielders would decoy them, pretending that they were about to make the catch. Speedy runners on first would barely make it to third on a legitimate double. An average runner would stop at first, believing that he'd hit a routine fly. Mauch countered by switching the Phillies bullpen from left to right field and ordering his relievers to wave a white towel whenever a fly ball was going to drop for a hit. Soon after, the Phillies began to capitalize on the strategy. A runner on first scored on a double, and the hitter occasionally stretched a double into a triple. Similarly, Mauch helped his young pitching staff by shaving the front of the mound down so they would keep their fastballs low, creating a better chance for ground ball outs or a strike out.[78]

Mauch's baseball genius and the expansion of the National League enabled the Phillies to climb out of the cellar in 1962. With the addition of the New York Mets and the Houston Colt 45s, the Phils were able to record their first winning season in nearly a decade. Because the schedule was expanded from 154 games to 162, New York and Houston suffered a combined 216 losses, allowing the Phillies to finish seventh instead of dead last.

Quinn also continued to improve the team by trading for proven experience. He acquired power-hitting first baseman Roy Sievers from the White Sox for third baseman Charlie Smith and pitcher John Buzhardt. Sievers struggled to hit above the .200 mark for most of the season, but he came alive in August and finished with a .262 average, 21 homers, and 80 RBIs. Pitcher Cal McLish, acquired from the White Sox in a separate deal, gave a bit more stability to a young pitching staff, contributing eleven victories.[79] The team's nucleus was also beginning to experience success.

Callison, who began the season on the bench, won Mauch's confidence and became the regular right-fielder by hitting .300 and contributing 23 home runs and 83 RBIs. Tony Gonzalez had an outstanding season at the plate, hitting .302 with a career-high 20 home runs, and in the outfield, where he handled all 276 chances without an error. Demeter, playing third base on a regular basis for the first time in his career, hit .307 with 107 RBIs and a team-high 29 homers. Covington (.283, 9 HRs, 44 RBIs) platooned in left field with Ted Savage (.266, 7 HRs, 39 RBIs). Even catcher Clay Dalrymple chipped in with 11 homers while batting .276. Bobby Wine, a sure-handed infielder with excellent range, took over at shortstop for Ruben Amaro, who was serving in the military. Tony Taylor (.259, 7 HRs, 43 RBIs) established himself as captain of the infield and a reliable leadoff hitter.

Mauch also had an up-and-coming pitching staff. Art Mahaffey enjoyed his best season in the majors (19–14, 177 K, 3.94 ERA) and was selected to the National League All-Star team. Jack Baldschun continued to be an effective reliever, going 12–7 with 95 strikeouts and a 2.95 ERA.[80] There were also some solid prospects. Chris Short (11–9, 91 K, 3.42 ERA) and Dennis Bennett (9–9, 149 K, 3.81 ERA) pitched brilliantly at times. Dallas Green (6–6, 58 K, 3.84 ERA), who was being groomed to start, could be just as impressive.[81]

In 1963, Mauch pushed his young team hard, believing that they had the talent to move into the first division. The writers were optimistic too. Hugh Brown of the *Philadelphia Bulletin* compared the young team to the 1950 pennant-winning Whiz Kids and predicted that they would surprise the fans.[82] Ed Richter asked Mauch if he could travel with the Phillies during the 1963 campaign so he could write a book on the trials and tribulations of a manager he considered to be the very best in major league baseball. Richter might have also hoped that *A View from the Dugout: A Season with Baseball's Amazing Gene Mauch* would prove to be the story of a pennant-winning season.[83] Regardless of his intent, Richter did provide some fascinating insight into Mauch's personality.

Noting that the Phillies manager was "quick to talk, quick to sulk, quick to feel hurt, quick to strike back and lash out," Richter also emphasized that his moodiness was tempered by "a complete knowledge of the game" and an "agonizing response to his own failures." Mauch demanded the same relentless drive from his players and would go out of his way to find out what motivated them. One of the hardest things about managing is learning the players—yours and the opposition's," Mauch told Richter. "A manager spends hours and hours—weeks and even months—learning about his players. I wonder how many players take even 15 minutes to learn what kind of manager they're playing for and exactly what his manager expected of him."[84] It was the kind of statement one might expect of a career utility-man who was now trying to make his mark as a manager. While Mauch almost seemed to resent the talent of his young players, he also realized that they were the ticket to whatever success he would enjoy at the big league level. He alternatively coddled and berated them, depending upon their performances, and he had good reason.

The Phillies stumbled out of the gate in 1963 and found themselves mired in last place until mid-July. But they rebounded to win 56 of their last 91 games to finish fourth, and they accomplished this feat largely without their ace, Art Mahaffey, who went down with a torn right ankle in July and did not pitch again until the final week of the season.[85] Instead, Mauch relied on twenty-two-year-old rookie Ray Culp, a $100,000 bonus baby who struggled for three seasons in the minors before reaching the big leagues.[86] Culp chalked up the most victories of any Phillies pitcher that season, and his 176 strikeouts and 2.97 ERA earned him the National League's Rookie Pitcher of the Year honors.[87] Veterans Cal McLish (13–11, 98 K, 3.26 ERA), Dennis Bennett (9–5, 82 K, 2.65 ERA), and Chris Short (9–12, 160 K, 2.95 ERA) also picked up the slack. Dallas Green collected seven key victories, walking only 38 batters in 120 innings. John Boozer, who began the season at Little Rock, was promoted to Philadelphia in mid-season and contributed 69 strikeouts in 83 innings of work. Jack Baldschun (11–7, 89 K, 2.29 ERA) continued to be effective out of the bullpen and got some help from veterans Ryne Duren (6–2, 84 K, 3.31 ERA) and John Klippstein, whose 1.93 ERA inspired the lyrical phrase: "There's still plenty of zip to Klip's flip!"[88]

The regulars were solid. Although veteran first baseman Roy Sievers slipped to .249, he also contributed 19 homers and 82 RBIs. Don Hoak, acquired from Pittsburgh during the winter, was the only other regular over age thirty. While his offensive totals were hardly impressive (.231, 6 HRs, 24 RBIs), Hoak gave the Phils the defensive stability they had lacked at

Fig. 14 Phillies Manager Gene Mauch was nicknamed the "Little General" because of an exceptional mind for strategy as well as for his surly, sharp-witted disposition. (National Baseball Hall of Fame and Library)

third base for some time. Similarly, Clay Dalrymple (.252, 10 HRs, 40 RBIs) was not a power threat, but his exceptional handling of the pitching staff and his rock-solid defense behind the plate were valuable assets to the club. Johnny Callison confirmed Mauch's decision to make him the regular right-fielder by hitting .284 with 26 home runs and 78 RBIs. Tony Gonzalez improved his batting average to .306 and collected career highs in doubles (36) and triples (12), while leading National League outfielders in fielding average (.986) for the second straight year. Tony Taylor's .987 fielding percentage also placed him among the leaders for National League second basemen, while at the plate he rebounded twenty-two points to .281 and collected twenty-three stolen bases.[89]

Mauch also used the platoon system at certain positions. "The schedule gets worse every year," he explained. "We fly thousands of miles, eat inadequately and play longer than we should. No ordinary player can work for 9 innings a game, 162 games a season and still perform at his best. All of the players need an occasional rest. Besides that, there are some players who do better against certain teams. The manager must get the most out of any given nine men on any given day. We have 25 players on this team and I intend to use them all."[90] Mauch was as good as his word. Although he was reluctant to divide playing time at shortstop because of the need for that position to learn opposing team's hitters, he platooned Bobby Wine (.215, 6 HRs, 44 RBIs) and Ruben Amaro (.217, 2 HRs, 19 RBIs). Neither player contributed much to the offensive attack, but both were mercury quick, with good hands, and had a knack for playing the opposing hitters. Aging veterans Wes Covington (.303, 17 HRs, 64 RBIs) and Don Demeter (.258, 22 HRs, 83 RBIs) were also platooned in left field and made the most of the opportunity at the plate.[91] Nor did Mauch forget "the poor guy sitting on the bench."[92] Cookie Rojas, Bob Oldis, and Frank Torre filled valuable roles as pinch hitters, base runners, and defensive replacements. In fact, Rojas eventually transformed the role of "utility player" into an imperative for any team hoping to contend for the pennant by learning to play all nine positions and doing so with the kind of relentless attitude Mauch demanded from his players.[93]

The Phillies played their final eleven games on the road in 1963. After winning two against the lowly Mets, the team split a two-game series at Houston. In the second game, Chris Short carried a 1–0 lead into the ninth when the Colt 45s rallied to tie the game. With two outs and John Klippstein on the mound in relief, rookie Joe Morgan knocked in the winning run with a single to right field. Mauch went berserk.[94] In one of his most memorable clubhouse temper tantrums, the Little General viciously berated his young players for allowing the 5-foot-7-inch Morgan, a "God-damned little leaguer," to get the best of them. To register the point, the infuriated manager proceeded to kick lockers and overturn the food tables.[95] "By the time I got to the clubhouse, the spread was on the floor," recalled Clay Dalrymple. "Half of it was in Covington's locker. I knew the shit had hit the fan. I didn't need anyone to draw me a picture. I looked over to see Covington sitting there holding his silk undershirt stained with chicken cacciatore grease. He didn't know what to say. It was actually kind of funny. But I guess Mauch felt he had to do something. After all, we had beaten Houston seventeen straight that season. If we had won that game, we would have set a major league record for totally dominating another team in a single season."[96]

Mauch's temper tantrum worked. The Phils went on from Houston to take two of three games from San Francisco and sweep the Dodgers in Los Angeles. Their five-game winning streak enabled them to nudge Cincinnati out of fourth place and gain a share of the World Series money.[97]

The player who created the most excitement during that streak, though, was a September call-up from Little Rock who batted .292 while playing seven games in the outfield and one at third base.[98] His name was Richie Allen, a prospect who would almost lead the Phillies to the pennant the following season.

3

THE SPRING OF '64

The Phillies were a long shot to capture the pennant in 1964. A poll of ten National League managers showed the team finishing fifth, while only 10 of the 232 members of the Baseball Writers Association picked them to contend. The consensus among writers, broadcasters, and the professional odds makers was that the Los Angeles Dodgers, behind the dominant pitching of Sandy Koufax and Don Drysdale, would repeat as National League Champions. San Francisco, St. Louis, and Cincinnati all enjoyed better odds of capturing the flag than the Fightin' Phils.[1] But the prognosticators underestimated the team's formidable pitching and defense.

Pitching would be the key to success for the Phils in 1964, and much of that success would depend on the right arm of Jim Bunning. A fierce competitor with the reputation of a "hot head," Bunning, along with catcher Gus Triandos, was acquired from Detroit in the off-season for outfielder Don Demeter and pitcher Jack Hamilton. On paper, the deal looked like a steal for the Phils. Bunning was a five-time All-Star who won more than 100 games over nine seasons with the Tigers and led all American League pitchers in strikeouts during the previous two.[2] He was a proven star. But after fourteen years in the Tigers organization, the native Kentuckian had worn out his welcome. While no one questioned his intelligence or dedication to the game, Manager Chuck Dressen believed that Bunning was through.[3] The fact that he was also the Tigers player representative did not help matters either.

Recognized by the Players' Association as a tough negotiator, Bunning was appointed as the American League pension representative. Together with the Phillies' Richie Ashburn, who was the National League representative, the Tiger hurler succeeded in forcing the owners to diversify the pension plan, making it part fixed income and part variable, which fluctuated with the stock market. Thus, Bunning had earned himself a reputation as a fighter for players' rights in the earliest stage of the union's ongoing— and increasingly antagonistic—battle with management.[4] Predictably, Tiger manager Charley Dressen, in 1963, bounced the thirty-one-year-old right-hander from the starting rotation to make room for a younger prospect, Denny McLain. Having been exiled to the bullpen, Bunning asked for a trade. The Tigers complied, sending him to Philadelphia.[5]

With the addition of Bunning, the Phillies enjoyed one of the strongest starting rotations in the league. Together with Dennis Bennett and Art Mahaffey, who had been hampered by injuries in 1963, the three pitchers could easily improve the team's 87–75 record of the previous year. Another ten or fifteen victories would place them in the thick of the pennant race. The Phillies also had depth at pitching with Ray Culp, who compiled the most wins on the staff (with fourteen in 1963), and Chris Short as the other starters. Dallas Green and John Boozer were projected as spot starters, while Ryne Duren, Jack Baldschun, and Johnny Klippstein anchored a strong relief corps. If the pitchers remained healthy, the Phillies would contend.

Just as critical to the team's success was its defense, and the Phillies enjoyed one of the strongest up the middle with their platoon system. Clay Dalrymple and Gus Triandos were experienced catchers with strong arms. Mauch planned to use Triandos behind the plate against left-handers, and Dalrymple against right-handers. Although the Phils' veteran catcher was not too happy about splitting time with the recently acquired Triandos, he understood the benefit of platooning. "Having Gus here ought to mean having a better year for the club and for me," he admitted. "A lot of injuries come from getting tired and falling into a rut. When I did get a rest last year, it was against a left-handed pitcher. This year we should get a solid .270 out of both catchers."[6]

Fig. 15 Jim Bunning was the ace of the Phillies pitching staff in 1964, but his active involvement in the Players Union resulted in a trade to Pittsburgh in 1967. (National Baseball Hall of Fame and Library)

Bobby Wine, who became the Phils' regular shortstop in 1962 when Ruben Amaro went into the military service, entered the 1964 campaign as the starter. While Amaro's bat might not have been as productive as Wine's, the Phils were better defensively with the slick-fielding Mexican at short. Amaro was not happy about his reduced role, but he was a team player and certainly wasn't going to complain about it either. "This team is going places and I want to go along," he told Ray Kelly of the *Philadelphia Bulletin* in spring training. "I want to be able to step in and 'pick up' some of the guys during the season."[7] Similarly, Tony Taylor, a .281 hitter, was the regular at second and would be spelled by Cookie Rojas, a scrappy infielder who hit at a .221 clip.

Tony Gonzalez gave the Phillies one of the best centerfielders in baseball, both offensively and defensively. The speedy Cuban had exceptional range and an accurate throwing arm, as evidenced by his .986 fielding average and eleven assists in 1963. Criticized by Mauch for not providing more power at the plate, Gonzalez still hit for a .306 average and promised to do even more in 1964. "Last spring I was still getting over a back operation," he said. "I got off to a bad start. I couldn't get a jump on the ball in the outfield, and I wasn't ready at the plate. For two months I felt weak. Then, when I was feeling better, I was hitting pretty good. I even had a chance to win the batting title, so I began to worry about my average instead of hitting home runs. This year I'll hit more, maybe twenty."[8]

The Phillies' biggest question marks going into spring training at Clearwater, were their rookies, especially Richie Allen and Danny Cater. Since the Phils lineup was loaded with left-handed hitters in Callison, Covington, Gonzalez, Dalrymple, and John Herrnstein, other teams would be throwing southpaws at them, so the team would go only as far as their right-handed hitters could take them. Allen and Cater would have to shoulder the burden, being younger than third baseman Don Hoak and first baseman Roy Sievers, aging veterans who had been the team's right-handed regulars.

So it is not surprising that all eyes focused on the competition between Allen and Hoak for the third-base job. Mauch did little to hide his choice for the position. "I want you to know that I've got real high hopes for Allen," the Phils' skipper told the sportswriters at the winter meetings in San Diego. "Any player who is good enough to be considered a prospect at shortstop should be able to play almost anywhere in the infield."[9] Ordering Allen to report early to spring training to "get over any nervousness" he might have, Mauch told the muscular rookie: "Third base is yours until you play yourself out if it."[10] When Allen was given the directive he was ecstatic.

"I love it!" he told the press. "I've been wanting to get back in the infield. In high school I was a shortstop for four years. But when the Phillies signed me I was moved into the outfield, where I became confused. It's good to be back where I belong."[11] Of course, Hoak was much less enthusiastic.

In the course of a single year, Hoak had gone from being Mauch's team captain to trade bait. Nagging injuries and a .231 batting average made the thirty-six-year-old veteran expendable. He even considered retiring after the 1963 campaign, but his never-say-die attitude forced him to return for another season. Realizing that his fate rested less with his own performance than with Allen's, Hoak spent most of the spring playing in B games, brooding about an uncertain future, and scrutinizing Allen's every move. When asked by the reporters why he seemed to be paying so much attention to his twenty-two-year-old competition, Hoak replied: "I just want to see what he can do. I like to know what every ballplayer can do. You never know when the information will come in handy. Whether I'm with this club or another club, it's good to know all you can."[12]

Allen wasn't fazed by the attention. "If he were in my shoes, would he be bothered?" said the highly touted prospect. "Look, there's nothing he can do that I can't do. The only edge he might have is experience. That's all."[13] When told of the remark, Hoak insisted that he held no animosity toward Allen. "Why should I?" he said. "My chance will come, then it's up to me. This is my eighteenth year in the game, and I've never been impressed by anyone who hits well in spring training. But if I were, I'd have to say that Allen is one hell of a prospect."[14]

Danny Cater's status also presented a dilemma. The 5-foot-11-inch 175-pound Texan hit .291 at Little Rock in 1963 and was voted Most Valuable Player of the Puerto Rican Winter League.[15] But when nineteen other clubs passed on him in the draft, he began to wonder if he'd ever make the majors. Cater could play both the outfield and first base, which should have made him a very attractive candidate, especially on a club in need of right-handed hitters. But Mauch was counting on twenty-six-year-old John Herrnstein to take over at first for the thirty-seven-year-old Roy Sievers, and the competition for the outfield was stiff.

Cater would be judged against two other right-handers—Alex Johnson and Adolfo Phillips—for a job as a part-time left-fielder and utility man. Johnson was a free-swinging twenty-two-year-old with a great arm who led the Florida State League with a .315 average in 1962, his first year in pro ball. The following season, he moved on to the Pioneer League, where he led the circuit with 35 homers, 128 RBIs, and 294 total bases, while stealing 28.[16] The numbers were those of a "superstar-in-waiting." Phillips, a slender, twenty-three-year-old Panamanian, was a natural leadoff hitter with speed. Often compared with Willie Mays, Phillips hit .306 with 15 homers at Double A Chattanooga in 1963.[17] Although Cater heard the trade rumors when he arrived in Clearwater, over the course of spring training he emerged as the best candidate of all four players.

Herrnstein impressed no one, going 6 for 29, including an 0-for-12 stretch in the final week when he substituted in the outfield for an injured Johnny Callison.[18] Johnson did better at the plate, but none of the coaches could figure out how to motivate him in the field. He rarely hustled, leaving the impression that he didn't care if he made the squad or not. Phillips performed better than either one, but showed that he still needed more seasoning in the minors, this time at the Triple A level. By the time the Phils headed north in early April, Johnson and Phillips were ticketed for Little Rock, and rumors were circulating that Herrnstein would be traded to the Mets for an aging, power-hitting first baseman, Frank Thomas.[19] Cater, who hit .454 and proved that he could be valuable at either first or in the outfield, won the job.[20]

Perhaps the most difficult decision looming over the Phillies camp, though, was which of their six bonus prospects they would retain: pitchers Dave Bennett, Rick Wise, Darrell Sutherland, Dave Roberts, Jim Miller; and/or outfielder Johnny Briggs. Because all six prospects signed for more than $8,000, they were considered "Bonus Babies" and subject to a special rule designed to reduce huge bonus payments. Any of the six who were not retained by the Phillies after spring training could be claimed by another organization, with the expansion teams—the New York Mets and the Houston Colt 45s—having the first pick. The Phils would have to trim their roster from forty to twenty-eight by opening day through trades, optioning players to the minors, or outright sale. Thirty days after the season began, the roster would have to be cut again to twenty-five.

Considering the circumstances, there was no chance that the Phillies could retain all six prospects. They could ask for waivers on two and subject the others to the draft, or they could sell the remaining four prospects to one of their minor league affiliates. If the Phillies exercised the latter option, though, it would not prevent other teams from securing the reassigned players, because they would be subject to the next winter's draft before being reacquired by the Phils. The only good news was that the rule allowed a team to option one first-year player to the minors in order to give him playing experience. That player could later be promoted to the majors and another first-year player sent down, as long as he remained on the farm for at least ten days. The catch was that the first-year player was still considered part of the twenty-five-man roster regardless of his major or minor league status.[21]

Bennett and Wise enjoyed the best chances of staying with the club. Bennett was the younger brother of starter Dennis Bennett. But at 6 feet 5 inches tall and 205 pounds, Dave was bigger and faster than his older sibling. With Bakersfield in 1963, the eighteen-year-old right-hander collected nine wins and struck out 102 batters, while walking only fifty-six in 124 innings of work.[22] The Phils outbid sixteen other clubs for his services, giving him close to $100,000 for signing.[23] With that kind of investment, management would pay close attention to his performance in spring training. Wise signed for $12,000 out of Madison High School in Portland, Oregon, where he led the baseball team to the Metropolitan State Championship in 1963. That same summer, he found himself in pro ball at Bakersfield, where his steady temperament and ferocious fastball allowed him to post ninety-eight strikeouts in only sixty-five innings. For an eighteen-year-old, Wise demonstrated the poise of a seasoned veteran, which made him an even more attractive candidate for the majors.[24]

Johnny Briggs had a good chance of making the team as well. Briggs was a three-sport athlete at East Side High School in Paterson, New Jersey, the same school that produced Larry Doby, the first African American to break the American League's color barrier. Briggs was a left-handed-hitting outfielder with excellent speed and a strong, accurate throwing arm. At Bakersfield, the year before, he hit .297 and collected 21 home runs and 83 RBIs. The Phillies brain trust believed that those statistics offered just a glimpse of the tremendous potential he possessed.[25]

The uncertainty created by the new bonus rule began to grate on some of the players as the spring unfolded. Dallas Green and John Boozer, two pitchers who were on the bubble, were most affected by the situation. Solid performances in the Grapefruit League would be necessary for them to remain with the Phillies. "I pick up the paper and read about Bunning, Short, McLish, Mahaffey, and Bennett starting," Green fumed. "I read about Baldschun, Klippstein, and Duren relieving. And I read about two bonus kids making the staff. It's the same in every paper, and I can't find my name anywhere. Well, I've got news for someone. I'm going to make it as a starter this season."

The outburst was uncharacteristic of Green, who did not sound off much in his playing days (something that would certainly change when he joined

Fig. 16 Johnny Briggs, a left-handed hitting outfielder with excellent speed, was one of the Phillies "bonus babies" who figured prominently in the club's future. (National Baseball Hall of Fame and Library)

management in the 1970s). The tall, handsome right-hander was also re-spected enough by his teammates to be elected player representative. Hav-ing posted a 7–5 record in 1963 and completing four of the fourteen games he started, Green deserved a little more respect than he was getting. "I hold no grudge against the [bonus] kids," he continued. "They can all pitch or they wouldn't be here wearing a big league uniform. But I'm wearing one too. I can pitch. But it's been the same thing every year. I've come down here and I haven't gotten a job. Opportunity is the greatest thing in the world. That's all I want—an opportunity. If I don't get the chance here, I'd like to see if some other club can use me."[26]

To be sure, Boozer performed better than Green when their opportu-nities came. Boozer gave up a single run in the twelve innings he pitched that spring, while Green surrendered eighteen runs in the twelve innings he pitched. Their last outing, which came on April 1 against the St. Louis Car-dinals in St. Petersburg, reflected their respective fortunes. Boozer started the game and surrendered only one run on two hits in the five innings he pitched. Green, on the other hand, entered the game in relief with a 5–1 lead. Two innings later the Phils were losing 6–5, which became the final score.[27] In the end, management's respect for Green's past performance prevailed. Shortly after the game, Mauch resolved the dilemma by keeping Green and Boozer on the big league roster as well as Rick Wise, Dave Bennett, and Johnny Briggs, by opening the season with Cal McLish on the disabled list.[28] By that time Mauch had also made Richie Allen the opening-day third baseman due to his prodigious .524 hitting and steady infield play. The Little General was content with his team as they broke camp for the final game of their exhibition season.

Standing in the dugout with pitching coach Al Widmar after the final workout in Clearwater, Mauch looked into the distance and saw Jim Bunning doing extra wind sprints in the outfield. "We're going to war with each other before the season is over," he told Widmar. "It will be a good thing, too. He's a great competitor, but he'll say something to me about not pitching him enough, or I'm taking him out when he doesn't think he should be taken out, and we'll just have to go at it."[29] What appeared to be a threat was actually Mauch's highest compliment.

On their way north the Phillies stopped off at Asheville, North Caro-lina, where Bunning pitched his last exhibition game against the Pittsburgh Pirates. Up to that point, Mauch made sure that the right-hander faced only American League teams, in order to prevent other National League teams from getting a close look at him.

"Just go out and take a little walk in the sunshine, Jim," Mauch ordered. "Don't show them anything, just get yourself loose. To hell with this game."[30] Bunning complied. The Bucs turned the contest into batting practice, pounding out twenty hits and four home runs, including prodigious blasts from Willie Stargell and Roberto Clemente. Pittsburgh also ran the bases so aggressively that Tony Taylor was bowled over at second base. Out of loyalty to his new teammate, Bunning drilled Donn Clendenon, the next hitter, and both benches emptied to join in the fisticuffs.[31] When the dust settled, the Pirates had crushed the Phillies 16–3, with their projected ace surrendering eleven runs on eight hits in just three and two-thirds innings. The fans back in Philadelphia were beginning to wonder just what kind of trade John Quinn had made with Detroit.[32]

The Phillies headed home with a 12–13 record and an eighth-place finish in the Grapefruit League. Despite its mediocre performance and an infamous history of race relations, however, the club would prove to be a bright spot in the midst of the racial turmoil that was surfacing in the City of Brotherly Love.

During the 1960s, Philadelphia witnessed the same hopes and frustrations of a civil rights movement that was unfolding across the nation. While the city continued to bask in the prosperity of the post–World War II economy, it also struggled with the currents of social and political change. Mayor Richardson Dilworth and the other liberal Democrats who controlled City Hall in the early part of the decade presided over a refreshing period of reform. Theirs was a welcome change from the corrupt Republican machine that had dominated Philadelphia politics for more than half a century. Dilworth's leadership also fostered public confidence that Philadelphia, though not without problems, was fiscally sound and that the Democratic Party would be able to fix any challenge that came its way. But when the mayor resigned to run for Pennsylvania governor in 1962, the white liberal establishment was challenged by other factions in the city's political landscape.[33]

Dilworth's successor was James H. J. Tate, president of City Council. Tate, more of a row-house politician than a friend to the downtown business and liberal communities, managed to earn enough public support to win election in his own right the following year. But his administration was plagued by ongoing racial conflict as it struggled with the painful truth that Philadelphia was two cities—one white, the other black.

While most white Philadelphians accepted the social integration of the races in theory, they had difficulty accepting the reality of it. In the years following World War II, the city's black population grew to be the third largest in the United States, at nearly 400,000, and residential patterns came to reflect the tacit principle of racial inequality.[34] African Americans newly arrived from the South, as well as those who were native to Philadelphia, settled on the fringes of Center City, residing in the cheap row houses once inhabited by first- and second-generation immigrants who relocated to the suburbs. North Philadelphia became the principal black residential area, especially the area from Twenty-ninth Street above Susquehanna, north along the Pennsylvania Railroad lines. At one time the area had been known for its working-class neighborhoods of Irish, Italians, and Jews, who were employed by the surrounding industries, such as Midvale Steel, Philco, Exide Batteries, Tastykake, the Budd Company, and Baldwin Locomotive. But now, as many of those businesses relocated outside the city limits, whites abandoned North Philadelphia. The Irish moved to the more spacious housing of West Oak Lane. Italian families migrated farther south and west of Center City. The Jewish population relocated to Oxford Circle, leaving West Philadelphia and Strawberry Mansion, which filled the growing need for black housing.[35] "White flight," or the migration of the white middle-class from the city to the Main Line communities of Bala Cynwyd, Merion, Haverford, and Swarthmore, or the outlying suburbs of Plymouth Meeting, Abington, and Bucks County, was also increasing, reflecting the desire for upward mobility as well as the racial stereotyping of African Americans as social inferiors.

Integration was largely restricted to Germantown, Mount Airy, Queen Village, and Fairmount, where liberal Jews and a rising black middle class employed in banks, insurance companies, law offices, and government agencies began to occupy the handsome houses along Lincoln Drive. Their example reflected the hopes of a small coalition of labor leaders, farsighted Democratic politicians, and minority leaders. Known as the "Americans for Democratic Action," this umbrella group was composed of political activists whose intelligence, idealism, and enthusiasm would lay the foundations of the momentous civil rights campaigns of the decade. With the exceptions of Germantown, Mount Airy, Queen Village, and Fairmount, the predominantly white middle-class northeastern section of the city, and the wealthy white enclave of Chestnut Hill, mostly poor blacks and low-salaried whites were left to fill Philadelphia's diminishing tax base.[36]

As expenses increased, City Hall was forced to make decisions on questions of education, employment, and public welfare for which it was ill-prepared. The "race factor" often became a rhetorical device for greater state and federal funding to meet those needs.[37] "There is disappointment at the slow progress of the civil rights bill through the Senate among Philadelphia's Negroes," wrote Bruce Biossat, a Washington-based editorialist, in the May 18 edition of the *Philadelphia Daily News*. "Yet a good many of the city's Negroes do not see the bill as central to their hopes, which focus on education and jobs; not on public accommodations. Philadelphia's Negroes want to end de facto segregation in the city's schools. Integration is not sought for its own sake, but as a path to better schooling for undertrained Negro children now crammed into overcrowded, run-down inadequate buildings. The city's job retraining program also flopped in 1963–64, with less than 400 persons said to have been trained for specific jobs."[38] Protest movements, focused on education and job training, erupted onto the city's streets. Together with Philadelphia's rising crime rate, black protest accelerated white flight to the suburbs. To his credit, Mayor Tate realized that the widespread unrest was fueled by both idealism and resentment, and he responded with a two-pronged approach by catering to the African American community's call for reform while also getting tougher on crime. It proved to be a mixed success.

To stem the tide of protest, Tate appointed Charles Bowser, a young African American lawyer, to head the Anti-Poverty Action Committee, an organization inspired by the federal government's "War on Poverty." The appointment curried favor with the African American community as Bowser worked hard to ensure local community participation on public-welfare issues. Bowser also represented the traditional leadership structure within the African American community. He was more comfortable working with moderates like the Reverend Leon H. Sullivan of Zion Baptist Church, who launched a successful self-help program called "Opportunities Industrialization Center," or jurist Leon Higginbotham, who in a methodical fashion effected change through the court system.[39] Bowser enlisted the support of these moderate leaders while tempering more radical ones who were vying for greater influence within Philadelphia's African American community. Chief among the latter group was Cecil B. Moore, a tempestuous defense lawyer who took over the local NAACP and launched a campaign to integrate all-white labor unions. Moore used protests and public rallies to create controversy and demand immediate change.[40]

"We are serving notice," he declared upon his election to the NAACP's presidency, "that no longer will the plantation system of white men appointing our leaders exist in Philadelphia. We will expect to be consulted on all community issues which affect our people. These issues have been settled by the Constitution. I will expect my people to stand up and be counted among the believers of the principles of the NAACP or have their names be listed as an enemy of democracy." Moore scoffed at the sit-ins and peaceful demonstrations organized by the Congress of Racial Equality (CORE) and the black clergy who organized boycotts and negotiated patronage quotas from the Tate administration. Instead, he accused the mayor and the city's municipal and construction trade unions of locking African Americans out of jobs. In May 1963 he followed up his accusation with direct action, organizing 200 pickets to block the entrance to the construction site for a new school in North Philadelphia. Tate ordered police to use human wedges to break the blockade and escort the white construction workers to the job site. Moore viewed the action as a reflection of the white-dominated Democratic Party machine and the police power it wielded to stay in power.[41]

Moore placed Philadelphia on a collision course between African Americans and whites in 1964 when Tate appointed Frank Rizzo deputy police commissioner in charge of the city's 6,000 uniformed police officers. Unfortunately, Rizzo's streetwise, shoot-from-the-hip, tough-cop style became synonymous with the public's image of Philadelphia—and it wasn't good. He antagonized the black community with his outspoken comments on race, voicing sentiments previously unthinkable among responsible public officials and couched in rhetoric of physical intimidation. Injecting the issue of race into rising crime rates, Rizzo ordered raids on black-owned nightclubs and looked the other way when police used excessive force in the city's black neighborhoods. The size of his charisma and personality inspired unreasoned loyalty among whites, and fear as well as violent opposition among African Americans. Predictably, Moore used Rizzo as a symbol for the white oppression inflicted by the Democratic Party machine, insisting that the future police commissioner made "crime control" a euphemism for "anti-black movements."[42] Their showdown would occur during the late summer of 1964 in the North Philadelphia neighborhood surrounding Connie Mack Stadium, where the Phillies played.

Located at Twenty-first Street and Lehigh Avenue, the Phillies ballpark was the only constant in a neighborhood that was rapidly changing in the postWorld War II era. Once a white, working-class neighborhood, the North Penn district was now integrated. African Americans and Hispanics were arriving in increasing numbers by 1964, inhabiting the row houses vacated by the Irish, the Polish, and the Germans.[43] The Phillies were making an earnest effort to court this more socially diverse fan base. It was good business, as well as common sense. Players like Richie Allen, Ruben Amaro, Johnny Briggs, Wes Covington, Tony Gonzalez, and Tony Taylor appealed to the minority groups who were moving into the neighborhood. In 1964 these players would provide the kind of exciting baseball that would bring white, African American, and Hispanic fans out to the ballpark, and they wasted no time generating fan enthusiasm.

The Phillies opened the regular season against the New York Mets at Connie Mack on April 14. A crowd of 21,016 braved a threatening sky to watch Dennis Bennett face the Mets' Alvin Jackson. The Phils took an early lead in the bottom of the first when Jackson issued a pair of walks and first baseman Roy Sievers followed with a three-run homer. The Phils added another run in the second when Dalrymple singled, took second on a wild pitch, and scored on a base hit by Bobby Wine. But the Mets launched a comeback when Joe Christopher hit a solo homer in the fourth and the New Yorkers rallied for another pair of runs an inning later.

A night of heavy rains had left the field slick and the area around third base waterlogged. For Richie Allen, the fifth inning proved to be a baptism by fire. It started with Allen charging Dick Smith's bunt. At the last second he slipped and had no play. When the next hitter, Amado Samuel, lifted a high pop in front of the plate, Allen called off catcher Clay Dalrymple, but slipped again and failed to make the play. The fans showered him with boos. Just as quickly the jeers turned to cheers for Allen when the very next batter, Ron Hunt, sliced a line drive to the rookie third baseman's right. Allen speared the ball and threw to first to double up Samuel. Frank Thomas followed with a single to left that scored Smith. By the time the inning was over, the Phils were clinging to a 4–3 lead. Fortunately, Johnny Klippstein came in to shut down the Mets and get the win, 5–3.

When asked about his performance after the game, Allen replied: "I feel like there's one down and 161 to go! Sure, I heard the boos, but they didn't bother me. Every time I slipped in that inning, I just forgot about it before the next play. It was history, and I couldn't do anything about it. I just wanted to get somebody out so Bennett could stay in there."[44]

The next day, Bunning won his first National League start, 4–1, against the Mets. Tony Gonzalez contributed a three-run homer to break a 1–1 deadlock in the eighth. Bunning went on to strike out the side in the ninth.[45] A five-game road trip followed with three games against the Chicago Cubs and two against the Mets. Mahaffey won the first game at Wrigley, 10–8, in a slugfest that saw home runs from Allen and Sievers. After the Phillies dropped the second game, 7–0, Bennett got them back on track with an 8–1 victory against the Cubs on April 19. Allen contributed two homers and 4 RBIs, and Cater singled to start the rally and later doubled and homered. Returning home with a 6–1 record, the Fightin' Phils found themselves all alone in first place, a full game ahead of the San Francisco Giants. The Dodgers, on the other hand, were in last place, having lost six in a row since Koufax shut out the Cardinals in the opening game of the season. It was their worst losing streak in two years and would foreshadow LA's inability to score runs as the season unfolded.[46]

The Phillies went on to win eight of their next nine games, including a come-from-behind 6–5 victory over the Pirates in the ninth, and a 10–0 rout of the Cubs. Allen was on fire, hitting .430 with five homers, and the Phillies gave Don Hoak his unconditional release.[47]

Bunning was just as impressive. After defeating the Mets in his first start, the slender right-hander threw a six-hit shutout against Chicago. In his second complete game in as many starts, Bunning chalked up nine strikeouts. In his third start, he held the Milwaukee Braves scoreless for eight innings before Chris Short and newly acquired reliever Ed Roebuck finished them off for a 5–3 win. In those three starts, Bunning surrendered just one earned run in a total of twenty-six and two-thirds innings of work.[48] He was even better during the month of May.

On two occasions, Bunning flirted with no-hitters. The first one came on May 18 at Houston when he faced just twenty-nine batters. Bunning carried a no-hitter into the fifth inning when the Colts' Jimmy Wynn singled past third for the only Houston hit of the game, a 4–0 Phillies win. Eleven days later, the Phils' ace faced Houston again, this time at Connie Mack Stadium. For six and two-thirds innings he pitched perfect baseball, retiring twenty in a row, and enjoyed a commanding 5–0 lead. But with two outs in the seventh, Colt third baseman Mike White lofted a fly to left field. Wes Covington got a late start on the ball and tried to make a diving catch, but the ball got past him for a double. Walter Bond followed with a clean single to right field to give Houston its first run of the game. Bunning lost not only the no-hitter but also his shutout. He was lucky to get the win after the eighth inning, when he gave up another four runs. But the Phillies rallied to win, 6–5. Bunning was determined never to allow the pressure of a no-hitter to get him again.[49]

While some of his success was due to the fact that none of the teams had ever faced him before, Bunning's competitiveness and experience gave him an edge over his opponents. "I've been around long enough to know that no league is easy," he admitted. "You just try to pitch like it's 1–0 every time you go out there."[50] As he forged a reputation as the Phillies' staff ace, Bunning also took nothing for granted, and neither did his teammates.

By mid-May, the Phils were locked in a seesaw battle with San Francisco for first place. Willie Mays, who was hitting at a .490 clip, and Juan Marichal, who entered the month with a perfect 4–0 record, kept the Giants in hot pursuit. But the Phillies, who had won fifteen of their first twenty-four games, refused to let up.[51] Covington, Callison, and Allen were leading the offense. In one of the most memorable performances—a May 9 game at Connie Mack against the Cincinnati Reds—Covington hit a mammoth home run to the far side of the Longines clock atop the 64-foot-high scoreboard in right center. He also collected two singles and 5 RBIs in that game, while Callison contributed two triples, a double, and a single in the 11–3 rout.[52] A week later, the Phillies defeated Marichel and the Giants at Candlestick Park, 7–2, a loss that dropped San Francisco into second place, eight percentage points behind the Phils. Once again, Callison made the difference in the game, going 5 for 5 with a home run and 5 RBIs.[53]

Allen was even more prodigious. Through May the rookie third baseman led the Phils in every major offensive category, with a .431 average, 7 home runs, and 13 RBIs.[54] "There's just no telling how good this kid can be," Mauch boasted. "He's got great hands, and a very quick, very short swing. But what impresses me most about him is his professional approach to the game. He doesn't get way up when things are going good, or way down when things are going bad. And that's the best approach to any professional sport."[55] Allen's numbers were so impressive for a rookie that the Pittsburgh Pirates hosted a "Richie Allen Night" two weeks later at Forbes Field to honor the local product.[56] By that time, the Phils had pulled one-half game in front of the Giants and one and a half games in front of the Braves, who were tied for third with the Cardinals. The Pirates were in fourth, only two games out.[57] It was an enchanted spring for the Phillies, their fans, and even the local sportswriters, who had grown accustomed to counting out the hometown team by June 1.

For better and worse, there were three daily Philadelphia newspapers that covered the Phillies: the *Evening Bulletin*, the *Inquirer*, and the *Daily News*. The *Bulletin*, published by Robert Taylor, enjoyed the highest circulation. It was the more staid and respectable newspaper of the three dailies because it refrained from taking controversial editorial positions. Instead, the *Bulletin* concentrated on an impartial printing of the news gathered by a highly competent staff of reporters. Sports editor Jack Wilson headed a staff of five writers who covered the Phils: Ray Kelly, Ed Pollack, John

Brogan, Hugh Brown, and Sandy Grady. Kelly was the regular, and his columns were also used by *The Sporting News*. He was regarded as a ball-player's writer, fair, concise, and reflecting a good, sound knowledge of the game. Grady, on the other hand, wrote a regular "Man About Sports" column in the 1960s that offered some of the best and funniest baseball writing on the East Coast. Nor was he afraid to offer his candid opinion to the Phillies brass, something that clearly distinguished him from his colleagues at the *Bulletin*.

The *Philadelphia Inquirer*, published by communications magnate Walter H. Annenberg, competed for the *Bulletin*'s readers by printing the news in the morning, and in a more colorful fashion. Frank Byrod was the sports editor, and Allen Lewis was the primary baseball writer. Frank Dolson, a columnist, often wrote on baseball, as did John Dell and Ron Smith.[58] Like Kelly, Lewis was a ballplayer's writer whose columns often alternated with Kelly's on the pages of *The Sporting News*. Because he grew up in nearby Havertown and attended Haverford College, Lewis was often accused of being partial to the Phillies in his writing. But he believes that he was able to emphathize more with the circumstances of the ballplayers. This stemmed from the fact that he played baseball through his college years at Haverford. "I honestly believe that if you didn't play the sport you were covering, it's very difficult to write about it," said Lewis. "I was passionate about baseball long before I was a writer. I played the game in grade school, prep school, and college. That experience taught me that baseball looks a lot easier than it really is."

One of the ways Lewis ensured his objectivity was to attend a dozen high school and college games each season. The experience reinforced his belief that the "routine play" in the majors is often extremely difficult for players at the lower levels of the game to execute. "Watching those games," he said, "reminded me that baseball is one of the most difficult sports to play, and you had better be careful before criticizing a professional ballplayer. I never believed in writing negatively if I didn't have to. Sure, if a guy wasn't hustling, I'd write about it. But I'm not going to rip a guy if he's not hitting well. I'd give him the benefit of the doubt that he's trying."[59]

For the sportswriters at the *Philadelphia Daily News*, however, Lewis's attitude was "old school." The *Daily News*, a satellite of the *Inquirer*, was a tabloid that made very little effort to cover national or international news other than what was made available by the wire service. Instead, the newspaper promoted itself as the "people paper" and concentrated on stories of local human interest with a high emphasis on sports. Often accused of sensationalizing the news, the paper's sportswriters tended to make ball-players flashier—and sometimes, more controversial—personalities than they really were. Stan Hochman covered the Phillies beat, while Larry Merchant wrote occasional columns on the team. Known as the "Chip-munks," Hochman and Merchant represented a new breed of aggressive young sportswriters who went beyond the statistics and narrative descrip-tion of the game to focus on the players' personalities and clubhouse con-troversy. The advent of television eliminated the need to rehash the events of the game, for fans had already watched the exploits of their heroes in the comfort of their own living rooms. Forced to adjust their writing, the Chip-munks resorted to intrusive questioning in their postgame interviews, and to scrutinizing the performances as well as lifestyles of the players.[60]

Hochman and Merchant could be tough on the players. When Ruben Amaro reported to spring training slightly overweight, for example, Hoch-man took the young Hispanic player to task on the sports page. "Amaro's feet no longer danced, his hands were a split second late, and his skills seemed to flee him," wrote the *Daily News* beat writer in a March 11 col-umn. "He should have come to Florida early and trim. Instead, he came on time and pudgy. He has a reason for that, too." Amaro explained that he had gained eleven pounds because he hadn't played winter ball. Play-ing year-round, he felt, hurt him during the regular season and taking the time off would be more beneficial. Of course, Hochman's interpretation was that Amaro "has built himself a whole house of deceit" and that if he didn't lose the weight he "may have to rediscover his skills somewhere else" even though the "demand has not been great so far."[61]

Still, Hochman was respected by the players for his knowledge of the game and because he, like the other beat writers, traveled with the team from spring training through September. "Stan tended to belabor some points, but he was always pretty fair," recalled Dennis Bennett. "He knew the game. He also had to put up with the same grind as the players—long days and nights, a lot of travel. As a player, you have to respect that."[62] Larry Merchant, on the other hand, was not well liked. Some of the players re-garded him as a "throat-cutter" who often sensationalized accounts of their off-the-field behavior.[63] Few trusted Merchant, because he was a colum-nist—not a beat writer, who traveled with the team. He was often accused of launching personal attacks.

One of Merchant's favorite targets was pitcher Art Mahaffey. "Art Mahaffey couldn't have thrown a baseball through wet tissue paper last night," wrote Merchant on June 10, after the Phils hurler pitched his team

Fig. 17 On April 23, 1961, Art Mahaffey struck out seventeen Chicago Cubs to tie a National League record held by Dizzy Dean of the St. Louis Cardinals. The following season, he won nineteen games and seemed destined to become the staff ace. But arm troubles cut his career short, and Mahaffey retired after the 1966 season. (Philadelphia Phillies)

past the Pirates for a 4–3 victory to improve his own record to 5–2. "He threw enough junk to open an antiques shop. Gene Mauch once said that Robin Roberts was throwing like Dolley Madison. All I've got to say to Mahaffey is: Hello Dolly. If he doesn't throw any harder, he may never see another win."[64]

On another occasion, Merchant printed a letter from a fan by the name of "Wilmington Phil," who allegedly wrote: "They should bore a hole in Mahaffey's head, suck out his brains and fill the cavity with custard. He would then become a 20-game winner. If any of the Phillies management is interested, I will loan them my Blue Cross card.[65]

To be sure, Mahaffey was struggling with a sore arm in 1964 and had to rely on his curveball and locating his fastball. He did everything in his power to regain the velocity he had in 1962, when he posted nineteen wins, including beating himself up mentally for the failure to do so. But it's hard to understand why Merchant continued to belabor the pitcher's troubles, especially in a season when he and the Phillies were enjoying so much success. Once, when a reader asked Merchant why he didn't have anything good to say about Mahaffey, he replied: "Okay, I think Art Mahaffey is the best washed up pitcher in creation."[66]

By today's standards, Hochman and Merchant were mild, but they also set a precedent for Philadelphia's sportswriters. No longer could the beat writer afford to sit in the press box and wax eloquent about the game. The "scoop" was in the postgame interview, and the writer had to get it, no matter how intrusive he became. Fans were more interested in the players' personalities and their off-the-field behavior. Over time, the players would distance themselves from the writers in what had become an antagonistic relationship. It is not surprising that Ray Kelly of the *Bulletin* and Allen Lewis of the *Inquirer* were most favored. "Kelly and Lewis were players' writers," said John Herrnstein. "They reported the game more objectively than anyone else in the media, and you could count on their integrity."[67]

Claude E. Harrison Jr., of the *Philadelphia Tribune*, had a reputation for taking the Phillies to task. Harrison's stories highlighted the achievements of the team's black players and, to a lesser degree, those of Hispanic players. Richie Allen provided a lot of press in the spring of 1964, some of it laced with social commentary about the Phillies' poor history of race relations. On May 2, for example, Harrison wrote:

> When the great white fathers decided to rip down the barriers and let the Negro athlete take a shot at major league baseball in the late

1940s, some of the senior circuit teams lagged behind in their search for Negro talent.

The Phillies were one of those teams, trying their best not to run across any Negro talent of value. They seemed happy to see their bank accounts hiked by the Negro fans who came to root against them. It was a natural thing for 10,000 to 15,000 non-white fans to stroll into Shibe Park and root for Jackie, Campy and Big Newk when the Dodgers rolled into town. And until this day the "old timers" still hold a grudge against the Phillies. They still root for the Giants and the Dodgers.

However, the Phillies have wised up to the facts of life and joined the "if you can't beat 'em, join 'em club" by bringing up Richie Allen, the hottest thing to hit Philadelphia since William Penn.

While Allen may not win back the old timers for the Phillies, he will surely groom the youngsters for the future. They'll pay the admission price to go out and root for the home club because they'll feel like a part of the team.[68]

Fans, both black and white, were indeed getting excited about the Phillies, and with good reason. The Phillies entered June with a 25–15 record and a .625 winning percentage. They were locked in a tight pennant race with San Francisco, which was only half a game out, and playing some of the most exciting baseball the city had witnessed in years.

On Tuesday June 2, the Dodgers, who had managed to regroup from their poor start but were still six games out, arrived in Philadelphia for a three-game series. The Phils won the first game, 4–3. A classic pitchers' duel followed the next night, with Bunning opposing Don Drysdale. Bunning struck out eleven before being lifted in the tenth inning of a scoreless deadlock. Cookie Rojas, who was hitting at a .500 clip, led off the bottom of the eleventh with a double. He advanced to third on a force play, and scored on an infield error by Jim Gilliam for the only run of the game.

Since replacing Tony Taylor in the lineup, Rojas collected sixteen hits in twenty-nine at-bats, including four doubles, a triple, and a home run. Despite all the media attention, the Cuban utility man downplayed his success. "I am only playing because Tony got a bad start and is tired," he insisted. "I like playing, but soon Tony will be back. He's the greatest."[69]

Chris Short faced Sandy Koufax on Thursday night, June 4. Koufax threw a no-hitter, defeating the Phils by a 3–0 margin. In the process, he struck out twelve, making it the fifty-fourth time in his career that he had whiffed ten or more batters in a game. Richie Allen, who walked in the fourth, was the only Phillie to reach base. All three of the Dodgers runs came on a mammoth Frank Howard homer in the seventh.[70]

Compounding the heartbreak were the Giants, who came into Philadelphia next and took all three games from the Phillies. The losses dropped the Phils one-half game behind San Francisco. But the league lead changed hands again within the week. On Saturday, June 13, Bunning beat the Mets, 8–2, for his sixth victory of the season. The following afternoon the Phillies swept a doubleheader. Ray Culp won the opener in relief, 9–5, and Mahaffey and Ed Roebuck combined for a 4–2 victory in the nightcap. Two days later, on June 16, the Phils beat the Chicago Cubs, 4–2, to regain sole possession of first place.[71]

A special chemistry was developing among the players during the spring of 1964. Most of them were young, in their early to mid-twenties, and had already weathered the adversity that came with being perennial cellar-dwellers, including a humiliating twenty-three-game losing streak. They could see that the future looked much brighter. They pulled for one another on the field and enjoyed a loose camaraderie off the field. But because they were so young, the Phillies lacked a proven leader among the regulars. Mauch wanted Johnny Callison to assume that role and, by 1964, Callison had come a long way from his early days in Philadelphia, when he was more concerned about impressing the fans. "I've read the stuff about leadership," he told Stan Hochman of the *Philadelphia Daily News*, "and I'm not sure I understand it. I don't do a lot of yelling, but when a guy boots one, I go up to him and say, 'Hang in there.' I think the guys respect me, though."[72] Callison had certainly earned the respect of his teammates as well as management, who awarded him a $9,000 salary increase from the previous year.[73] But he still wasn't comfortable accepting the mantle of leadership. Though he wasn't a position player, the leadership role fell to Bunning, whose success in the American League and whose fiercely competitive style served as a warning to opponents and teammates alike that he had come to Philadelphia to do business.

Just as important was Mauch's role in molding a talented group of individuals into a *team* with a budding sense of pride. "I think Gene was a great manager for younger players," said Dennis Bennett, reflecting on the 1964 team years later. "He created a camaraderie among us in the clubhouse. After a Sunday afternoon game, he'd sit around with myself, Chris Short, and Ray Culp and talk about the hitters around the league. It was quite an education. He was the finest manager I ever played for."[74]

Like his players, Mauch, at the age of thirty-nine, was also young, and hungry to be part of a winner. That insatiable desire motivated him to get the edge in any way possible. Some of his methods were constructive: using the double switch, replacing a pitcher and a fielder at the same time; or inserting a relief pitcher into a deeper slot in the batting order so he could squeeze more innings out of him. Other tactics were simply ruthless. Once, Mets catcher Jerry Grote ventured into the Phillies dugout in pursuit of a pop foul. Mauch karate-chopped him across the forearms, forcing Grote to drop the ball. On another occasion, Mauch's callousness backfired. Standing behind the batting cage at Wrigley Field to study the Cubs during batting practice, the Little General began to agitate the hitters. Chicago manager Leo Durocher, who never passed on the opportunity to get an edge himself, began lining fungos off of Mauch's legs to chase him away.[75] Whether it was the "scratch-and-claw" attitude he developed as a career utilityman, or a fundamental desire to gain some respect in the baseball world, Mauch cultivated a sense of pride in his players. "For years," said the Little General, when asked about his team's quick start, "we've been kicked around. But last year we finished in the first division and gained the respect of the league. Now we have the rest of the league believing we're a good team and the kids have pride. It'll take us a long way."[76]

It certainly would ... at least for 150 games.

4

ON TOP OF THE NATIONAL LEAGUE

On Sunday June 21, Jim Bunning faced New York's Tracy Stallard in the first game of a doubleheader at Shea Stadium. The night before, the Phils lost to the cellar-dwelling Mets, 7–3, when reserve catcher Robert "Hawk" Taylor led New York's sixteen-hit assault.[1] Now Philadelphia was clinging to a half-game lead over the second-place Giants. Mauch turned to Bunning for a win, just as he had three days earlier when he used the lanky right-hander in relief to seal the Phillies' 6–3 victory against the Cubs.[2]

It was also Father's Day, and Mary Bunning, accompanied by her twelve-year-old daughter, Barbara, drove up from Philadelphia to be with her husband. The couple's other six children stayed behind at their apartment in Cherry Hill, New Jersey, with their babysitter, Mary Fran Hoffman.[3]

Mauch would split the catching duties on this hot summer afternoon. Triandos would be paired with Bunning in the opening contest. He was easy to catch. The Kentucky hurler was always around the plate, and threw a lot of strikes. Triandos was also familiar with him because the two had been battery mates with Detroit. Dalrymple would catch rookie Rick Wise, who would be making his first big league start in Game Two. Mauch felt more comfortable with Dalrymple catching the younger hurlers, who needed more guidance.[4]

No one in the crowd of 32,026 that packed Shea that afternoon could have predicted that they would witness baseball history in the making. Johnny Briggs, pressed into service because of Gonzalez's pulled groin, opened Game One with a leadoff walk. Herrnstein sacrificed him to second, and, after Callison struck out, Allen singled to left to score Briggs and give the Phils a quick 1–0 lead. They picked up another run in the second when Triandos doubled Tony Taylor home.

The Phillies' big inning came in the sixth, though. Callison opened the inning with his ninth home run of the year, a towering 371-foot shot to right center. After Allen struck out, Covington walked and was replaced on the base paths by Bobby Wine. Taylor singled to center, advancing Wine to second. Rojas flied to right. Triandos followed with a single to left, scoring Wine and sending Taylor to second. The Phils now had a 4–0 lead. Bunning was next. He doubled to left center, scoring Taylor and Triandos. The Mets lifted Stallard for Bill Wakefield, who retired Briggs on a fly to left. But the damage was done. The Phillies had given Bunning a commanding 6–0 lead.[5]

The Mets, on the other hand, couldn't get anything started. No one reached base against Bunning through the first four innings. He retired all twelve batters he faced, striking out four of them. The lanky right-hander baffled the New Yorkers with an assortment of pitches, his most effective being the slider.

But the Mets threatened in the fifth. After right-fielder Joe Christopher popped up to short, Jesse Gonder, the Mets' left-hand-hitting catcher, hit a hard shot into the hole between first and second. Tony Taylor, diving to his left, somehow managed to spear the ball and throw him out.

"I thought the ball was going by me," Taylor admitted after the game. "Then I dive and I catch it in the pocket of my glove. I dropped it when I hit the ground, but I threw him out on my knees."[6]

Bunning was unstoppable after that, refusing to allow another no-hit bid to be spoiled. But instead of following the customary ritual of silence, he talked freely with teammates on the bench. After each inning, he counted down the number of outs remaining. "It was the strangest thing," recalled Johnny Callison. "You don't talk when you have a no-hitter, right? But Jim was going up and down the bench telling everybody what was going on and telling us to dive for the ball so nothing would fall in for a hit. We just hoped like hell that nobody would hit the ball to us. The pressure was incredible. We tried to get away from him so we wouldn't jinx the thing, but he kept following us around."[7]

On the field, Bunning directed shortstop Cookie Rojas to play closer to second base against the left-handed-hitting Mets. He realized that his awkward delivery, which thrust him in the direction of first base on his follow-through, prevented him from getting to a ball that was hit back through the middle. So Bunning often asked his shortstop to cheat up toward the second-base bag.[8] Today, it was more of an order than a direction.

"Sure, I started thinking about a no-hitter around the fifth inning," admitted Bunning, who had previously thrown a no-hitter against the Boston Red Sox on July 20, 1958, when he was with Detroit. "I knew I had a chance after Tony made that play on Gonder." When asked why he defied one of baseball's oldest superstitions—never discuss a no-hitter in progress—the Phillies' ace reasoned, "If you talk about it, you're not as disappointed if you don't get it."[9]

Mauch refused to leave anything to chance. Remembering Wes Covington's miscue that cost Bunning a no-hitter in Houston three weeks earlier, he made a defensive change in the fifth. Covington was replaced in left field by Cookie Rojas, and Wine came in to play short.[10]

Bunning almost lost the perfect game with two outs in the eighth when Mets left-fielder Bob Taylor worked a full count. Triandos signaled for a slider, and the lanky right-hander threw it at the outside part of the plate. Taylor took the pitch, thinking it was ball four, and headed toward first base. But home plate umpire Ed Sudol bellowed, "Strike Three!"[11]

In the top of the ninth, Bunning received a standing ovation from the Mets fans when he came to bat. Back in Philadelphia, Hoffman, who was babysitting the other six Bunning children, had them all sitting in front of the television to watch the final inning, as the Phils went down in order. Before he left the dugout for the bottom of the ninth, Bunning turned to Triandos and deadpanned: "I'd like to borrow Koufax's hummer for the last inning." It wouldn't be necessary.

Shortstop Charley Smith fouled a 2–2 pitch thatwas gobbled up by Wine for the first out. New York Manager Casey Stengel then decided to pinch hit for Amado Samuel. As George Altman came out onto the on-deck circle, Bunning, sweltering in the 90-degree heat, called time and motioned for Triandos to come out to the mound.

"Tell me a joke or something," Bunning asked his battery mate, trying to muster the energy to face the last two hitters.

Triandos couldn't think of anything, so he just laughed and went back behind the plate. "I'd never seen him so gabby," he said later. "Jim was really silly. I guess he wanted a breather. I just wanted to get back behind the plate and end the game, especially since his curve has a habit of hanging in the late innings. As it turned out, he didn't make a wrong pitch all afternoon."[12]

Altman took two quick strikes and then whiffed on a low curveball for out number two. John Stephenson would be the final batter. He swung and missed a curveball for strike one, then took a curve for strike two. The next two pitches were outside for balls. Bunning threw him a 2–2 curve and struck him out swinging, to end his perfect, no-hit gem.

It was the first perfect game in the National League since John M. Ward of Providence accomplished that feat against Buffalo on June 17, 1880. Bunning's was also the first perfecto in all of major league baseball since 1956, when Don Larsen of the Yankees threw his gem against the Brooklyn Dodgers in the Fall Classic.[13]

Pounding his fist into his glove, Bunning was mobbed by his teammates as his wife and daughter rushed out of the stands to join the celebration. Even Mets fans took to their feet, chanting: "We want Bunning! We want Bunning!"

The Phillies' ace was more subdued in the clubhouse afterward. "When it was over, he didn't entertain the sportswriters with giddy stories of his youth or share bubbly champagne with his teammates," wrote New York sportswriter Maury Allen. "Instead, Bunning remained in character: intense, a little angry, proud, and contentious as he was being questioned. Only Bunning and Bob Gibson [of the St. Louis Cardinals] seemed to intimidate hitters as well as sportswriters with their violent pitching and abrasive interview style."[14] Bunning must have been in a better mood before too long, because he accepted a $1,000 invitation to make a thirty-second appearance on the Ed Sullivan Show that evening.[15]

June 21 was also a special day for Rick Wise. The eighteen-year-old rookie collected his first major league victory against the Mets in the second game of the twin bill that afternoon. Frank Lary started for the Mets and took the loss. Briggs and Callison hit home runs, and veteran Johnny Klippstein sealed the 8–2 win in relief.[16] Wise's three-hit victory also set a major league record for fewest hits allowed for a doubleheader. "In the third inning, I walked a batter, and all the fans started cheering," recalled the rookie Phillies hurler. "I couldn't figure it out until a teammate explained that it was the first Met to reach base all day."[17]

Johnny Briggs was also creating quite an impression. The twenty-year-old outfielder showed flashes of brilliance. In his first major league start, on June 14 against the Mets, Briggs, batting leadoff, collected three hits including a double, and 2 RBIs, scored two runs, and stole a base, pacing the Philles to a 9–5 win.[18] A week later, in New York, he went two for three with a homer to help Wise cap his first big league victory. "There's no telling how highly I regard Johnny," said Mauch. "He goes out and works before a game. He plays seven or eight innings of outfield in batting practice. He doesn't cut or slash in batting practice, trying to knock down the fences. The kid's going to be a great ballplayer. He's got talent to go with desire."[19] Briggs was a quiet, introverted player. Like all rookies in those days, he made sure to be seen and not heard. He understood that his primary responsibility was to learn how to play the game at the big league level, and he went about his business without any fanfare. "Being a rookie, I was just happy to be in the major leagues," admitted Briggs, years later. "Just to have the prestige of being a major league player. I had no reason to complain. It was a dream come true for me."[20] Briggs was the kind of African American player that white-controlled Major League Baseball appreciated at a time when the civil rights movement was encouraging African Americans to become more assertive in the workplace. Together with his special blend of speed and power, Briggs's quiet nature and youthful desire to improve made a more outspoken black veteran expendable.

Wes Covington had worn out his welcome in Philadelphia by the summer of 1964. His hitting wasn't the problem. After arriving in Philadelphia in 1961, Covington hit .303 and replicated that performance in 1963 when he collected 17 homers and 64 RBIs in just 353 at-bats. But the black slugger was a liability in the outfield and in the clubhouse, where he gave long interviews that often criticized management.[21] Some of the criticism addressed the segregated accommodations that still existed in the early 1960s at the Phillies' spring-training base in Clearwater. Because Covington invested his money wisely, he enjoyed greater financial independence than most ballplayers of the era, as well as the security of being able to speak out against social injustice when he saw it. While he was with Milwaukee, Covington purchased a home in St. Petersburg so he didn't have to live in segregated quarters during the spring. When he came to Philadelphia, he championed the campaign to have the Phillies housed together in Clearwater. "Many people asked me why I was worried about the players moving in together since I have a house just fifteen miles away from Clearwater," he told Claude Harrison of the *Philadelphia Tribune* in an effort to explain

Fig. 18 Wes Covington, who came to the Phillies from the Milwaukee Braves in 1961, was one of the few veteran players with postseason experience. (Philadelphia Phillies)

his actions. "I told them that they couldn't expect [black players] to cross the picket lines the Philadelphia NAACP was planning to throw in our faces at Connie Mack Stadium when we went North. So [management] finally came around and now all of us stay together."[22]

As admirable as Covington's stand was, his remarks to the press did not sit well with the Phillies brain trust, especially when the organization was making a conscious attempt to distance itself from a poor history of race relations. Predictably, General Manager John Quinn spent most of the spring trying to work a deal that would send Covington either to the New York Mets for left-hander Al Jackson, or to San Francisco for hard-hitting first baseman Orlando Cepeda. But both deals fell through by the time the June 15 trading deadline passed, and the only transaction of any note that Quinn could make was to sign Ron Allen, the twenty-year-old brother of Richie.[23] Ron, a catcher, was assigned to Bakersfield of the California League to learn first base.[24] With Harold Allen playing at Chattanooga in the Southern League, the Phillies had both of Richie's brothers in their farm system. Covington would remain with the Phillies through the 1965 season, often trying what little patience Mauch had for clubhouse politics.

Never known to take anything for granted, Mauch continued to be a taskmaster, even though his team was in first place. On June 29, for example, the Phils were on the losing end of a whitewashing by the seventh-place Colts, and the Little General let his disappointment be known. "There was no place worse in baseball to play before the Astrodome was built," recalled Clay Dalrymple. "The old stadium was cut right out of a cow pasture. Every inning, when you'd come in from the field you had to spray the bugs off your clothing and body, and the heat was stifling. It was especially bad on that day. Every inning we'd come in complaining about the bugs and the heat."[25]

By the sixth inning, Mauch had heard enough.

"I'm sick of your griping about horseshit conditions," he yelled. "They have to play in this shit too. The next guy who complains gets fined a hundred bucks!"

The next inning Callison returned from the outfield sweating profusely and covered with bugs.

"God, it's fuckin' hot out there," he moaned, forgetting himself.

Mauch glared at him, ready to slap him with a fine. But the shrewd right-fielder corrected himself, quickly adding: "Good'n hot, just the way I like it!"[26]

The Phillies entered the month of July dropping a heartbreaker to Sandy Koufax and the Dodgers. After taking a 2–0 lead in the fourth on a two-run homer by Johnny Callison, Dennis Bennett lost the lead, and the game, 3–2. Koufax went on to post ten strikeouts, allowing him to reach the career total of 1,600.[27] The Phillies fared better in San Francisco, where they headed for a first-place showdown. Ray Culp threw a six-hitter in the opening game to clinch a 5–1 victory, and Bunning raised his record to 9–2 the following day, defeating the Giants, 5–3. The Phils completed the three-game sweep on July 5 with a 2–1 victory behind the combined pitching of Bennett and Baldschun. Allen turned in brilliant performances in all three games. He hammered out five hits in ten plate appearances in the first two games, including his sixteenth homer of the season. In the third game he made two remarkable plays in the field that saved the game for the Fightins'.[28]

At the All-Star break in early July, the Phillies were on top of the National League with the Giants one and a half games behind. Cincinnati was a distant third, six games out, followed by fourth-place Pittsburgh (seven games out) and the fifth-place Cardinals (ten games out). Four Phillies were among the league-leaders as well: Cookie Rojas, with a .326 batting average; Richie Allen, with 16 home runs; Chris Short, with a 1.58 ERA; and Jim Bunning with 99 strikeouts and 125 innings pitched.[29] Despite the team and individual success, no one was selected to the National League's All-Star Game starting lineup. Only Bunning, Callison, and Short made the team as reserves. Instead, the major league players, who made the selections in those days, named the following starters for the mid-summer classic that would be played at New York's Shea Stadium:[30]

Roberto Clemente, Pittsburgh Pirates, right field
Dick Groat, St. Louis Cardinals, shortstop
Billy Williams, Chicago Cubs, left field
Willie Mays, San Francisco Giants, center field
Orlando Cepeda, San Francisco Giants, first base
Ken Boyer, St. Louis Cardinals, third base
Joe Torre, Milwaukee Braves, catcher
Ron Hunt, New York Mets, second base
Don Drysdale, Los Angeles Dodgers, pitching

"It's the damnedest lineup card that's ever been on this dugout wall," said Casey Stengel, manager of the hapless Mets, who was named by National League Manager Walter Alston as one of the coaches. "Look at them extry [sic] men—Aaron, White, Koufax, Bunning."[31]

A crowd of 50,850 was on hand at Shea on July 7 to watch Don Drysdale face Dean Chance of the American League's Los Angeles Angels. The American League took the lead in the top of the first when the Angels' Jim Fregosi singled, took second on a passed ball, and scored on a long single to left by the Twins' Harmon Killebrew.[32] After that, Drysdale did not allow another base runner in his three innings of work. When Bunning relieved him in the top of the fourth, the Phillies' ace made All-Star history by being the first player ever to pitch for both leagues in the mid-summer classic. Bunning had made six appearances for the American League while he was with Detroit.[33]

In the top of the fourth, Bunning faced Mickey Mantle, who popped up to second base while trying to bunt for a base hit. Killebrew came up next. Bunning threw him a high, inside fastball that nicked his bat and rolled toward third base for an infield single. Orioles third baseman Brooks Robinson followed with a single to right. But the Phillies' ace stranded both runners by striking out the next two batters to end the inning.[34]

In the bottom of the inning, the National League took the lead on a pair of solo homers by Billy Williams and Ken Boyer. Bunning preserved the 2–1 lead by retiring the side in order in the top of the fifth to complete his scoreless two-inning stint with four strikeouts and surrendering just two hits. The National League added another run in the bottom of the fifth when Roberto Clemente got an infield single and Dick Groat of the Cardinals scored him on a double to right.[35] When Alston sent Johnny Callison to bat for Bunning, the Phils outfielder popped out and returned to the bench, believing he had made his cameo appearance. But Alston sent him out to play right field in the bottom of the sixth. Chris Short, the only left-handed pitcher on the National League squad, was also sent into the game.[36]

Short began the sixth by striking out Tony Oliva, the hot-hitting Minnesota outfielder. But Mantle and Killebrew followed with singles. After Twins first baseman Bob Allison flied out to center field, Brooks Robinson hit a triple to deep right field, tying the game at 3–3. Short, who was hampered by a muscle pull in his side, retired the side on a comebacker by Bobby Richardson of the Yankees, but the damage had already been done.[37]

"I felt good out there," said Short after the game. "But I could feel this [muscle pull] in my side and I was sort of afraid to throw hard. I threw my breaking stuff hard but I didn't let go on my fastball. I told Alston after the inning I wasn't right, and he took me out. In a way I'm glad it happened. It's better to find out now than it would have been in a Phillies game."[38]

The American Leaguers took the lead in the seventh inning when Fregosi hit a sacrifice fly to score Brooks Robinson. In the bottom of the

inning, American League Manager Ralph Houk gave the ball to Boston's
Dick Radatz, a 6-foot-6-inch 250-pound sidearmer who was averaging two
strikeouts an inning that season. Radatz held the National League team
scoreless through the next two innings, striking out four of the six hitters
he faced. The game entered the bottom of the ninth with the American
League clinging to a 4–3 lead, and Radatz in command.

Willie Mays led off for the National League with a walk. Cepeda followed. On Radatz's second pitch to the Giants' first baseman, Mays stole
second, beating Yankee catcher Elston Howard's throw. Cepeda hit Radatz's
third pitch off the handle of his bat for a bloop single into right field. When
Mays saw the ball drop, he ran for third. Rightfielder Rocky Colavito of the
Kansas City Athletics threw home. The ball bounced ten feet in front of the
plate and skipped past the outstretched arm of Howard. Radatz, confused
as to whether he should back up third or home on the throw, hesitated and

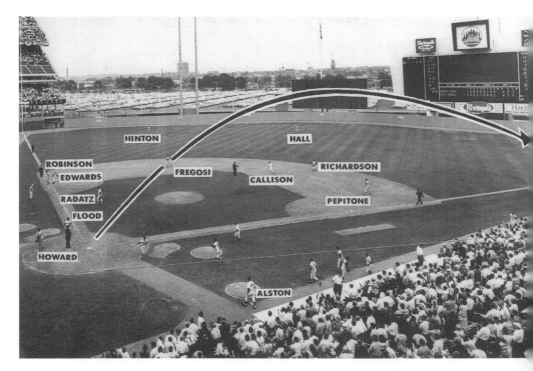

Fig. 19 and Fig. 20   Johnny Callison crosses home plate *(opposite)* after hitting the
game-winning homer in the 1964 All-Star Game at New York's Shea Stadium, and
the trajectory of that home run. *(Philadelphia Daily News)*

Fig. 20

found himself running toward the play. When the dust cleared, Mays had scored, Cepeda was standing on second base, and the game was tied at 4–4.

Ken Boyer, the Cardinals third baseman, came up next. Radatz retired him on a pop foul near the plate. John Edwards of the Reds was intentionally walked to set up a double play possibility with Cepeda still on second. Braves star Hank Aaron, who was sitting out the game with a stomach virus, was called on to pinch hit for second baseman Ron Hunt. But Radatz struck him out on four pitches.[39]

With two outs and two men on, Johnny Callison came to bat. "I remember how hard Radatz threw in the seventh," said Callison, recalling the long fly ball out that he hit to center field in his earlier at-bat. "So I decided to switch to a lighter bat. I borrowed one from Billy Williams and went up to the plate thinking 'Don't strike out!'"[40] Radatz's first pitch was a high fastball. Callison drove the ball into the right-field grandstand for a climactic three-run homer, and the National League walked off the field with a 7–4 come-from-behind victory. "As soon as I swung, I thought it was a homer," admitted Callison. "I saw Colavito move three steps to his left, and then I watched the ball bounce off the seats in the upper deck. I was on cloud nine as I floated around the bases. By the time I'd rounded second I saw Radatz throw his glove into the dugout. Curt Flood, Johnny Edwards, and the rest of the National League All-Stars mobbed me at home plate. It was a real thrill for me."[41]

The Phillies opened the second half of the season on July 9 with a six-game home stand against the Cincinnati Reds and the Milwaukee Braves. The Phils defeated the Reds, 4–3, in the first game but lost the next two games, including a 3–1 heartbreaker on Saturday July 11. The game, played in stifling 90-degree heat, was a scoreless duel between Bunning and Cincinnati's Joe Nuxhall, until the Reds scored all three of their runs in the sixth. Worse, the loss knocked the Phillies out of first by one-half game as the Giants swept a four-game series against the Chicago Cubs. Milwaukee came into Philadelphia next, and won both ends of a Sunday doubleheader, 4–3 and 6–2, before the Phillies finally defeated Warren Spahn on July 13 to snap a four-game losing streak. Allen was the star of the game, hitting a triple and a double while scoring two runs.[42]

In an unusually generous column, Larry Merchant of the *Philadelphia Daily News* wrote: "There is no way that Richie Allen can have anything but a big, big year." Comparing Allen's start with the debuts of such sluggers as Frank Robinson, Orlando Cepeda, and Mickey Mantle, Merchant predicted that the Phillies rookie would hit "around .300" and "drive in and score 100 runs, get 190 to 200 base hits with 30–35 home runs, 35–40 doubles and 10 triples." Of course, Merchant also predicted that Allen would "strike out 160 times." Never one to give much credit to management, the *Daily News* columnist attributed the rookie's success to the fact that the Phillies coaches "leave him alone and let him play ball."[43]

If Allen was letting his success go to his head, he certainly did not show it. His mother made sure of it. "All of this [success] is nice," Era told her son, "but being a baseball player isn't everything. I want you to do right, to be a right kind of man."[44] Allen, who had purchased a new house for his mother shortly after he signed with the Phillies, paid close attention to her advice. "If I made a million dollars in baseball and gave it all to her, it wouldn't be enough to repay my mother for what she did for me," he admitted. "If you wanted to play ball at our house growing up, you had to get up before daybreak and do your homework. She didn't stand for any nonsense. Outside of baseball, I think she was the best hitter I ever saw!"[45] Richie Allen was a dream come true, not only for Philadelphia's growing pool of African American baseball fans, but also for the Phillies management, who appreciated his exceptional maturity, both on and off the playing field.

The Phillies regained first place on July 16 by defeating the Pittsburgh Pirates, 7–5. Coupled with the Giants' three-game losing streak against sixth-place Milwaukee, the Phils held first by four percentage points. Cookie Rojas was the hero, with two doubles and a single. Art Mahaffey raised his record to 8–4 with three innings of two-hit relief from Jack Baldschun.[46] The Phillies went on to Cincinnati, where they dropped three of five games against the Reds. On Friday, July 17, the Phils defeated the Reds, 5–4, to gain sole possession of first. On Saturday, Ray Culp faced Cincinnati's John Tsitouris in a day game. Covington, who had been partying hard the night before, showed up at the ballpark with a bad hangover.

"Hey, Bro—you don't look so good," said Allen, greeting his black teammate as he stumbled into the clubhouse. "You know you're starting today?"

"Noooh problem!" said Covington, as he pulled on his uniform.

When the Phillies left-fielder went to bat in the first, Tsitouris threw him high and tight to back him off the plate. But the pitch got away from the Reds' pitcher. Covington was like a deer caught in the headlights. He couldn't move, and the pitch hit him squarely on the head.

As Covington was being carried off the field on a stretcher, Allen went over to him and joked: "Noooh problem, Bro. Noooh problem!"[47]

Fortunately, Covington made a quick recovery.

The Phillies also got pummeled that afternoon in a seventeen-hit assault. A young Pete Rose served as a one-man wrecking crew for Cincinnati, pounding out four hits, including the very first grand slam of his career. Deron Johnson and Don Pavletich also hit home runs. Tsitouris hurled a complete game for the 14–4 victory, while Ray Culp took the loss for the Phillies. The win allowed the Reds to move within three and a half games of the first-place Phils.[48] The next day, Sunday, July 19, a near-sellout crowd of 27,245 saw the Reds and Phils split a doubleheader. Bunning started the opener and had a 4–0 lead going into the sixth when he surrendered two unearned runs. Chris Short came into the game in relief and gave up another run. Jack Baldschun and Ed Roebuck were hit hard for four more tallies, and the Phils ended up losing, 7–4. John Boozer got the win in the nightcap in a come-from-behind, 4–3 victory.[49]

Clay Dalrymple, exhausted from catching both ends of the double-header, went out on a Cincinnati riverboat that night to unwind. Dennis Bennett went along for the ride. After a few beers, Bennett bet his battery mate that he couldn't swim across the Ohio River. Dalrymple countered with the same bet. Stripping down to their underwear, the two teammates dove off the riverboat and headed for the Kentucky shoreline. Halfway across, Dalrymple turned to Bennett and said: "I know we can both make it to the other side. But I don't know if we'll both be able to swim back. We just might be stuck in Kentucky in our underwear! Let's just swim back to the boat. I think we've proved our point."[50]

Years later, Bennett recalled Allen's remarks to Covington and his own bet with Dalrymple as signs of the close chemistry on the team. "There was no bickering or clubhouse escapades on that team," he said. "There was no racism that I could see. We all liked each other and joked around with each other. It was one of the tightest group of guys I ever played with."[51] Tony Taylor agreed. "There was great chemistry between the Hispanic, black, and white players on the team in '64," he said. "We were all very young, plus we had a young manager in Gene Mauch. He knew the importance of team chemistry on an integrated club. He had already been through integration in the Dodger organization as a player and saw all the things Jackie Robinson went through to break the color barrier. Gene also played in Cuba. So he kept all the players together, to function like a team."[52]

Cookie Rojas also credited Mauch for the team's winning chemistry. "In '64, no one gave us a chance to contend," he noted. "But under Gene Mauch we learned a lot about baseball. We had strong defense, good hitting, and strong pitching. You'll never hear me complain about Gene Mauch. He gave me the opportunity to play. It didn't matter where he put me, I went out and gave him the best I had."[53]

Rojas had his reasons to be supportive of Mauch. He had been relegated to the bench in Cincinnati before he arrived in Philadelphia. The Little General resurrected his career. Credited with popularizing the platoon system, Mauch made Rojas his chief utility player. Although Rojas's best position was second base, the Phillies skipper made him the first player in the history of the National League to play all nine field positions.[54]

Others were less complimentary of Mauch. Frank Dolson, a columnist for the *Philadelphia Inquirer*, believes the Little General had less to do with the cohesion of the team than the Hispanic players themselves. "It's impossible to think that the '64 Phillies were a real tight-knit group because of the way Mauch treated them," he said. "The ones who were important, like Callison, Bunning, and Allen, were made to feel important. Those who weren't that important were made to feel that way. Sure, the players respected him, but they didn't like him. Mauch was divisive." Instead, Dolson credited the Hispanic players like Taylor, Gonzalez, and Rojas for the team's special chemistry. "The Hispanic players were all class acts," said Dolson. "They thought and acted in terms of *team*, not individual achievement."[55] Art Mahaffey, whose hatred for Gene Mauch was compulsive, agreed with Dolson's assessment. "When I first came to the Phillies in 1960, we were a bad team," said the Phillies veteran pitcher. "Everybody agitated each other in those days. Every player had been a superstar in high school, but now they were thrown together with twenty-five other 'superstars' on the same team. You were just one of many, and you had to live together for seven or eight months out of the year. It wasn't pretty, and Mauch didn't make it any easier. Once, he got us into the clubhouse and reamed us out. He ended his tirade by screaming, 'I hate everyone on this team, except Callison!' But in '64, things were different. I guess we succeeded in spite of Gene. Basically all the players respected each other's abilities. It didn't matter if you were black, white, or Latino. We heckled each other a lot, but it wasn't malicious. It was just the way we kept each other loose, a way to have fun in the clubhouse."[56]

Dallas Green was more diplomatic. "Gene knew the rule book better than the umpires," recalled Green, who admits that he adopted many of the lessons Mauch taught his players when he managed the Phillies in 1980. "He knew the rules inside and out. He also introduced us to a lot of trick plays, such as pickoffs and different defenses. In fact we used the squeeze play twenty-five times one season to score some runs. But Gene was *not* a people person. He was terrible to his players—except maybe for Callison, who appeared to many of us to be his favorite."[57]

Regardless of their feelings for the manager, the members of the 1964 club had positive feelings about their teammates. "When I put the uniform on, I didn't think about anything but playing the game," said Tony Gonzalez. "I think all of us got along all right. Sure, players kidded around with each other. One of my teammates called me a 'Cuban monkey.' But that didn't bother me because that kind of stuff went on in all the clubhouses back then. Besides, he didn't mean anything by it. Everybody— white players, black players, Hispanic players—got along fine."[58]

In today's "politically correct" atmosphere, baseball players are much more hesitant to use racial vocabulary as terms of endearment, but that certainly was not the case in the 1960s. Racist language was a natural part of clubhouse culture throughout the majors. In Philadelphia, white veterans often used the term "nigger" to demonstrate their acceptance of an exceptional young black player. "Richie Allen and I were very close friends," insists Clay Dalrymple. "We'd walk down the street with our arms around each other's shoulders. I'd call him 'nigger, ' he'd call me 'white trash,' and we'd be laughing like sons-of-bitches. But he trusted me because I was Pat Corrales's roommate, and Pat was one of his closest friends on the team."[59]

"There was no racism on the '64 Phillies because everybody was in the same boat," added Rick Wise. "We weren't making much money as players in those days, and that was the major gripe. It certainly wasn't race relations. As far as race relations were concerned, I never saw any racist attitudes on the Phillies." Then again, Wise admits that he "probably wouldn't have recognized racism if it did exist" among his teammates at that point in his life. Having just come out of high school in predominantly white Portland, Oregon, he had not been exposed to segregation until 1964, when the Phillies charter flight arrived at Atlanta's airport and he saw segregated restrooms. Like all rookies, Wise understood that he was up with the big club to learn and contribute whenever he could. "Back in those days, it was rare for a veteran player to take a rookie under his wing," he recalled. "But even then, players like Tony Taylor were wonderful to me. Tony showed me a lot of things about big league life, on and off the field."[60] Rookies looked out for each other as well.

Richie Allen was a valued mentor to other young African American players who were promoted to the Phillies during the season. Grant Jackson remembers being called up to the big club with Ferguson Jenkins late in the 1964 campaign. "Richie looked out for us because we weren't making much money," he said. "He and his wife, Barb, invited me to stay at their house in Germantown, and they refused to take any rent. They even let me use their car."[61] Similarly, Allen took Briggs and Alex Johnson under his wing.[62] Briggs was genuinely liked both by teammates and by ownership, and he relied on Allen's encouragement to realize his own potential. Johnson was more difficult to understand or like. "Alex called everybody 'dickhead,' recalled Allen. "To him, baseball was a whole world of dickheads. Teammates, managers, general managers, owners. Everybody was a dickhead to him. That was just his way. But the front-office types took it personally. They said he was surly. But Alex was also the kind of guy who would come over to my house and play with my kids, or jump into his car and drive out to the Schuylkill Expressway to help a clubhouse attendant fix his broken-down car. People just didn't understand him. All Alex wanted to do was be left alone to play ball."[63]

Allen also looked out for the veterans. In one of the unwritten rules of baseball, pitchers retaliate when an opposing hurler throws at a teammate. Often, the benches clear after a knockdown pitch in a show of loyalty to either the victim or the offender. Allen made it clear to all the Phillies pitchers that he would be the first to protect them in such cases, and he followed through on his promise whenever such an incident occurred.[64]

The 1964 Phillies also endeared themselves to the fans, both on and off the field. Many of the players made their year-round home in the Philadelphia area: Callison and Dalrymple lived in suburban Glenside; Baldschun and Taylor, in Yeadon; Wine, in Norristown; Green, in nearby Wilmington, Delaware; and Mahaffey, Short, Allen, Amaro, Covington, and Gonzalez all lived within the city limits.[65] Players mixed with the fans outside the ballpark. "I'd walk to the ballpark from the North Philadelphia station," said Dallas Green, who traveled on a train between Connie Mack and his hometown of Wilmington, Delaware. "After the game, I'd walk back along with the crowd and catch the latest train that stopped. It was really no big deal. At that time, train stations were still pretty safe, and you also got to know some of the regulars who came to the park."[66] Neighborhood kids had access to their heroes. "The early '6os were good times," said Michael Fitts, who lived on the 2700 block of North Twentieth Street, bordering the stadium's right-field wall. "Us kids, we'd wait outside the Twenty-first Street exit for the players and get their autographs—Richie Allen, Chris Short, and Tony Taylor would always stop and sign. Of course, Johnny Callison was my boy!"[67]

Fig. 21 Dallas Green, a hard-luck pitcher for the Phillies from 1960 to 1964, made his mark in 1980, managing the team to its only world championship. (Philadelphia Phillies)

"Most of the fans were pretty good," recalled Baldschun. "There were regulars in the box seats who would bring us newspapers and magazines to read in the bullpen. They knew their baseball too. Once in a while, you'd have someone give you trouble if you made a bad play. But that's because they knew the game so well."[68] A special bond developed between the players and the fans that summer, and it was based on more than mutual admiration. There was a genuine affection between the Phillies and the hometown crowd that sometimes translated into lifetime memories for both parties. "I'll never forget this little blind girl who used to come to the games and sit in a box seat near home plate," said Clay Dalrymple, in a recent interview. "She called herself my biggest fan, and I just fell in love with her. It got to the point that the ushers would always tell me when she came to the park. One time, after a game, I offered to take her onto the field. It was just something I wanted to do for her. I walked her over to home plate, and she knelt down to feel it. Then we walked to first base so she could feel the bag. Then to second and third. She was just so overjoyed." Dalrymple was so moved by the experience that he failed to notice a small crowd that had gathered to watch the scene. Suddenly, he heard an appreciative applause from the stands. "It was probably the biggest ovation I ever received," recalled the Phillies backstop, who is still overcome with emotion at the memory nearly forty years later. "Fans like that little girl made my entire career worthwhile."[69]

When the Phillies returned home from the West Coast on July 24, more than 5,000 fans turned out to greet them at Philadelphia International Airport. Placards and bumper stickers with the words "CALLISON FOR PRESIDENT" and "GO PHILLIES GO" began to surface throughout the city. Pennant fever was raging in Philadelphia for the first time in more than a decade. But Mauch knew better than to take his club's first-place standing for granted.[70]

The Phillies had managed to hold on to first by beating the weaker National League teams. Their cumulative record against the Mets, the Colts, the Cubs, and the Dodgers at that point in the season was 30–11. The Mauch men had been less successful against the Reds, who had taken six of eleven games from them, and the Cardinals, who won nine of the sixteen contests between the two teams. Both those teams were sending left-handers to the mound against the Phillies, who were in need of a right-handed power hitter.[71] If the Phils were to contend in the second half, they would have to have more success against the first-division teams. They would also need to trade for a right-handed power hitter. Roy Sievers tried to convince Mauch that he could fill that void. But the thirty-seven-year-old first baseman was hitting just .183 with 4 homers and 16 RBIs through early August. "My offensive numbers were down because I had a pulled muscle in my right leg," Sievers explained, years later. "I told Gene that I'd be able to play in September and October. But they had other plans and sent me back to Washington in late August."[72] Unfortunately for the Phillies, Sievers was good to his word. In the month of September he collected four home runs and 11 RBIs as the Senator's regular first baseman.[73] Instead, Quinn acquired power-hitting first baseman Frank Thomas from the New York Mets in exchange for minor leaguer Wayne Graham, rookie pitcher Gary Kroll, and cash in early August.[74]

Thomas, a strapping 6-foot-3-inch 200-pound slugger, was a three-time all-star who up to that point had hit 272 home runs in an eleven-year career with the Pirates, the Reds, the Cubs, the Braves, and the Mets. A dead pull-hitter who crowded the plate, Thomas attracted the attention of John Quinn in 1962 when he hit thirty-four homers and 94 RBIs for the expansion Mets.[75] Thomas carried the Phillies for his first two weeks with the club. In his first game as a Phillie, he played first, drove in two runs with a double and a single, then started a double play from first base to cap a 9–4 victory against his former teammates.[76] The victory increased the Phillies' lead to two and a half games over the second-place Giants. The Phillies would go on to win twenty of their next thirty-two games, with Thomas leading the charge. During that span, the veteran first baseman hit .302 with 7 homers and 26 RBIs. He became so popular that WFIL Radio gave him a morning show in which he would play the most recent hit records and talk baseball.[77]

With Thomas in the lineup, Allen and Callison became even more dangerous at the plate. By mid-August both players were tied for the club lead in home runs with twenty each, while Callison led the Phillies in RBIs with 70 to Allen's 61. Both players were leading candidates for Most Valuable Player, with Allen favored to capture the National League's Rookie of the Year Award as well.[78] "We have a ball club that has the will to win," said Allen. "We have no long ball hitters like the Giants and the Braves, but we have a scrappy team.[79] Bunning agreed. "I thought all along in spring training that we had a chance to win the pennant," he admitted. "Then once around the league, I was more convinced than ever that we can win the pennant."[80]

Having been in contention since opening day, the Phillies seemed to be favorites to capture the flag. Heading into the dog days of August, they were getting excellent pitching from Bunning, Bennett, and Short. Baldschun was an extremely effective closer, and Roebuck and Boozer were the other consistent relievers. Quinn added depth to the bullpen by acquiring veteran left-hander Bobby Shantz from the Chicago Cubs.[81]

After defeating Milwaukee, 6–1, on August 26, the Phillies held a commanding seven-and-a-half-game lead over San Francisco, with a hot Cincinnati club in third, eight games behind, and the Cardinals in fourth, ten games out.[82] Their enchanting summer had continued through the dog days, a make-or-break period for most contenders. But when the team returned home from the Midwest on the August 28 to face the Pirates at Connie Mack Stadium, they were confronted by one of the most devastating race riots of the civil rights era.

On Friday night, August 28, a black police officer approached a black female motorist whose car had stalled at the intersection of Columbia Avenue and Twenty-second Street in North Philadelphia, just a few blocks away from the ballpark. Refusing to move her car, the motorist and her husband, a passenger, stepped outside the vehicle to confront the officer. The couple were intoxicated. Tempers flared. Suddenly the woman slapped the police officer and shoved him out of her way. A crowd gathered as the police officer radioed for support. As the disorderly motorist was being arrested, the police were attacked by a hailstorm of bricks and bottles. By 10:30 P.M., the incident had erupted into a full-fledged riot with as many as 2,000 people looting, destroying storefronts, and setting fires.[83]

Just before dawn, 600 policemen converged on the North Penn District, but the looters continued their rampage. Police Commissioner Howard Leary refused to allow his officers to wade into the hostile crowd and ordered them not to use their weapons unless directly threatened. When the rioters began shooting at firefighters and police, Deputy Police Commissioner Frank Rizzo confronted Leary, warning that the incident had spiraled out of control. Leary ignored him, refusing to do anything more drastic. At dawn Cecil Moore, president of the Philadelphia NAACP, arrived and tried to reason with the rioters. "I understand your problems," he shouted to them, "but this is no way to solve them!" Disc jockey Georgie Woods, an NAACP deputy officer, drove through the neighborhood with a loudspeaker, pleading for rioters to "get off the streets." Judge Raymond P. Alexander, a respected African American jurist, stood on the hood of Wood's car and promised that the police would leave if the crowd dispersed.[84] Nothing worked, until 9:00 A.M., when Mayor Tate arrived to announce a curfew on a 410-block square of North Philadelphia. Accompanied by another 600 police officers, Tate finally managed to restore some semblance of order.

"I remember driving to the ballpark that Saturday," said Jack Baldschun, who commuted with Tony Taylor from their suburban Yeadon homes. "We were worried about a brick getting thrown through the windshield of my car. But we had no choice. They didn't cancel the game. We had to play."[85] To be sure, the ball game against the Pittsburgh Pirates went on before a near empty stadium that night. Allen tripled and hit his twenty-fourth home run, knocking in four runs, while Callison hit his twenty-third homer and collected 3 RBIs. Art Mahaffey, who enjoyed a 10–0 lead, was knocked out in the eighth when the Bucs rallied for four runs. Boozer replaced him, but surrendered another four runs before Baldschun could finish the game, a narrow 10–8 victory.[86]

During the game, the mob, ignoring Tate's curfew, resumed its rampage. Marching west on Columbia Avenue, the rioters destroyed white-owned businesses one by one. The rioting continued all day Sunday as the Pirates humbled the Phillies, 10–2, at Connie Mack. Not until Monday evening, after all the stores on Columbia had been looted, did the riot end. When it was over, 2 people were dead and 339 were wounded, including 100 police officers. Another 300 people were arrested, and more than 600 businesses, many owned by white Jewish merchants, were destroyed, with damages estimated at $3 million.[87] North Philadelphia's neighborhoods were now blocked off from the rest of the city by police barricades.

The fans stayed away from Connie Mack Stadium for days after the riot. Black rage had increased the fears of the whites who lived in the North Penn District, hastening their flight to the suburbs. It also increased police presence around the ballpark. Between 50 and 60 officers surrounded the stadium, an additional 100 patrolled the neighborhood, and another 1,000 could be found across North Philadelphia.[88] Gerald Early, a professor of African American Studies at Washington University in St. Louis, remembers as a youngster walking with friends from his South Philadelphia neighborhood to Connie Mack. Not only was it a fifty-block journey, but to watch the Phillies they had to pass through the newly created "police state" as well as the territory of some of the worst black street gangs in the city. Members of the Zulu Nation, the Twenty-first and Tioga Street Gang, the Master Street Gang, and the Anthill Mob did not share the earlier generation's interest in baseball and would jeer those African American youngsters who did: "Y'all niggers *walking* to Connie Mack Stadium to watch the Phillies? Y'all must be crazy. I wouldn't go see no ball game, especially the Phillies, if they paid me."[89]

Like African Americans across the nation, Philadelphia's blacks were becoming more race conscious. They had grown tired of being second-class citizens and were demanding integration into the American mainstream. The struggle involved black self-assertion, or expressing dissatisfaction— actively, if not militantly—with the status quo. Blacks resented white dominance of the businesses in a neighborhood that was increasingly populated by African Americans. In North Philadelphia, the Phillies were one of those white-owned businesses. "The only thing I regret about the riot," said one black resident, speaking on the condition of anonymity, "was that we didn't burn down that goddamn stadium. They had it surrounded by cops, and we couldn't get to it. I just wish we could've burned it down and wiped away its history that tells me I'm nothing but a nigger."[90]

North Philadelphia's residents were not the only ones awakened by the Black Rage sweeping across their neighborhoods. Richie Allen also became acutely aware of the fact that he was a black superstar on a team that had never been accepted by the city's African American residents and, as such, became a symbol for the racial unrest that was consuming Philadelphia. "Racial tensions were at the boiling point," recalled Allen, years later. "The neighborhood around Connie Mack looked like a bomb had just hit it. The streets were empty. People stayed indoors. Police cars patrolled the streets. Stores were boarded up. And whites blamed blacks for that. I guess being the star black player for the Phillies also made me a threat to white people, especially since I said what was on my mind. They weren't used to a black athlete like that."[91]

What was happening in Philadelphia, however, was happening in other major league cities as well. Tim McCarver, currently a broadcaster, was a catcher for the St. Louis Cardinals in the mid-1960s. He points out that "race riots also took place in New York, Chicago, and Los Angeles as well" and that to "single out Philadelphia is just unfair."[92] And racial tensions were not restricted to city streets. In San Francisco, Giant manager Alvin Dark, frustrated with his team's inability to catch the Phillies in the pennant race, was quoted as saying, "We have trouble because we have so many Negro and Spanish-speaking players on this team. They are just not able to perform up to the white players when it comes to mental alertness. One of the biggest things is that you can't make them subordinate themselves to the best interest of the team. You don't find pride in them that you get in a white player."[93] Dark, a native Southerner, denied making the remark, but his nonwhite players still threatened to revolt. Team captain Willie Mays saved Dark's job and averted the strike by insisting that while he had nothing but contempt for Dark's racism, it did not interfere with his decisions as a manager.[94] Nor were the Giants' racial tensions limited to African American ballplayers.

Concerned by Fidel Castro's takeover of Cuba, Major League Baseball viewed itself as a diplomatic vehicle to prevent the spread of communism. It donated baseball equipment to the Peace Corps in the Dominican Republic, for example, so the game would "keep a bunch of kids out of the clutches of Castro's agents." At the same time, baseball restricted the freedom of Hispanic players who wanted to return to a native country threatened by the spread of communism. Accordingly, Commissioner Ford Frick fined Giants pitcher Juan Marichal and outfielder Felipe Alou for playing winter ball in the Dominican Republic. "These are our people," protested Alou, demanding that a Hispanic representative be appointed to the commissioner's staff. "We owe it to them to play for them."[95] Therefore, as dismal as the state of race relations appeared in Philadelphia, the Phillies certainly had none of the clubhouse tensions the Giants were experiencing. On the playing field, things were even better.

In order to win the pennant, the Phillies, on September 1, would have to win just half of their remaining thirty games. They enjoyed a five-and-a-half-game lead over Cincinnati, who had knocked the Giants out of second. San Francisco was in third, six and a half games out, and St. Louis was in fourth, seven games back.[96] The Phils opened the month with a three-game home stand against the Houston Colt 45s. In the first game of the series, Jim Bunning and Colt knuckleballer Hal Brown were locked in a scoreless tie through six innings. Callison broke the deadlock in the bottom of the seventh with a homer. Thomas and Covington followed with solo shots. Allen hit an inside-the-parker in the eighth to give the Phils a 4–0 lead, which allowed Bunning to coast to his sixth straight victory and fifteenth of the season. Chris Short earned his fifteenth victory the following night, throwing a four-hitter and collecting ten strikeouts. The Phils blew scoring opportunities in the first three innings, but Tony Taylor picked them up in the fourth. After Covington singled to right and Dalrymple singled up the middle, Taylor followed with a two-run base hit. Houston almost came back in the ninth. With one out and one run across, Bob Aspromonte hit a bouncer to Allen at third. The Phillies rookie backed up on the ball and threw it past Frank Thomas at first for a two-base error. It was his thirty-fourth miscue of the season. But the Phillies managed to eke out a 2–1 win.[97] After the game, Mauch said that he never panicked. "Shoot, we've been in games like this all year long," he insisted. "If we don't beat 'em one way, we beat 'em another. We knew we were going to win. This year is the most fun I've ever had in my life. Nobody worries. We don't worry about the Giant or Cincy scores. It doesn't matter what they do if we win."[98]

On Thursday night, September 3, Dennis Bennett faced Houston's Don Larsen in the final game of the series. With two outs in the fifth inning, Giant shortstop Eddie Kasko smashed a hard ground ball off Richie Allen's chest. The scorer ruled it a base hit. Bob Lillis followed with a bunt down the third-base line. Allen charged, trying to scoop the ball with one hand, but he bobbled the play. Again, the scorer ruled it a hit. The fans were much less charitable, showering both Allen and the scorer with a hailstorm of boos. It didn't matter that the Phils' star rookie tripled in the eighth. The Phils dropped the game, 6–0, but still retained a five-and-a-half-game lead over the Reds, who were defeated by the Cubs, 3–0.[99] In a postgame interview, Allen told Stan Hochman of the *Philadelphia Daily News* that he was not bothered by the fan reaction. "Let them boo," he said. "They can't play third base for me. They paid to get in, so they can boo if they want to. It doesn't bother me a bit."[100]

On Friday, September 4, the third-place San Francisco Giants came to Connie Mack Stadium. Tickets were in demand for the critical three-game series, with sellout crowds for the first time since the August riot. The fans were treated to some of the most exciting baseball of the season. In the first game, the Phils were trailing the Giants, 3–1, in the fourth when Willie Mays robbed Ruben Amaro of an extra-base hit by leaping against the scoreboard for a sensational catch. The score remained 3–1 Giants until the sixth, when Frank Thomas blasted a two-run homer off the roof in deep left field to tie the game. Gus Triandos followed with a double. Callison, batting seventh, drove in the slow-footed catcher with a bloop single, and the Phillies walked off with a 4–3 victory.[101] The Phillies beat the Giants again, 9–3, the following night. Bunning won his seventh straight game, and his sixteenth of the season. But the Giants came back to win the final contest, 4–3, on Sunday, September 6. Juan Marichal pitched brilliantly, striking out thirteen. Considering that the Phillies surrendered six extra-base hits and committed five throwing errors, the Phils were lucky to keep the game within one run.[102]

On Labor Day, September 7, the Phillies found themselves still enjoying a five-and-a-half-game lead over second-place Cincinnati and a seven-and-a-half-game lead over both St. Louis and San Francisco. With a crowd of 26,390 on hand to see the Phillies play a doubleheader against the seventh-place Dodgers, the club set a new season attendance record of 1,224,172.[103]

Dennis Bennett started the opener and snapped a personal seven-game losing streak by defeating the Dodgers, 5–1, for his tenth victory of the season. Rick Wise lost the nightcap, 3–1, but the Phillies were encouraged by the pitching of Bobby Shantz, who hurled seven strong innings in relief and allowed only three hits.[104] The following afternoon, the Phils hosted the Dodgers in a make-up of an August 3 contest that had been postponed due to "threatening weather." In fact, Mauch and Quinn had manipulated the postponement at a time when the Phillies were on a losing streak and when Koufax, who was scheduled to pitch, was at his best. It was no coincidence that both men wanted to make up the game as a doubleheader during the Jewish New Year in early September so the Phils would once again avoid Koufax, a devout Jew who refused to pitch on holy days.[105] Although the Phillies had avoided Koufax, facing twenty-six-year-old left-hander Jim Brewer instead, they still lost the game, 3–2.

They also lost Frank Thomas to a freak injury. In the fourth inning, Allen tripled and broke for home when Thomas hit a chopper back to the mound. Caught in a rundown between third and home, Allen was tagged out by Brewer while Thomas advanced to second base on the play. Alex Johnson came to the plate next and hit a grounder to shortstop Maury Wills. Thomas, who had broken from second, tried to slide back to the bag, but Wills tagged him out and threw to first to complete the twin killing. On the play, Thomas broke his right thumb sliding into second base. The injury forced the hot-hitting first baseman out of the lineup.[106]

Quinn tried to fill the void for a power-hitting first baseman by acquiring Vic Power from the Los Angeles Angels. Power, who began his career with the old Philadelphia Athletics in 1954, was a four-time all-star at first base. Known for his showboating style of play and colorful personality, the thirty-three-year-old Puerto Rican directed much of his humor at the racist treatment he experienced in the majors. Once, while playing in Little Rock, Arkansas, a waitress told him she was sorry but the restaurant did not serve blacks. "That's all right," replied Power, "I don't eat them!" On another occasion, Power was ticketed for jaywalking in Orlando, Florida. The judge dismissed the case, however, when the Hispanic ballplayer explained that he thought the "Don't Walk" sign was for whites only because he saw "so many signs in Florida that read 'For Whites Only.'"[107] Between his quick wit and timely hitting, Power was immediately accepted by his new teammates. In his first game in Phillies pinstripes, on September 10, the Puerto Rican first baseman got a hit and knocked in a run as the Phillies defeated the second-place Cardinals, 5–1.[108]

After the game, the Phillies, with a comfortable five-game lead over St. Louis, left for the West Coast on a ten-day, ten-game road trip. The first stop was San Francisco, where the Giants would try to break out of a three-way tie for second with the Reds and the Cardinals. The Phillies, on the other hand, were relaxed and confident as they dressed for the game at Candlestick Park on Friday, September 11.

"What's the magic number?" asked Richie Allen.

"Seventeen," Callison replied.

"It'll be sixteen after tonight," said Bennett, who was scheduled to start that night's game. "And you know something, I just might hit one out tonight, too."[109]

The Phillies southpaw did not get a round-tripper, but he did collect the first of the Phils four hits off the Giants' Juan Marichal. He also struck out Willie Mays three times with runners in scoring position. Amaro, who started at short, doubled home the game's only run in the fifth to give Bennett the 1–0 victory and boost the Phils' lead to six games.[110]

Before the next night's game, Baldschun and Boozer were standing in the outfield at Candlestick shagging fly balls. Baldschun asked his fellow reliever for a plug of tobacco, knowing that Boozer always carried a bag of Red Man in his back pocket. Boozer, who was known for spitting tobacco juice onto the clubhouse ceiling and catching it in his mouth as it dripped back down, gave him the bag and went to chase down a fly ball.[111] As Baldschun dug his fingers into the Red Man, he felt something moving inside.

"Hey, Booz," he called out, holding up a chaw filled with white maggots. "C'mere and look at this!"

When Boozer saw the maggots, he spit out his own plug and wailed: "Shit! I just chewed most of that bag last night and didn't see any of those things!"

Turning to track down another fly ball, the comic reliever added: "It sure was good and juicy, though."[112]

No one was laughing a few hours later as the Giants pounded the Phillies, 9–1. Art Mahaffey started the game and surrendered a two-run homer to Jim Hart. Boozer replaced Mahaffey in the third and immediately hit two batters and walked a third before giving up a 380-foot grand slam to Orlando Cepeda. Ryne Duren came in to relieve Boozer. Duren, who wore coke-bottle glasses because of his poor eyesight, sent chills down the spine of Willie Mays, who was standing outside the batter's box waiting to hit. Noticing that Duren was squinting to see Dalrymple's target, Mays asked the Phillies catcher: "I don't care if he can see the plate or not. I want to know: Can he see me?"[113] Duren somehow managed to get through the Giants order before surrendering another home run to Cepeda. Despite the shelling, the Phillies retained their six-game lead because the Cubs defeated the Cardinals, 3–2, and they rebounded the very next afternoon defeating the Giants, 4–1, behind the masterful pitching of ace Jim Bunning.[114]

On September 15, the Phillies announced that they would begin to accept applications for World Series tickets beginning on September 23 at noon. Because Connie Mack Stadium had a seating capacity of only 34,000, the Phillies restricted sales to sets of two each, enabling the maximum number of fans to see at least one game. Box seats went for $25 a set. Reserved seats were $17 a set, and bleachers were $9 a set.[115] In Houston to play a three-game series, the Phillies were so confident of going to the World Series that some players began spending their bonus money. Cookie Rojas bought a pistol with a Wyatt Earp holster. Chris Short bought a pair of matching shotguns, and Wes Covington bought a rifle. Showing off their new purchases in the clubhouse, Covington brandished his firearm and said: "This is for the sportswriters."

"You must be crazy," said Art Mahaffey. "How can you take a gun into the same clubhouse with Gene Mauch?"

Covington, wearing little more than lemon-colored undershorts and Rojas's gunbelt and holster, marched to within ten feet of Jim Bunning and crouched into a quick draw stance.

"Hey, Bunning," he challenged, "whenever you're ready!"

Before the Phillies' ace could respond, Johnny Callison snuck behind Covington, grabbed the pistol, and jammed it into the outfielder's back.

As George Kiseda of the *Philadelphia Bulletin* witnessed the bravado, Vic Powers explained: "We're relaxed. The last time I was in a pennant race I was with the Twins in '62. Everybody there was afraid of something or somebody. This club is so relaxed. They're always jumping around. They play the radio real loud. They make jokes. Sometimes it drives me crazy."[116]

Later that night, Dennis Bennett and Jack Baldschun teamed up to beat the Colts 1–0. Callison was responsible for the only run of the game, knocking in Richie Allen from second on a base hit in the sixth inning. Despite the victory, the Phils still lost one-half game to the Cardinals, who swept a twi-night doubleheader from Milwaukee.[117] Anxious to extend his team's lead in the standings, Mauch scheduled Bunning to pitch the next night on just two days' rest. It looked like a sure bet. Bunning had won his last eight decisions, and he would be facing a Houston team that was mired at the bottom of the second division. Besides, by pitching his ace on Wednesday night in Houston, he could use him again with a full three-days' rest against the Dodgers the following Sunday in Los Angeles, the final game of the road trip.[118] The decision backfired. Bunning lasted just four and a half innings against the Colts, who defeated the Phillies, 6–5.

Mauch was furious. "How did we let those bastards beat us?" he fumed. "I don't expect them to score on us. Get eleven runs in a game and the Phillies are supposed to win."[119] Even though his team's lead over second-place St. Louis remained at six games, as the Cards lost to the Braves, 3–2, Mauch was desperate. Going into Dodger Stadium on September 17 for the final series of the road trip, the Little General was so eager to clinch the pennant that he began to juggle the rotation. Instead of going with Mahaffey, who had failed to survive the first inning in three of his last six starts, Mauch went with Rick Wise in the opening game. This time, Wise failed to survive the first inning. But Bobby Shantz pitched seven and a half strong innings, holding the Dodgers to just one run on three hits. The Phillies defeated Don Drysdale, 4–3, to reduce their magic number to ten games, with fifteen remaining in the season.[120]

Mahaffey was bypassed again the next night, this time for Dennis Bennett, who was suffering from a sore left shoulder. Bennett agreed to start, but he did not make it past the third inning and the Phillies lost the game, 4–3. Chris Short pitched on Saturday night, taking a 3–2 lead into the eighth before surrendering a game-tying homer to Frank Howard. The game went into extra innings deadlocked at 3–3, until the bottom of the sixteenth. With two out and no one on, Willie Davis lashed a line drive that bounced off the chest of first baseman John Herrnstein. Herrnstein recovered the ball and flipped it to pitcher Jack Baldschun, who was covering the bag. Davis reached first the same time as the Phillies reliever, his foot landing on top of Baldschun's. When the umpire signaled "safe," Mauch stormed out of the dugout to argue the call.

Baldschun was so infuriated by the play that he threw a wild pitch to Tommy Davis, the next batter, as Willie Davis was breaking for second. When the ball was finally recovered, the speedy centerfielder was standing on third. Baldschun walked Tommy Davis, bringing Ron Fairly, a left-handed hitter, to the plate. Mauch went to the bullpen. He called on twenty-one-year-old Morrie Steevens, who had just been brought up from Little Rock. Steevens's first two pitches were strikes. Dalrymple called for a curveball, and as the young pitcher went into his delivery Willie Davis broke for the plate. Fairly, who certainly hadn't been given a squeeze signal with two outs, could not believe what he saw out of the corner of his eye.

The absurdity of stealing home took everyone on the field by surprise. If Fairly had swung at the pitch, he could have killed his teammate. It was all he could do to back himself out of the batter's box to make space for the charging Davis. Steevens, caught by surprise, threw a fastball low and in the dirt to the third-base side of the plate. Dalrymple somehow managed to catch the ball and dove toward Davis to apply the tag. But the aggressive base runner knocked the ball loose, and the Dodgers won, 4–3.[121]

"All Steevens had to do was throw strike three over the middle and the inning was over," explained the Phillie catcher afterward, in disgust. "Instead, he threw the son-of-a bitch four feet up the third-base line. I just strained the ligaments in my right knee and I'm trying to dive at the ball and tag the runner at the same time."[122] Mauch was even more incredulous. "All he had to do was throw a strike," he moaned to the sportswriters. "But what the hell does Morrie Steevens know? It's so absurd. Of course, Leo Durocher was coaching at third, and apparently he thought that Fairly wasn't going to get the run in, so let's take a chance. See, that's one of the things I always try to do—eliminate the surprises for my players. But I can't prepare for two-strike steals of home. I can't handle that."[123]

Fortunately, the Phillies salvaged the final game of the series, 3–2, on Sunday afternoon, but just barely. Jim Bunning took a 3–1 lead into the ninth. With two out and a runner on second, first baseman Vic Power mis-played a hard-hit grounder, and the runner scored from second. Now the tying run was on base with LA's hot-hitting catcher, John Roseboro, at the plate. But Bunning struck him out on a 2–2 fastball to end the game and notch his eighteenth victory of the season.[124]

The Phillies had managed to survive the West Coast trip. That evening they boarded a charter flight to Philadelphia with a six-and-a-half-game lead and only twelve games left to play. The magic number was down to seven games, with the next seven to be played at Connie Mack Stadium. What looked to be a sure thing would turn into a nightmare of historic proportions.

5

SEPTEMBER SWOON

Mayor James Tate and a crowd of 2,000 well-wishers greeted the Phillies when their plane arrived at Philadelphia International Airport in the early morning of September 21. Fans were confident that the Phils would capture their first National League flag in fourteen years. With twelve games remaining and a six-and-a-half-game lead, the Phillies' magic number was down to seven. Only St. Louis and Cincinnati—both tied for second place—stood in their way and, as luck would have it, both those teams were mired in losing streaks. The Phillies ticket office was just as optimistic.

World Series tickets had already been printed.[1] Ruben Amaro was so sure he would be playing in the Fall Classic that he had already ordered $1,800 worth of tickets and telephoned his father in Mexico asking him to make plans to come to Philadelphia in October.

"I don't want to sound pessimistic," the elder Amaro told his son, "but I wouldn't be sure of playing in the World Series until I know you have clinched the pennant." The father knew better, having been in some tight pennant races himself as a professional player in Cuba.[2] So did Gene Mauch. When his players arrived at Connie Mack Stadium that afternoon, he called a clubhouse meeting. "Just remember," he told them, "the 1950 Phillies had a seven-and-a-half-game lead with only eleven games to play. But they lost eight of their next ten and had to win the last game to save the pennant."[3] Mauch was cynical by nature. On the desk in his clubhouse office was a sign that read "Isn't this a beautiful day? Just watch some bastard louse it up."[4]

The Phillies opened their final home stand against the Reds that night. More than 21,000 fans packed Connie Mack to see Art Mahaffey face the Reds' John Tsitouris, a pitcher with an infamous reputation as a "Phillie Killer" in spite of his 7–11 record. The Phillies wasted three scoring opportunities through the first five innings, and the game was a scoreless pitchers' duel until the sixth.[5] With one out, Chico Ruiz, the Reds' rookie third baseman, singled to right. Vada Pinson followed with a line-drive base hit to right, but when he tried to stretch it into a double, Callison nailed him at second. Ruiz went to third on the play. With two outs, Cincinnati's best hitter, Frank Robinson, came to the plate. Mahaffey had had good luck against Robinson in the past, so Mauch decided to let his hurler go after him. Common sense dictated that Ruiz would stay put at third and wait for Robinson to drive him in. But Ruiz, a utility player who usually entered games in the late innings as a pinch hitter or pinch runner, went against the

Fig. 22 The 1964 Philadelphia Phillies held a six-and-a-half-game lead with twelve games left to play, and then lost ten straight games to finish in second place. It was the worst collapse in major league history. (Philadelphia Phillies)

Fig. 23 The "ghost" program the Phillies ordered in anticipation of clinching the National League pennant in 1964 is a sad reminder of the worst collapse in the history of major league baseball. (Philadelphia Phillies)

odds. Dancing down the third-base line during Mahaffey's first pitch, he noticed that the Phillies' right-hander was paying no attention to him and was taking a leisurely windup. Robinson took the first pitch for a strike. Mahaffey took the sign from Dalrymple and went into his windup.[6]

Gordy Coleman, who was kneeling in the on-deck circle, saw his teammate take off. "Uh oh," he thought, "I hope Chico makes it or he just better keep running right up the tunnel and out of the ballpark." Ruiz hadn't even bothered to flash Robinson a sign; he just broke for home. "Frank could've taken his head off if he swung," said Coleman.[7]

Dick Sisler, the Reds manager, couldn't believe it either. He jumped off the bench screaming at the top of his lungs, "NO! NO!"[8] Robinson, in disbelief, froze at the plate. Mahaffey was also taken by surprise. "At the exact fraction of a second that I'm going to throw the ball, I see him running," he admitted afterward. "My arm tightened, and I threw the ball wide, up the third-base line."[9] Catcher Clay Dalrymple jumped at the wild pitch. His glove deflected the ball and it rolled to the wall. Ruiz scored. The run proved to be the margin of victory in the game as the Phils lost, 1–0.

"I was pissed at Mahaffey," said Dalrymple. "Just a few days before, Willie Davis of the Dodgers had stolen home on us. After that game I told all our pitchers to throw the ball over the middle. When that guy is breaking from third, the hitter's concentration is broken. Just get me the ball! In that situation with Ruiz, all Art had to do was throw me the ball and we had his ass. But he threw it ten feet to my right and away from the runner. We didn't have a chance."[10]

Mauch, incensed by the play, was convinced that Mahaffey had cracked under pressure, so he refused to pitch the right-hander in his next scheduled start.[11]

Even though the Phillies' lead was trimmed to five and a half games over Cincinnati, few of the Phillies appeared concerned. World Series tickets went on sale the following day. More than 52,000 fans flocked to their local post office to mail in their orders.[12] That night the Phillies felt assured of a victory as their seventeen-game winner Chris Short went to the mound.

But Short suffered his worst outing of the year. With one out in the third, he loaded the bases on walks to pitcher Jim O'Toole and to Ruiz, and on a single by Pete Rose. Pinson grounded into a fielder's choice at second, and O'Toole scored on the play. With two outs and runners at the corners, Frank Robinson came to the plate. On Short's third delivery, Pinson broke for second on a delayed steal. Phils catcher Gus Triandos threw wildly into center field and Rose scored. With first base open, Mauch could have ordered an intentional pass. Instead, he directed his battery to continue to pitch to Robinson, and the Reds slugger smashed a 3–2 slider into the left-field upper deck, giving the Reds a 4–0 lead. Reds first baseman Deron Johnson drove in two more runs in the fifth, on a bases-loaded single to right. Short was lifted for rookie reliever Morrie Steevens, who surrendered a pair of unearned runs in the sixth on a throwing error by Richie Allen and two passed balls by Triandos.[13]

Ed Roebuck relieved Steevens in the seventh, with Cincinnati leading, 9–1. Chico Ruiz was the first batter. In an attempt at vindication, Roebuck nailed the Reds utility man with a fastball between the shoulder blades. Ruiz responded by stealing second. When he jogged out to play third base in the bottom of the inning, someone from the Phillies dugout threw a ball that whistled past his head. Both benches emptied.[14] When the dust finally settled, O'Toole had gone the distance, scattering eight hits, and the Reds defeated the Phillies, 9–2. The Cards also won that night, defeating the Mets, 2–1, behind the pitching of former Phillie Curt Simmons. Now the Reds were only four and a half games back and the Cards were just five back.[15] "Everything's fine," insisted a hoarse Mauch, speaking to the sportswriters after the game. "Except I can't talk loud enough to cuss anyone out—if I wanted to, which I don't."[16] In fact, Mauch was beginning to panic.

September 23 was "Richie Allen Night" at Connie Mack Stadium. Organized by the local business community, the special night was opposed by the Phillies front office, which did not believe in honoring rookies. Nevertheless, Allen was presented with a television, snow tires, luggage, a stereo, and a $1,000 scholarship for his infant daughter's education. The rookie third baseman was noticeably touched by his mother's presence. After the pregame ceremonies, he posed with her for a photograph and joked, "I guess all those years of cutting class at Wampum High to play ball have finally paid off." Of course, Era Allen didn't find the remark very amusing, but she was extremely proud of her son.[17]

An hour before game time, the Little General approached Dennis Bennett, who was nursing a sore arm, and asked, "Can you give me six good innings?" Bennett, never one to refuse, said, "Yes." Somehow he managed to take a 3–2 lead into the seventh against the Reds' Billy McCool. But Cincinnati came back. Johnny Edwards began the rally with a single to left. Leo Cardenas followed with another base hit. Pinch hitter Marty Keough forced Cardenas at second, but on the play Edwards advanced to third. The Reds had runners at first and third when Pete Rose lined a base hit to center, scoring Edwards and tying the game at 3–3. One out later, Vada Pinson stepped to the plate. Mauch called for time and went out to the mound.

"Do you think you can get Pinson?" he asked Bennett.

"Yeah," replied the sore-armed right-hander.

But Pinson slammed Bennett's second pitch over the right-field fence for a three-run homer.[18] The Reds, leading 6–3, brought in reliever Sammy Ellis to pitch the bottom of the seventh. After striking out Alex Johnson, Ellis walked the bases full. Callison came to the plate with the crowd of 23,000 chanting "Go! Go! Go!"

Callison struck out on a 3–2 slider that caught the outside corner of the plate. Ellis struck out Tony Taylor on a 2–2 slider, killing the rally. The

Fig. 24 On September 23, 1964, in the midst of the Phillies collapse, Philadelphia merchants held a "Richie Allen Night" to honor the rookie third baseman. (Temple University Urban Archives)

Phils picked up another run in the eighth when Allen led off with a double and scored when Ruiz made a throwing error on Alex Johnson's infield single. But it was not enough, as the Reds went on to win, 6–4, and trim the Philles' lead to just three and a half games.[19]

Mauch was desperate. His team had just created a three-way pennant race with the Reds and the Cardinals, and their magic number remained stalled at seven games. Instead of riding out the storm, he began to second-guess himself. Juggling his starting rotation for the next home series against the Milwaukee Braves, Mauch decided to pitch Bunning on two days' rest. It would be his fourth start in twelve days. Once he learned that the Braves intended to start Wade Blasingame, a cocky twenty-year-old rookie, Mauch inserted rookie outfielders Alex Johnson and Adolfo Phillips into the starting lineup. The Little General had learned that Phillips and Johnson had fared well against Blasingame in the Pacific Coast League earlier in the season, so Mauch pinned his hopes on a repeat of those performances. As it turned out, Mauch had been misinformed.

Both Johnson and Phillips went 0 for 3. Phillips made a costly error in the outfield that led to the Braves' first run, and Johnson's poor base-running might have cost the Phils the game in the seventh. With one out in that inning, the Phillies ran themselves out of a potential rally. After Richie Allen singled, Johnson hit a bouncer back to Blasingame. The young pitcher fired high to second, pulling shortstop Santos Alomar off the bag. Allen, barreling into second to break up the double play, overslid the bag and was tagged out. Vic Power came up next and grounded to third baseman Eddie Mathews, who juggled the ball. Realizing that Johnson rounded second on the play, Mathews threw to second baseman Denis Menke for the third out.

The Phillies finally rallied in the eighth when Johnny Callison hit a bases-loaded two-run single and Allen drove in another run with a two-out infield hit. But Chi Chi Olivo struck out Tony Gonzalez to kill the rally and re-tired the Phillies in order in the ninth, as the Braves went on to win, 5–3.[20]

When asked about the wisdom of starting Johnson and Phillips after the game, Mauch defended his decision. "If Mathews fielded the ball cleanly and threw it away, Johnson scores," he insisted. "Then it's no blunder. If the ball that's hit to Phillips doesn't take a bad bounce, he throws out the runner trying to score. Then it's no blunder."[21]

On September 25 the Phillies were clinging to a two-and-a-half-game lead. Mauch could see the pennant slipping away and became more intent than ever on halting the four-game losing streak. Before the game, injured first baseman Frank Thomas ripped the cast off his broken thumb against doctor's orders and asked the Little General if he could play. Desperate for the offense, Mauch agreed. He also started Chris Short on two days' rest, instead of the scheduled starter, Art Mahaffey, who had three.

Short pitched well, holding a 1–0 lead at the end of the sixth, allowing only one earned run and six hits. The Braves rallied to score two runs in the seventh and extended their lead to 3–1 in the eighth. Callison hit a two-run homer to tie the score in the bottom half of that inning. In the tenth, the Braves rallied for another pair of runs on a two-run homer by Joe Torre to regain the lead, 5–3. Allen tied the game up in the Phillies' half of the inning with a two-run inside-the-park homer. With one on, he drove a ball off the scoreboard catwalk and scored standing up when Ty Cline missed the cutoff man.

The heartbreaker came in the twelfth. The Braves' Gary Kolb led off the inning with a scratch infield hit, and Gene Oliver walked. With runners on first and second, Eddie Mathews hit a hard ground ball to the right of first baseman Frank Thomas. The ball bounced off Thomas's glove and into right field, scoring the tie-breaking run. Before the inning was over, the Braves put another run across the plate, and the Phillies dropped their fifth straight game, 7–5.[22] The Phillies lead was down to one and a half games.

After the game, Mauch pointed to his decision to pitch to Joe Torre with first base open in the tenth as the turning point in the contest. "My choice of who to pitch to wasn't very good," he said in a rare admission of error. "Managers in these situations don't think in terms of hanging curves." Mauch, thinking two batters ahead, was more concerned about Mathews, and Torre made him pay with a two-run homer.[23]

On September 26, Mauch reluctantly started Mahaffey. The game, which appeared on national television, began promisingly enough when Cookie Rojas opened with a single, Allen tripled, and Johnson homered to left field. The Phils knocked Braves starter Denny Lemaster out of the game in the second, adding a fourth run on singles by Amaro and Rojas and a sacrifice fly by Callison. Mahaffey kept the Braves off the scoreboard until the fifth, when Denis Menke homered and Alou and Lee Maye hit back-to-back doubles. Still, the Phillies took a 4–2 lead into the eighth inning, when their luck suddenly changed. After Joe Torre and Rico Carty opened the inning with back-to-back singles, Mauch brought in Jack Baldschun to face Menke.

"The way I was pitching that day, I couldn't believe he was taking me out," recalled Mahaffey, still angered years later by the move. "I believe in my heart that I would have won that game if Mauch hadn't taken me out."[24] Menke's attempt to advance the runners on a bunt backfired, and Torre was forced at third. Mike de la Hoz came to the plate next and hit a hard grounder to third. The ball skidded off Allen's glove for a hit, and the bases were loaded. Ed Bailey, a left-hander, was sent up to pinch hit for Chi Chi Olivo. Mauch waved to the bullpen for lefty Bobby Shantz. Coach Peanuts Lowrey asked him if he wanted to make a double switch and replace Triandos with Clay Dalrymple, a better defensive catcher. But Mauch said, "No, my daughter could catch Shantz."

That was a mistake. Shantz's fourth pitch to Bailey was a high change-up that glanced off Triandos's glove. Carty scored on the passed ball. Shantz struck out Bailey, walked Alou intentionally, and got Lee May on a pop-up for the third out. But the passed ball cut the Phillies' lead to one run, 4–3. In the ninth, Hank Aaron and Eddie Mathews opened the inning with back-to-back singles. Frank Bolling, batting for the starting pitcher Blasingame, grounded to Amaro at short, but Tony Taylor couldn't handle his throw to second, loading the bases. With the hot-hitting Rico Carty coming to the plate, many of the Phillies expected that Mauch would go to the bullpen for a right-hander. However, he stayed with Shantz, and Carty smashed the first pitch off the center-field wall for a bases-clearing triple.[25] What followed was a bizarre series of events that illustrated more than anything the Phillies' frustration with a season that was suddenly falling apart.

Mike de la Hoz followed Carty with a sinking liner to left. Rojas, who was playing left field, made a running shoestring catch, but third-base umpire Ed Vargo missed the call and ruled it a safe hit. Rojas threw home too late to nail Carty, and then charged Vargo. Mauch and Amaro tried in vain to calm the fiery utility man down. After Vargo ejected Rojas, he consulted with second-base umpire Shag Crawford and reversed the call. Now de la Hoz went crazy and was thrown out for charging Crawford. After order was restored, the Phillies made an appeal at third base, and Carty was called out for failing to tag up. Braves manager Bobby Bragan was tossed, and the Braves finished the game under protest.[26] It didn't matter much for the Phillies, who lost their sixth straight, 6–4.

"The slumping Phillies have run out of room as NL leaders," wrote Allen Lewis in the next morning's *Philadelphia Inquirer*. "Their advantage over second-place Cincinnati reached the minimum of half a game yesterday. The defeat extended the Phillies' longest losing streak of the season to six games and was the ninth setback in their last eleven contests. The team, which appeared to have a safe six-and-a-half-game advantage upon their return from the West Coast early last Monday, is struggling to stay

Fig. 25 Some 63,000 applications for World Series tickets were received at Connie Mack Stadium on September 23, 1964, three games into the Phillies' ten-game collapse. (Temple University Urban Archives)

on top. The magic number has, at least temporarily, lost its significance in the pennant race."[27]

Johnny Callison points to the 6–4 defeat as the turning point of the season. "It seemed as if Gene didn't know what to do to stop the losing streak," he said. "The panic set in after that game. We had lost our confidence. After that, we played as if we were waiting to lose."[28] Dalrymple put it more bluntly: "There were some seriously tight asses in our clubhouse."[29]

After the game, Jim Bunning walked into Mauch's office and said, "I'll take the ball tomorrow." Mauch realized that his ace would be pitching on only two days' rest, but he gave him the start anyway. Bunning lasted just three innings, surrendering seven runs on ten hits—most of which were the result of bad hops, bloopers, and misplayed balls. The tragic comedy unfolded in the fourth with the Phillies leading, 3–2. Joe Torre led off with a grounder toward short that Allen deflected into center field. Carty came up next and hit a double-play grounder that took a bad bounce over Tony Taylor's head. Menke followed with a punch shot to Amaro's right that skidded under his glove. Cline doubled, and Cloninger hit a blooper that fell between Amaro, Gonzalez, and Covington in short left. By the time Dallas Green came on to relieve Bunning, the Braves had rallied to lead, 5–3. Green, who surrendered five more runs on seven hits, only added to the Phils' miseries.[30] With the Braves leading 12–3 in the sixth, Callison was desperate. Before going to the plate, the Phillies' superstitious all-star packed his jaw with chewing tobacco and bubble gum in the hope that the nauseous mix would bring him some luck. Callison, who promised his wife that he'd stop chewing because of the risk of cancer, stepped up to the plate and nailed Tony Cloninger's first-pitch fastball over the right-field wall. He repeated the feat in the eighth off Chi Chi Olivo, and again in the ninth. The last homer was the most impressive as it glanced off the light tower to the left of the scoreboard.[31] Despite Callison's heroics, the Phillies lost the game, 14–8.

The fans had finally lost their patience. Whatever remained of the crowd of 20,569 that came out that Sunday afternoon showered the Phillies with such a fuselage of boos that the players were glad to be heading out of town for the final five games of the season. In the clubhouse, Sandy Grady of the *Philadelphia Bulletin* mentioned to Mauch that some of the Braves thought his players appeared to be "tight."

"Tight?" Mauch snapped, indignantly. "When did they notice that? After the score was 12–3? Did we look tight when we went ahead, 3–2? No, we came back. But no one mentions that."

Grady, realizing that the Reds had bumped the Phils out of first by sweeping two games from the Mets, mustered the courage to ask the infuriated manager, "What do you think of your chances [to capture a pennant] now?"

"We've got to do in five days what Cincinnati took five and a half months to do," Mauch replied, matter-of-factly. "There's a good chance we're better going after something than holding on to something."[32]

Over in the visitor's locker room, the Braves were relishing their four-game sweep. These were lean years for Milwaukee. After finishing in the first division throughout the mid- to late 1950s, the Braves were headed for another fifth-place finish. Sweeping the Phillies was regarded as a moral victory, especially because of the team's hatred of Gene Mauch. "You didn't feel sorry for Mauch in those days," admitted Joe Torre. "Gene was an arrogant bastard. He'd scream at you from the dugout, anything to get an edge."[33]

Outside in the parking lot, Diane Callison was all smiles when she met her husband after the game. "You hit three home runs!" she gushed, giving him a congratulatory hug. "One was the one-hundredth of your career."

"But we lost" were the only three words the all-star outfielder could manage.[34]

Once loose and mischievous, the Phillies clubhouse was now, in the words of beat writer Sandy Grady, "an accident ward teeming with victims of an earthquake," all of whom were "asking in hushed tones: 'What had happened?'"[35] The shell shock had even consumed Mauch, the most unlikely victim. "All he does is sit there like Mahatma Gandhi," wrote Larry Merchant of the *Philadelphia Daily News*, commenting on the eerie composure of the Phillies manager. "For Mauch, being calm is a sign of panic."[36]

Some believed that Mauch saved his fury for his players, revealing little more than a chain-smoking facade for the writers. Not so, according to reliever Jack Baldschun. "Throughout the season, Gene acted like the 'Little General' he was called," said Baldschun. "He was all over our asses. If we lost during the season, you'd want to be the last one into the clubhouse because you didn't want to get hit by any flying debris. But during that losing streak, there was none of that. You'd go into the clubhouse after a loss and his door would be closed. I think if he'd have stayed on our tails—more door slamming, fist pounding, and cussing—we'd have gotten fired up and clinched it."[37]

But Richie Allen had different memories of Mauch's behavior during the collapse. "Mauch was only thirty-eight years old, and he wanted to win so badly," Allen explained. "He would have done anything to win. But during the skid, he forgot the most elementary rule of baseball: to have fun. Instead, he became a wild man. After losses, he would close the clubhouse door and start dressing us down, throwing things around. All we really needed was for him to pat us on the fanny and say, 'Thanks fellas, good effort, we'll get 'em tomorrow.' Instead we got ranting and raving, and all that did was make us feel more tired than we already were."[38]

Indeed, Mauch vented his frustration on September 28, before the first game of a three-game series against the Cardinals in St. Louis. Calling a clubhouse meeting, the Phils skipper tried to fire up his players by accusing them of "letting the flag slip away."

"Go start a fight!" he fumed. "Do something, before it's too late!"

But Mauch's tirade fell flat. "He tried to enrage us," said Jim Bunning. "I can remember Gus Triandos and I walking out of the clubhouse saying, 'I think he meant for us to start a fight with somebody on the Cardinals.' That's the only thing I got out of it. He could've started the fight. Mauch was better at that than anyone else."[39]

In fact, the Phils' skipper went looking for a fight before the game. During batting practice, Mauch saw *Inquirer* beat writer Allen Lewis standing near the first-base coaching box. "What's wrong with my team?" he asked, almost daring the Philadelphia sportswriter to tell him.

"Gene, you don't want to know what I think," said Lewis, who had grown accustomed to Mauch's prickly temperament.

"Yes I do," Mauch shot back, arms crossed in a defiant pose.

"Gene," Lewis began, "for 150 games I don't think anyone could have managed better than you did. But every pennant that's blown is blown because the manager screwed up the rotation by pitching guys out of turn."

Lewis proceeded to give Mauch a litany of specific examples, and Mauch grew angrier and angrier with each one.

"If you would have said to yourself 'All we have to do is play .500 ball with twelve games to go to win the pennant and planted that thought in the minds of your players, you'd have clinched it," added Lewis. "But you insisted on winning every damn game, and that was a serious error in judgment."

Mauch had heard enough. "Aw, that's a bunch of bullshit!" he said, throwing up his hands in disgust. With that, the Little General turned and walked away. He refused to speak with Lewis for the rest of the season.[40]

Mauch started Chris Short that night. It was Short's fourth start in eleven days. The Cardinals took a 1–0 lead in the second on a sacrifice RBI by Mike Shannon. They added another run in the fourth when Ken Boyer doubled, advanced to third on a base hit by Bill White, and scored on Julian Javier's bounced to second. Short, visibly weary, was knocked out in the sixth when Boyer doubled and White singled him home. Bob Gibson and Barney Schultz combined on a five-hitter for the 5–1 Cardinal victory. The Phils' losing streak was now at eight. The Cards were in first place by one-half game over second-place Cincinnati, and the Phillies followed in third, one and a half games out.[41]

Sitting in front of his locker after the game, Dennis Bennett dismissed any notion among the sportswriters that he was through for the season. When asked about his sore shoulder, now noticeably discolored, he said he was "a little concerned" about the internal bleeding, but not to worry. "I'll beat 'em tomorrow night," Bennett added, "and Jim will beat 'em the next night. We're a long way from dead."[42]

Bennett started the next night and did not last through the second inning. In the first, Curt Flood singled, was bunted to second by Lou Brock, and scored on a double by Dick Groat. When Javier opened the second with a double and McCarver drove him in on a base hit, Mauch yanked Bennett. The Cards picked up a third run when Flood scored Shannon on a grounder to Tony Taylor. The Phillies managed to cut the Cardinal lead to one run in the fourth when Redbird starter Ray Sadecki walked the bases full and Gus Triandos slashed a two-run single to center. In the sixth, Bill White added an insurance run with a homer off John Boozer. Down 4–2 in the seventh, Mauch tried to rally his team by calling on Callison to pinch-hit. Weakened by a viral infection, the Phillies right-fielder had spent most of the game on his back in the trainer's room, but he somehow managed to connect for a base hit. After reaching first base, Callison was shivering so badly that Mauch asked the home plate umpire for permission to give him a warm-up jacket. But the right-fielder's fingers were shaking so much that Bill White, the Cardinals' first baseman, had to help him button it.[43] "J.C. was sumbuck," said Richie Allen of Callison. "He was the man of the year in '64. He refused to quit, and his example pushed me to be a better ballplayer. If we'd have won the pennant, he would have been the MVP that year."[44]

With two outs, Cards pitcher Ray Sadecki walked Tony Taylor, and Barney Schultz came in to get Richie Allen on a pop-up to end the rally. The Cards won, 4–2, dropping the Phillies two and a half games out of first.[45] "Maybe it sounds ridiculous," said the Cardinals' Bill White after the game, "but I think everyone in our clubhouse feels sorry for the Phillies."[46]

Jim Bunning started the last game of the series on Wednesday night against a former Whiz Kid, Curt Simmons. Tim McCarver started the scoring for the Cardinals in the second with a two-run homer. Flood led off the third with a double, and Brock advanced him to third on a bunt that was misplayed by Tony Taylor. White followed with a double, scoring Flood, and Boyer singled, driving in Brock. By the time Bunning was relieved in the fourth, he had surrendered six hits and six runs, five of them earned. Simmons, on the other hand, was throwing a no-hitter until the seventh, when Richie Allen broke it up with a base hit. Still, the Cards went on to win, 8–5, recording their eighth straight victory, while the Phillies dropped their tenth in a row. After the game, Simmons was asked if he enjoyed defeating the same team that had released him four years earlier. "No," he replied, tactfully. "That story is four years old. I feel for them a little bit. I just hope it never happens to us like that. Something like that would stay with you for the rest of your life."[47]

Despite their ten-game losing streak, the Phillies could still force a three-team playoff. It would depend on their defeating the Reds in their final two games of the season and on the Mets sweeping the Cards.[48] At the same time, the Phils no longer controlled their own destiny, having to rely on the Mets in order to create that scenario.

The Phillies arrived in Cincinnati on Thursday, October 1. They finally had an off day, as they were scheduled to play the Reds the next night. During the Thursday afternoon workout, Fred Hutchinson, who was forced to retire as Reds manager earlier in the season because of a losing battle with cancer, approached Mauch near the batting cage.

"I wish there was something I could say to help," remarked Hutchinson.

Mauch was stunned. Here was a man whose body was ravaged by cancer and he was offering him his sympathy for little more than plain bad luck.[49]

The next night, the Little General sent Chris Short to the mound. Again, the Phillies found themselves losing, 3–0, until the seventh inning. Cincinnati first baseman Deron Johnson led off the bottom of the inning with a base hit and moved to second on Tommy Harper's bunt. Shortstop Leo Cardenas followed. When Short's first pitch grazed his left shoulder, Cardenas started toward the mound, waving his bat at the Phillies southpaw. "You son-of-a-bitch," he cursed. "I'll hit you next."

Clay Dalrymple jumped up and grabbed the angry shortstop from behind, "You're not going to hit anybody," he said, as both benches emptied.

Short had his teammates fired up. After order was restored, the Phillies rediscovered their offense and rallied to win on a two-run triple by Richie Allen and a run-scoring single by Alex Johnson in the eighth. While the Phillies were downing the Reds, 4–3, the Mets were routing the Cards,

Fig. 26 Chris Short was the number-two pitcher in 1964. On three separate occasions, he started games on just two days' rest during the collapse. (National Baseball Hall of Fame and Library)

15–5. The defeat left the Cards with just a half-game lead over Cincinnati, with the Phils only a game out.[50]

With a three-way tie for first becoming a distinct possibility, the National League held a lottery to determine a round-robin playoff based on a two-loss elimination. In the first round, Cincinnati would play at Philadelphia on Monday, October 5; St. Louis would play at Cincinnati the following day; and Philadelphia at St. Louis on Wednesday, October 7. In the event that each of the three teams was 1–1, another draw would be held to determine which two teams played next, with the third team drawing a bye. The loser of that game would be eliminated, and the winner would go on to play the idle team in a one-game playoff for the pennant.[51]

In the end, the round-robin playoff never happened. On Sunday, October 4, the last day of the regular season, the Phillies defeated the Reds, 10–0. But the Cardinals also beat the Mets, 11–5, and in so doing won their first pennant since 1946.[52] St. Louis, led by third baseman and league MVP Ken Boyer, went on to defeat the New York Yankees in the World Series in seven games. The final National League standings were:

Team	Won	Lost	%	Games Behind
St. Louis	93	69	.574	—
Philadelphia	92	70	.568	1
Cincinnati	92	70	.568	1
San Francisco	92	72	.556	3
Milwaukee	88	74	.543	5
Los Angeles	80	82	.494	13
Pittsburgh	80	82	.494	13
Chicago	76	86	.469	17
Houston	66	96	.407	27
New York	53	109	.327	40

The fact that ninety-two victories set a new franchise record for wins in a season, or that the 1,425,891 fans the Phillies drew that season set a new attendance record, meant little for a team that had watched the pennant slip through its grasp.[53]

Owner Bob Carpenter blamed himself for the collapse. "If only two or three years ago I had invested more in the farm system, then I would have been able to replace Frank Thomas when he got hurt and maybe brought up one or two pitchers to take the pressure off Bunning and Short," he speculated.[54] In fact, the only team in major league baseball capable of rejuvenating itself with talent from the farm system in the heat of a pennant race during the 1960s was the New York Yankees. So while Carpenter's belief was rather naive, he did identify two significant factors resulting in the swoon.

The injury to Frank Thomas was a critical loss for the Phillies. After he had been acquired from the Mets in early August, Thomas, a power-hitting first baseman, went on a tear. In thirty-nine games, he drove in twenty-six runs. When he broke his thumb sliding into second base on September 8, the first-place Phillies had a six-and-a-half game lead. Quinn traded for Vic Power, another slugging first baseman, to replace Thomas. But Power was a disappointment. In eighteen games with the Phillies, he hit an anemic .208, with only 3 RBIs and no home runs.[55] Some of the players, and even Mauch himself, believed that Thomas's injury was the main reason the Phillies did not win the pennant.[56] The more compelling explanation is Mauch's overuse of pitchers Jim Bunning and Chris Short.

On three separate occasions during the swoon, Mauch started his two top pitchers on just two days' rest, which only served to exhaust them. "I don't know if it's humanly possible to pitch effectively on two days' rest more than once," admitted Bunning, years later. "I was at my best with three or four days."[57]

In fact, there was no reason to do it. Mauch could have gone with Art Mahaffey on any of those occasions. The twenty-six-year-old right-hander already had twelve victories to his credit before the collapse, including two complete game shutouts. Bunning himself was bewildered by Mauch's decision to ignore Mahaffey. "Art should have been starting right along with Shorty and myself, because he was sound and willing," said the Phillies' ace. "If Gene had had a little more confidence in Art, he'd have won seventeen or eighteen. He should have been pitching in the last ten days of the season. Art should have started the second game of the Cardinals series instead of Bennett, who was seriously hurt and couldn't pitch well, or the Houston game that I pitched on short rest."[58] When reminded of Mauch's belief that Mahaffey had cracked under pressure, Bunning quickly rejected the notion. "Art lost a 1–0 game to Cincy on a suicide squeeze," he said. "That's not cracking under pressure, it's a fluke. Within the next week, he also took us into the eighth inning against the Braves and pitched very well."[59]

If Mauch did not trust Mahaffey, he might have started Ray Culp. In June, Culp just missed a no-hitter against the Chicago Cubs by one pitch, which Len Gabrielson hit for a single. By late August, the twenty-two-year-old right-hander had chalked up eight victories, but when he developed a sore arm in a game against the New York Mets, Mauch refused to use him. "He doesn't want the ball," the Little General told inquiring sportswriters.[60]

But Culp defended himself at the end of the season. "It wasn't that I didn't want to pitch," he insisted.[61] Clay Dalrymple believes that Mauch had a personal vendetta against Culp. "Gene wouldn't pitch Ray because he gained ten pounds during the season and Mauch was a bitch about gaining weight," said the Phillies' veteran catcher. "I thought to myself, 'What the hell does that have to do with his pitching ability?'"[62]

But if Dalrymple had problems with the way Mauch was handling the pitching staff, why didn't he voice his opinion? Pitcher Dennis Bennett claims that Dalrymple and Mauch "thought so much alike that if you cut off the top of Clay's head you'd see another Mauch walking around in there."[63] Not so, according to Dalrymple. "Mauch was bull-headed," he said. "His greatest weakness was his handling of the pitching staff. But you sure couldn't tell him that. I knew he was panicking when he was starting Bunning and Short every two days. I knew that he gave up on Culp and Mahaffey because he thought they didn't have any guts. If he didn't like them, then why didn't he trade their asses and get somebody who could help us? Instead, Gene just stayed mad at them."[64]

Mauch might even have considered starting rookie Rick Wise and then going to his bullpen early. Roebuck could have pitched the fifth and sixth innings, John Boozer or Dallas Green could have pitched the seventh and eighth, and Baldschun could close. The theory of such a "staff game" still would have served the same purpose of giving Bunning and Short an extra day's rest so they could have been more effective when they did start the next game.

John Herrnstein disagrees. "People seem to forget that out of those ten straight games we lost, we were really in seven of them and could have won them," insisted the rookie first baseman. "Why throw a staff game if you don't have to? I know Gene was criticized for pitching Bunning and Short on only a few days' rest. But I'm not sure that's fair. Some of the guys had bad arms and refused to take the ball for fear of extending the skid. Mauch did the only thing he could do, which was go with the live arms."[65]

Baldschun agreed. "I don't think it's fair to criticize Mauch for using Bunning and Shorty as often as he did during the losing streak," said the reliever. "Nor would it be fair to speculate about what he should have done. Gene was a sharp manager. He knew what he was doing. I offered to start and relieve for him during the skid. I had a rubber arm. But he said that I was more valuable to him as a reliever when the nut-cutting time came in

Fig. 27 Clay Dalrymple was made the Phillies' first-string catcher in 1961, and for the next seven years he caught at least 101 games a season for Gene Mauch. He finally made it to the World Series in 1969 with the Baltimore Orioles. (Philadelphia Phillies)

the seventh, eighth, and ninth innings. He came to me every day before the game during the losing streak and told me that I'd be the first man out of the bullpen if we were tied or ahead in the game. Well, during the losing streak we were rarely ahead by the seventh inning and Gene wasn't going to call on me for mop up duty. He was going to save me for the next game."[66]

But Dallas Green believes that Mauch was "mad at both Baldschun and Roebuck" for "cracking under pressure" and "refused to pitch them." Instead, he went with "guys like myself, Bobby Shantz, and Morrie Steevens, who just couldn't get the job done. Gene wasn't a people person. He was terrible to his ballplayers."[67]

Frank Dolson of the *Philadelphia Inquirer* was more objective. "I didn't agree with the way [Mauch] handled his players," said Dolson. "He treated his superstars one way and all the rest of the players another. He was also damn stubborn. There's no question in my mind that Mauch blew the pennant by the way he handled the rotation. But you also have to credit him for putting the Phillies in a position to win. For 150 games, the Phils were a good team having an incredible year, and that was because of Mauch's genius for the game."[68]

Whatever the case might have been, it staggers the imagination to think that Mauch did not use Baldschun during the swoon. He was as good a reliever as there was in the National League. Baldschun had saved twenty-one games, won six, and had an ERA of 3.13. Baldschun had already established himself as the staff's closer by pitching in pressure situations. To be sure, Gene Mauch possessed an exceptional knowledge of baseball, but he certainly did not know how to manage his players.

Perhaps the most compelling reason for the September swoon, though, was simply bad luck. For example, if the Phillies had played under the previous 154-game schedule that year, they would have clinched the pennant on September 24. Under the new, 162-game schedule, established in 1961, however, the additional eight games cost the Phillies the pennant. Then there was the Phillies' decision to release Curt Simmons in 1960, which also came back to haunt them in 1964. Simmons, a former Whiz Kid, was picked up by the St. Louis Cardinals. During the last two months of the 1964 season, he compiled a 6–0 record—including a key 8–5 victory against the Phillies on September 30—helping the Cardinals win the pennant. It seemed that "cruel fate" was the deciding factor in the Phillies' failure to clinch the flag.

Gus Triandos called 1964 "the year of the blue snow," his own peculiar reference to describe the freak nature of the swoon.[69] Jim Bunning was more explicit. "Our defense, which had been unbelievably good for 150 games, was terrible," he said. "A pop fly would go up, we'd drop the ball. A ground ball, a normal double play, we struggled to get one out. When we pitched well, we didn't hit. When we hit well, we didn't pitch. We had our losing streak at the wrong time of the season."[70]

Callison was also staggered by his team's sudden reversal of fortune. "We had a six and a half game lead with twelve to go," he said, trying to explain the inexplicable nearly forty years later. "What could look better? If we would have won six of twelve, we'd have clinched it. If one of the contenders would have lost six of twelve we'd have clinched it. What happened to us was against all odds—we didn't win and they didn't lose. You can blame the manager, you can blame yourself, you can blame everyone else on the team—and we were all to blame. But let me tell you, there was also some really freaky stuff going on during those ten games. There was a double-play ball that would have taken us out of an inning, but the ball hit a rock and went over Tony Taylor's head. There were bad bounces, missed plays, and just plain bad luck. It was just a damn shame. And the players had to live with the sad, painful anger."[71]

To be sure, the players were devastated by what had happened. Dalrymple was completely spent. After the season, all he could do was return to his suburban Philadelphia home and sleep on the couch for three days. "It didn't really hit me, though, until I was lying there watching the first game of the World Series on TV," he admitted. "My daughter, who was in first grade at the time, came home from school, saw me watching the game, and said, 'Daddy, how come you're not playing today?' It was an innocent question, but it really hurt."[72]

For rookie Rick Wise, the swoon was "like watching a horror film unfold." "So many strange things happened in the final twelve games," he said. "I guess it taught me that baseball can take you to great heights, or it can crush you."[73] Art Mahaffey, who still has difficulty talking about the swoon nearly four decades later, said that it "destroyed everyone inside" and that the "abuse [he] took during the off-season was unbelievable."[74] Callison refused to discuss the swoon for months afterward. But the hurt kept returning. "I think one of the saddest days of my life came after the season," recalled Diane, his wife, recently. "In early October, the check I sent the Phillies for $1,100 worth of World Series tickets came back in the mail, and the pain of all those losses came right back."[75] Only Gene Mauch could understand what Callison was going through.

The Little General's biggest regret to this day is that the Phillies' collapse

Fig. 28   Johnny Callison hit the game-winning home run in the 1964
All-Star Game and would have been the National League's Most Valuable
Player had the Phillies won the pennant. (National Baseball Hall of
Fame and Library)

prevented his all-star right-fielder from winning the National League's Most Valuable Player award that season. "I always compared Johnny to Mickey Mantle," he said. "Mickey had more bulk, but their styles were pretty much the same. In '64, I never saw anyone play harder and perform as well in 162 games as Johnny did. If I could have figured a way to win a couple of those ten games we lost at the end, he would have had the MVP for sure. He should have had it. I think I would give up about anything I ever accomplished to have that happen for him."[76]

Despite all the disillusionment, there were some players who managed to find a silver lining in the season. Richie Allen captured the National League Rookie of the Year Award with a .318 batting average, 29 home runs, and 91 RBIs. Three other Phillies also finished among the league leaders: Callison finished fifth in home runs (31) and RBIs (104); Bunning finished fourth in victories (19) and winning percentage (.704) and fifth in ERA (2.63); and Short finished third in ERA (2.20) and seventh in winning percentage (.653).[77]

There were other, more endearing achievements as well. "There is no question that what we went through as a team was such a heartbreaking experience for so many of us," said shortstop Ruben Amaro. "That team had lived through the good and the bad together. A trying experience like that brings you closer together as a team. For some of us, 1964 was memorable for a good reason. Players like Bobby Wine, Richie Allen, Johnny Callison, Tony Taylor, and myself became fathers for the first time that season. All our wives gave birth to their first child in '64. That was the biggest blessing that we could have had after losing such a heartbreaker."[78]

Cookie Rojas has also managed to put the swoon in a proper perspective after the distance of forty years. "Looking back, it's easier to understand what happened to us," he admitted. "We were a very young ball club. Nobody gave us a chance to be a contender. But we had the right mix of guys, and Gene was a great manager. We put together a club that was very exciting and executed the fundamentals well. We played beautifully for 150 games. That was a real achievement, considering the tremendous teams we were playing against. Every opponent had three, four, or five good hitters and several good pitchers. In addition, the Dodgers, Giants, Cardinals, and Reds had had experiences with pennant races. Of course, we hadn't [had that experience] and it would show. It wasn't even that we played poorly. It's just that we never had the pressure of a pennant race put on us before. The way I choose to look at it these days is that in 1964 the Phillies had a fantastic year, a great run at the pennant, but it just didn't happen."[79]

Phillies fans took the collapse the hardest. It was difficult enough to root for a team whose only successes had come in 1915 and 1950, when they captured pennants. In Philadelphia, National League championships came once a generation. Philadelphians had been spoiled by Connie Mack, the storied manager of the American League's Athletics who put together two championship dynasties, first in 1910–14, and then again in 1929–31. Those teams compiled nine pennants and five world championships during their half-century in the City of Brotherly Love, inspiring the belief that the wrong team had left town in 1954 when the A's moved to Kansas City.[80] Just as important, the A's set a precedent for the kind of team Philadelphians adored. The players on the A's two championship dynasties were sharp-witted and strong, reckless and carefree, brutally candid and shamelessly self-indulgent, much like the early twentieth century in which they played.

The Phillies, on the other hand, were perennial losers who received the sympathy of self-respecting fans in other cities. But in Philadelphia, the Phils were alternatively loved and vilified. The love came from fans like Matt Wilson, a North Penn barber, who attended forty games in 1964 only to be sorely disappointed. "Oh, well, forget it," he sighed after the collapse. "It's all gone now, just another part in the life of Phillies baseball."[81] Those were the kinds of fans that greeted the Phillies at the airport at the end of the season with banners that read, "We Still Love You," "Thanks for the Memories," and "We'll Get 'em Next Year!"

Vilification came from others, who gave Philadelphia a more infamous reputation. These too were diehards, but of a distinctly different breed. They judged the players on a "what-have-you-done-for-me lately" attitude where nothing less than winning was acceptable. Losses, poor play, and unemotional performers were greeted with disapproving jeers that often bordered on the obnoxious if not the profane. These so-called "Boo Birds" loved swaggering, trash-talking ballplayers who wear their emotions on their sleeves. They wanted their players to show their humanness—warts and all—with no apologies to anyone, to function in the same black-and-white world of heroes and bums as they do. If they don't, the Boo Birds will let them know it loud and clear. These are the fans that never forgave the Phillies for the '64 swoon, fans like Steve Wulf, a writer for *Sports Illustrated* who was just thirteen years old in 1964. "I cursed Mauch and the Phillies," he admitted. "Why did they have to come so far, only to come so close?" The pain was so unbearable for Wulf that he compared the collapse to "swimming in a long, long lake, and then you drown."[82]

"I can only imagine what the fans went through," said Frank Dolson of the *Philadelphia Inquirer.* "I grew up in New York, a Yankees fan. So when the Phillies blew the pennant, I could really care less as a fan. It was great stuff to write about, though. All those losses made the National League race a little closer, setting up a dramatic finish. That was great stuff to write about. It underlined for me the fact that there's no sport like baseball. You have to play it day after day, and just when you think you know it all, you find out that you don't know a damn thing."[83]

Larry Merchant of the *Daily News,* on the other hand, summed up the collapse with a moribund eloquence. "Future generations will be told this incredible horror story September after September, that the Phillies of Philadelphia led the league by six and a half games—and couldn't win another game," he wrote in his Monday October 5 column. "Children will shriek, adults will shiver, managers will faint. The legend will take its place alongside such classics as the Dodgers of '51 and Frankenstein and the Wolfman."[84] Merchant could feel the pulse and the anger of the Boo-Birds. His words proved to be a bitter but accurate prophecy that continued to haunt Philadelphia until 1980, when the Phillies finally captured another pennant and their only world championship. It's more difficult to explain what happened to Gene Mauch and his team after that fateful September.

6

SEASONS OF FRUSTRATION

Spring training is usually an elixir for a team that suffered through a disappointing season the previous year. The Grapefruit League offers not only another chance for glory but also revival of the spirit. But when Gene Mauch walked into Jack Russell Stadium in Clearwater in February 1965, he was forced to confront the painful reminder of a blown pennant. The messenger came in the person of Howard Cosell, a brash, egotistical sports journalist who achieved nationwide admiration and hatred for his penchant for uncovering a scoop.

Cosell came to the Phillies spring-training camp to interview Mauch on camera. The Little General said he would talk, on condition that there would be no discussion of the collapse. Cosell agreed, and the camera began to roll.

"What was it like to lose the pennant after being six and a half games up with only twelve to go?" asked Cosell in his very first question, violating the pact he had just made.

Mauch, noticeably angered, glared at the obnoxious journalist and replied: "Fuck you, Howard." Then he turned and walked away, ending the interview.[1]

During the next three seasons, Gene Mauch was determined to clinch the pennant that had eluded him in 1964. The quest bordered on a personal obsession that eventually proved to be his downfall as a manager. Each year his efforts were frustrated by bad trades, injuries, and a growing distance between himself and his players, especially the team's enigmatic superstar, Richie Allen. Desperate to land the veterans who could make the difference, Mauch and General Manager John Quinn traded away talented young prospects for seasoned veterans, all of whom failed to deliver the elusive flag.

In 1965, Quinn acquired Dick Stuart, a power-hitting first baseman from the Boston Red Sox, for pitcher Dennis Bennett; pitcher Bo Belinsky, a free-spirited hurler with a lively arm, from the Los Angeles Angels for first baseman Costen Shockley and pitcher Rudy May; and pitcher Ray Herbert from the Chicago White Sox for outfielder Danny Cater.[2] All three of the trades proved to be busts. Stuart was inconsistent at the plate, and his wacky defense earned him the nickname "Dr. Strange Glove." Belinsky had great ability but very little understanding of how to pitch. He won only four of thirteen decisions and argued constantly with Mauch. Herbert, a junkballer, surrendered 162 hits in 131 innings and finished the season with a 5–8 record.[3] Although Bunning (19–9, 260 K, 2.60 ERA) and Short (18–11, 237 K, 2.82 ERA) had good seasons, the Phillies pitching wasn't nearly as good as the year before. In addition to the poor performances of Belinsky and Herbert, Art Mahaffey was plagued with arm troubles and finished a disappointing 2–5. Jack Baldschun and Ed Roebuck could not hold leads, and rookies Ferguson Jenkins, Grant Jackson, Morrie Steevens, and Gary Wagner were too inexperienced to help.[4] In the clubhouse there were growing signs of discontent as Wes Covington and Tony Gonzalez openly complained about being platooned in the outfield.[5] It is not surprising that the Phils struggled to play .500 ball for most of the season.

As so often is the case in Philadelphia when the Phils are out of contention early, the fans found some consolation in the exploits of individual stars, and there was no greater star than Richie Allen. The young third baseman picked up where he left off in 1964, entering the month of May with a twelve-game hitting streak and closing it with a 529-foot shot over the left-field roof at Connie Mack Stadium in a dramatic 4–2 come-from-behind victory against the Chicago Cubs. It was one of the longest home runs in baseball history.[6] By the end of June, Allen was hitting .348 and had been named to the National League All-Star team. This African American superstar—the first in Philadelphia's infamous baseball history—appeared to have captured the hearts of the fans. Then suddenly, on July 3, things changed for the worse.

Allen was taking ground balls at third base before that night's game against the Cincinnati Reds, while Frank Thomas was in the cage taking his cuts. Johnny Callison, who stopped by to visit with Allen, suggested that they taunt Thomas for his poor showing at the plate during the previous night's game against the Giants. With runners on first and third and one out, Thomas tried to avoid hitting into a double play by bunting the ball. After three failed attempts, the thirty-six-year-old slugger struck out. His own teammates found the scene hilarious, unable to control their laughter in the dugout. Now, Allen and Callison—both of whom had been the object of Thomas's own ridicule several times before—were ready to get even.

Down in the cage, Thomas took a big swing and missed. "Hey Donkey!" yelled Callison, referring to the veteran by his nickname, "Why don't you try bunting?" Instead of responding to Callison, Thomas glared down the third-base line at Allen and shouted: "What are you trying to be, another Muhammad Clay, always running your mouth off?" Insulted by the comparison with Cassius Clay, the colorful but controversial heavyweight boxing champion who had recently changed his name to Muhammad Ali, Allen charged the cage, and the two players went at each other. Allen hit Thomas with a left hook to the jaw, sending him to the ground. When he got to his feet, Thomas was wielding his bat and connected with Allen's left shoulder. By now the rest of the team was at home plate trying to restrain the two players.

According to Allen, Thomas "knew it was Callison who had taunted him." But Thomas's response was, once again, directed at him. "The 'Muhammad Clay' remark was meant to say a lot," insists Allen. "It reminded me of how Frank would pretend to offer his hand in a soul shake to a young black player on the team. When the player would offer his hand in return, Thomas would grab his thumb and bend it back. To him, it was a big joke. But I saw too many brothers on the team with swollen thumbs to get any laughs. So I popped him. I just wanted to teach him a lesson. But after he hit me with the bat, I wanted to kill him."[7]

One of those "young black players" to whom Allen referred was his best friend on the team, twenty-one-year-old outfielder Johnny Briggs. A speedy base runner who played the outfield with an exceptional instinct, Briggs was a player from whom the Phillies expected too much, too soon. With less than 200 games experience in the minors, the Phils had promoted Briggs to the majors for the pennant race in 1964. He played the outfield so

Fig. 29 After he was acquired from the Mets in August 1964, Frank Thomas drove in twenty-six runs in thirty-four games for the Phillies. But an injured hand put him on the disabled list in September before the Phillies collapse. (National Baseball Hall of Fame and Library)

effectively for twenty games that they decided to keep him on the roster in 1965. It was a mistake.

Briggs platooned in center field with Tony Gonzalez and was made the leadoff hitter as well. But he struggled to hit .230 for most of the season and never really felt comfortable with his role on the team, even stating that he would prefer being sent back to the minors just to play on an everyday basis.[8] Ironically, the Phillies found themselves in a no-win situation with Briggs. While Briggs was a part of an earnest attempt to integrate the team, the Phillies only damaged his self-confidence by not sending him down for more seasoning. Perhaps their decision was based on potential, or simply a genuine desire to protect a young black player from discrimination at the hands of the Little Rock fans; something they learned from Allen's experience. Whatever the case might have been, the Phillies failed on both counts. In fact, Thomas only made matters worse for Briggs in Philadelphia. "Frank Thomas often made racially inflammatory comments," recalled Briggs, years later. "As a rookie, I'd never say anything when he made those remarks to me. I might tell Richie about it, just like some of the other black players. That's about all I could do."[9]

According to Pat Corrales, reserve catcher for the Phils, Thomas "had been picking on Johnny Briggs all season, saying 'Boy this' and 'Boy that.'" Allen "didn't go for that." He came to the defense of Briggs time and again. Finally, Thomas turned on Allen.[10] Callison added that hard feelings between the two players had been building for quite some time. "I knew that Thomas had been riding Richie and that a fight was only a matter of time," he said. "Richie was under control until Thomas took that swing at him with the bat. After that, it took five guys to keep Allen off Thomas. Our shortstop, Ruben Amaro, took a shot in the chops trying to restrain Richie."[11]

Amaro, who found himself in the middle of the brawl, also called it "a racial situation." But he remembered it a bit differently than either Allen or Callison. "Thomas liked to intimidate his teammates," recalled Amaro, "especially the young players, who called him 'Donkey' because he had a knack for saying the wrong thing at the wrong time. But Richie wasn't completely innocent either. He was taking ground balls at third before the game and started taunting Thomas, saying, 'Hey Donkey, you can't hit a ball past me!' Thomas yelled back: 'Okay, Richie X, see if you can catch this one!' Of course, Thomas was referring to Malcolm X, a very controversial African American leader at the time. Allen got mad. He went over to the cage and told Thomas: 'I won't call you Donkey anymore and you better not call me Richie X.' Allen returned to third base, and Thomas hits a

Figs. 30 & 31 From 1964 to 1968, Ruban Amaro and Bobby Wine *(opposite)* provided the Phillies with strong defense at shortstop. (Philadelphia Phillies)

Fig. 31

screaming line drive in his direction that goes all the way down the line. Before you know it, Thomas is yelling at him: 'Hey, Richie X, how come you didn't catch that one?' That did it. Allen stormed the cage and the fight began."[12]

During the game that followed, Allen hit two triples, one a 400-foot shot off the Ballantine Beer scoreboard in right-center field in the seventh, and Thomas followed it with a pinch-hit home run an inning later. But the Phillies lost to the Reds, 10–8, dropping them in the standings to fourth place, four games behind the league-leading Dodgers.[13] After the game, Quinn placed Thomas on irrevocable waivers, denying that the fight was the sole reason for his decision. "We had talked with one club in particular," the general manager explained to the press. "We were trying to work out a deal without success—even before the trade deadline—so it just isn't the incident that occurred between Thomas and Allen. This is what we thought we should do for the best interests of the ball club."[14]

Mauch threatened Allen with a $2,000 fine if he discussed the incident with the press. When sportswriters asked the black slugger to give his side of the story, he said published versions of the fight were "false" but refused to go into any detail about it because "it might hurt Thomas's chances of getting a job with another team." "I'm sorry about the whole thing," Allen told them. "I'm really sorry. I should have thought it over.... I know in the heat of a pennant race tempers flare. I'm also sorry they put Thomas on waivers, but I don't work in the front office."[15] Allen pleaded with Mauch to spare Thomas, who had a large family to support. But the Phillies skipper refused to listen.[16] When asked about the decision by the press, Mauch replied: "I had to choose between a thirty-six-year-old veteran who was hitting .250 and a twenty-three-year-old power hitter who was hitting .348, the kind of player you see once in a lifetime."[17] It was the worst thing he could have said.

Thomas took his case to the press, exploiting the role of a victim. "I've always liked Richie," he insisted. "I've always tried to help him. I guess certain guys can dish it out, but can't take it." Thomas also told the sportswriters that he had apologized to Allen and to management for his part in the incident, but that the front office refused to reinstate him on the team. "I think you're being unfair," Thomas reportedly told Gene Mauch, before leaving the team. "We're always agitating each other, and he hit me first."[18] Some sportswriters were sympathetic. While Sandy Grady of the *Bulletin* did not exonerate Thomas for "breaking baseball's code by using a bat in a ballgame brawl," he wrote that General Manager John Quinn "made a more impulsive decision" by putting Thomas on "irrevocable waivers" after the fight. According to Grady, Quinn made "a glaring mistake" by preferring "clubhouse harmony" to "loud, late-inning rallies" that could bring the Phillies a pennant.[19] Other writers made Allen the culprit.

George Kiseda of the *Bulletin* wrote: "Allen's refusal to tell his side of the story made him the villain in the eyes of the fans." Insisting that he was more concerned about the implications of the Thomas waiver on the Phillies' bid for a pennant, Kiseda explained that the fans were not "booing out of compassion for Thomas, but out of self-pity because they suspect they might have lost a pennant."[20] Larry Merchant of the *Daily News*, however, was relentless in his condemnation of the young Phillies slugger. For one full week after the incident, Merchant continued to hammer out columns that fueled rumors of racial divisiveness in the Phillies clubhouse. "If you want to give, you should be ready to take the agitating that goes on among ballplayers," wrote Merchant in his July 6 column. "Allen gave but didn't take. He lost his cool. His skin wasn't so tough after all." Allen "resents authority and he admits it." When Thomas told him he was "mouthing off" it was a "fatal putdown, a kick in the gut." It was like "telling him he was still a punk kid, mind your manners." But Thomas's release only "exposes Allen as a kid who caused a veteran to lose his job." Merchant suspected that "an unspoken resentment must smolder between Allen and his teammates because they know he was wrong. To protect themselves, they will instinctively withdraw from him. Who wants to kid with a kid who might blow up?" While Merchant wrote that the incident had "no racial connotation whatsoever," he did predict that "rumors of racial strife" would arise, as they "always do during losing streaks."[21] He did not have to write anything more; he had already planted the seed for controversy.

When Allen fans came to their hero's defense, Merchant categorically refuted them. "Why don't you give Richie Allen a chance?" asked thirteen-year-old Nancy Peahm. "His popularity is certainly stunted now. I am very disappointed for the reputation of Richie." "You have every reason to be disappointed, Nancy," replied Merchant. "But it wasn't the sportswriters who started the brawl. If anyone hurt Richie Allen's reputation, it was Richie Allen."

Charles Liebman, a Temple University sophomore and editor of the *Temple News*, also took exception to Merchant's "comments on the Allen-Thomas slugfest." "Who cares about Frank Thomas?" he asked. "If I was a manager, I'd personally ship out any third-string outfielder who has the nerve to look cross-eyed at a budding superstar." "If I was your journalism professor," replied Merchant, "I'd ship you out. Your values stink."

Another fan cut to the core of the controversy when he wrote: "I don't think you're being fair to Richie Allen when you write one version of the incident. Allen protected Thomas and hurt himself by not revealing what was actually said. I'm sure you can guess what was really said. I also feel that the fans are being unfair to Allen because Thomas is white. I wonder if they would have booed if the fight was between Allen and Covington and Covington was released." Merchant, in his response, tried to avoid any complicity in creating a racial controversy. "The difference between you and I is that I don't have to guess," he wrote. "Players who were on the scene—white and Negro—have verified Thomas's version. If Allen interpreted remarks made previously by Thomas as racial (whether they were or weren't), then why did he start agitating him on fight night? The only element that has been omitted in this story has been omitted to protect Allen. I think the boo-ers are protecting an injustice—which, again, was perpetrated by the front office—although there are undoubtedly bigots among them. I don't think it would make much difference if Covington was involved."[22]

With petty sarcasm and a patronizing style, Merchant launched a nasty character assault on Richie Allen. He might have denied fueling the flames of racial animosity that already existed in the city, but he did give greater credence to the rumors of racial divisiveness on July 9 when he wrote: "There is a mild form of hysteria sweeping [Philadelphia], sweeping with a dirty broom." The Richie Allen–Frank Thomas incident has "surfaced a lot of underground whispers of fights and racial strife among the Phillies," wrote Merchant. "Ordinarily, one doesn't dignify this sort of trash with a reply," he added, trying to absolve himself of any complicity, "but it's apparent that this wasn't an ordinary case. There is a latent bigotry involved that dates to the 1940s, when the Phillies were a lily-white club."[23]

At the same time Merchant was vilifying Allen in print, the *Tribune*, Philadelphia's most popular African American newspaper, worsened the controversy by making it headline news.[24] Allen had been the paper's top baseball story since he signed with the Phillies in 1960, and its writers were quick to come to his defense. They were also quick to resurrect the Phillies' racist history in order to explain the discriminatory treatment of the team's first black superstar.

In one of the most damning columns, sportswriter Claude E. Harrison Jr. criticized the Phillies and Philadelphia for its shameful history of race relations. Pointing out that Philadelphia was the "last National League city to hire Negro ballplayers" and that San Francisco, Chicago, Los Angeles, St. Louis, and Cincinnati all had marquee players who were black, Harrison insisted that Phillies fans "seem to rebel at the idea of a Negro being one of the team's superstars" and that the "booing of Allen seems to bear this out." Allen, according to Harrison, "certainly can't be blamed for the firing of Thomas, who committed one of the biggest sins in baseball: striking an individual with a bat. Had Thomas hurt Allen and put him out of operation, would the boos still be bouncing off the center-field wall? Doubtful! Very doubtful!"[25]

Harrison's column only reinforced the racial animosity that already existed in Philadelphia. It was bad enough to resurrect the Phillies' poor history of race relations at a time when the club had turned the corner on integration. But to underscore Allen's problems with the fans, Harrison also wrote, that Johnny Callison, the white fans' hero, was only an "average player" who "can't live up to the press he receives." In doing so, he undermined a growing friendship between the two players. To add insult to injury, Harrison, in a subsequent column, facetiously identified all the reasons why Allen "is an annoying fellow." Harrison wrote that Allen "annoys Phillies fans because he refuses to buckle under"; he annoys "General Manager John Quinn at contract time by holding out for what he considers a good salary"; and he annoys "sportswriters because when asked a question, he usually thinks twice and says nothing."[26]

While Harrison's column intended to show how Allen had vindicated himself with his critics, it also suggested that he was a spiteful individual who purposely stirred controversy. The column certainly did not help the slugger's precarious situation. Both Harrrison and Merchant should have allowed the incident to die a natural death.

Frank Dolson of the *Inquirer* disagrees. He insists that it was impossible for the city's sportswriters to dismiss the racial implications of the Allen-Thomas incident. "When Allen and Thomas got into their fight, the writers had to address it," he said, in a recent interview. "It happened in full view. We couldn't just sit on it. Since one of the players was black and the other white, it was hard not to perceive it as a racial issue. But I don't think any of us consciously dredged up the story to stir controversy. After we reported it, the story took on a life of its own in a town that was experiencing racial problems."[27]

To be sure, the Allen-Thomas fight reinforced, in the minds of white Philadelphians, the racial stereotyping of African Americans as "troublemakers." Whites pointed to the rise of the Black Mafia, a street gang based

around Twentieth and Carpenter Streets, as a justification for the stereotype. Led by Benjamin Coxson and "Big Sam" Christian, this organized
band of black gangsters controlled gambling, prostitution, and drug-dealing
in the city's African American neighborhoods.[28] They gradually displaced
the traditional "Pop system," where older black men who were respected
members of the community mentored black youth, encouraging clean living and education as the keys to success.[29] Like churches and schools, the
Pop system was overwhelmed by a dramatic increase in the juvenile population in the post–World War II era. These socializing institutions were
beginning to crumble at the very moment when Philadelphia's African
American youth needed them most.[30] The Black Mafia and the several black
gangs that were sprouting up across the city in the late 1950s and 1960s
offered a quick—and illegal—way to make money. In a study of 10,000 male
adolescents who were born in 1945 and lived in Philadelphia, more than
one-third had been arrested at least once by the age of eighteen, and half
that number were arrested more than once. A later study of male adolescents born in 1958 revealed similar findings.[31] For white city-dwellers, the
statistics reinforced the negative stereotype of African Americans and, in
the mid-1960s, colored their perception of the civil rights movement itself.
Cecil B. Moore's fight to overturn the will of nineteenth-century banker
Stephen Girard, giving black youth the right to attend the all-white Girard
College, fueled white animosity toward the city's African Americans.

Moore, president of the Philadelphia NAACP and a controversial political figure, launched a campaign to integrate the college preparatory school
in 1957. In that year, the United States Supreme Court ruled that Girard
College, established in 1848 to educate orphaned white males, was "publicly aided to a sufficient degree to require non-discriminatory entrance
policies admitting minority candidates." When the Board of City Trusts,
responsible for oversight of the school, prepared for integration, a separate governing body was created to overrule them. Moore argued that the
act was a blatant evasion of the Supreme Court's decision, and organized
large-scale pickets to protest it. The longer the school refused to integrate,
the more heated the African American community became. The situation
became so severe by 1965 that 1,000 police had to be deployed in the
neighborhoods surrounding the school to preserve order. Even the Reverend Dr. Martin Luther King Jr. attended a rally urging nonviolent pressure for open admission.[32]

In Philadelphia's racially charged atmosphere, Allen's own situation was
inevitably distorted, not only by the press but also by the city's baseball

fans. Even though the Phillies star was hitting .328 and was named the starting third baseman for the National League's All-Star team, fans continued to blame Allen for the fight. They labeled him a "troublemaker" and scrutinized his every act. Playing in Philadelphia became an increasingly hellish experience. Allen was "sucker punched" by one fan, others screamed "darkie" or "monkey" at him, and, in one especially painful act, a white father held his little boy up in the air with one hand and pointed at the black slugger with the other, teaching his son to boo.[33]

There were times Allen admitted to "feeling the anger at the plate, ripping through [his] veins." On July 9, for example, he hit a grand slam in the nightcap of a doubleheader against the San Francisco Giants at Connie Mack. The blow proved to be the margin of victory for the Phils, who defeated the Giants, 4–2. After hitting the homer, Allen saw the crowd of 37,110 giving him a standing ovation when just thirty seconds earlier they were calling him a "monkey." He called the scene "the ultimate mind game."[34] Off the field, Allen received hate mail regularly. The front lawn of his Mount Airy home was strewn with trash, compliments of the neighborhood's disgruntled fans. The abuse became so bad that Era Allen pleaded with her son to tell his side of the Thomas story.[35] Some of Allen's friends even urged him to hire a bodyguard. But the young third baseman took it in stride. "The fans are not the ones I want to beat," he stated. "If I paid my money to see a ball game, I guess I'd raise a little hell too."[36]

But years later Allen admitted that all the abuse had taken its toll. "After the Thomas fight, I started playing angry baseball," he confessed. "It seemed the whole city of Philadelphia blamed me for what happened. They hung banners from the bleachers at Connie Mack Stadium in support of Thomas. I began getting hate mail and lots of it. Most of the letters I got started off with 'nigger.' None of them were ever signed. Racists are cowards. After a while, I just dumped the mail in the trash, unopened."[37]

The negative press and the "mind games" the fans were playing with him inevitably affected Allen's performance, as well as the badly bruised shoulder he suffered from the fight with Thomas. He hit only .271 in the month of July, but he refused to be taken out of the lineup. Still, he completed the 1965 season with a very respectable .302 average, 20 homers, and 85 RBIs for a team that finished sixth, eleven and a half games behind the pennant-winning Dodgers.[38]

The Richie Allen soap opera may have been the focal point of the Phillies' disappointing season, but it was part of a much larger race problem the nation was experiencing in the mid-1960s. That point was made clear when the Phillies traveled to Los Angeles to play the Dodgers that summer. On August 11 a Los Angeles Police Department officer patrolling the neighborhoods of Watts arrested a young black male on the suspicion of drunk driving. An ugly confrontation ensued, escalating into a full-fledged race riot. Over the next three days, 35 people lost their lives, 1,200 were seriously injured, more than 4,000 were arrested for civil disobedience, and property damage was estimated in the millions.

The Phillies flew down from San Francisco to play the Dodgers on Sunday evening, August 15, shortly after order had been restored. As their plane began its descent, the captain announced that he would be "forced to make a steeper than normal approach" to the airport due to the "fires and other difficulties that exist in the riot area."

"Son—of—a—bitch," murmured Gene Mauch, as he peered out the window at the black plumes of smoke and still burning fires below. "Those folks really mean business down there."

The players saw a war zone as they traveled through downtown Los Angeles on a chartered bus from the airport to the Ambassador Hotel on Wilshire Boulevard. Sirens blared. Police were on the lookout for random snipers. More than 13,000 national guardsmen occupied the streets to prevent further looting.

"Tonight's going to be the crucial night as far as riots go," observed Wes Covington. "I hear there is talk of them reorganizing."

Covington's prediction proved to be accurate. That night there was rioting in Long Beach and San Diego, 100 miles away. None of the players had the courage to go out. Instead they remained glued to the television set, watching the drama unfold.[39] The experience must have been especially traumatic for Richie Allen, Johnny Briggs, and Alex Johnson, young black players who were struggling to establish an identity, not only as professional athletes but also as African American men in a white mainstream society. They were in early adulthood, a difficult period for anyone starting out on a career path. But the process of resolving the dilemma was especially difficult for them because of the much greater visibility of a professional athlete. They were not only encountering racism but also immersed in an environment in which they were forced to grapple with what it means to be a member of a group targeted by racism.

To eliminate any involvement in civil rights demonstrations, some clubs wrote clauses into the contracts of their black players forbidding them to "participate in any freedom marches." *Ebony* magazine, a national African American periodical, attacked the clause, condemning the "handful of owners who believe that Negroes should be forever grateful that they were finally admitted to the majors and should never complain."[40] According to Ruly Carpenter, son of owner Bob Carpenter, the Phillies never required such a restrictive clause in the contracts of any of their black players. However, he did understand the position of the clubs that did resort to the clause. "Civil rights demonstrations could often be pretty dangerous," he said. "If you had a good player, you certainly didn't want him to get hurt. It was a way to protect your investment in the player."[41] The Phillies' problems, on the other hand, had to do with with team chemistry, although they were beginning to be cast in a racial context.

During the final series of the 1965 season against the Mets, Wes Covington, a black veteran outfielder who had grown tired of being platooned, sat in front of his locker at New York's Shea Stadium and lambasted the Phillies organization.

"This club should have won the pennant the last couple of years," he told a group of Philadelphia sportswriters. "I've been on a pennant winner in Milwaukee, and I know what it takes to win a pennant. The club we had a year ago, one guy would break his back for the other one. Why, over one year, did we become a club of guys who just think about themselves? We lost twenty-three in a row in 1961 and we had better spirit than we have now. What happened in the last year? If you were the manager, and if you had managed a club the year before with the spirit we had, and something happened, would you as manager take charge then, or would you turn your back? There's a damn good reason why this club is in the second division."[42]

Covington stopped just short of saying that Gene Mauch had lost control of the club. It did not matter. The veteran outfielder had worn out his welcome in Philadelphia and was traded to the Chicago Cubs for outfielder Doug Clemens.

There were other trades too. On October 27, Quinn sent the moody but talented young outfielder Alex Johnson, along with Art Mahaffey and backup catcher Pat Corrales, to St. Louis for veteran first baseman Bill White, shortstop Dick Groat, and catcher Bob Uecker.[43] Shortly afterward, Ruben Amaro was traded to the New York Yankees for infielder Phil Linz.[44] Finally, on April 21, 1966, Quinn sent twenty-two-year-old pitching prospect Ferguson Jenkins, first baseman John Herrnstein, and outfielder Adolfo Phillips to the Chicago Cubs for veteran right-handers Larry Jackson and Bob Buhl.[45]

Allen was devastated by the trades. He had lost three of his best friends at a time when he needed their support most. Allen had mentored both

Johnson and Jenkins when they first came up to the Phillies, teaching them how to deal with the precarious racial climate of Philadelphia baseball. They became close friends. But Corrales was Allen's confidant. The two players were roommates at Little Rock and came up together through the Phillies organization. "As a Chicano with Indian blood raised in a tough neighborhood, I had already been through all the racial crap that Richie hadn't as a kid," said Corrales, reflecting later on the trade. "In Little Rock I had him laughing at all that crap. I could reach him. We were like brothers." The trade, he added, was the "dumbest thing the Phillies could have done, as far as Richie was concerned."[46] At the time, however, the trades appeared to favor the Phillies' bid to capture a pennant in 1966.

Larry Jackson and Bob Buhl were seasoned veterans who could give the Phils 200 or more innings of work each. Jackson was a twenty-four-game winner in 1964, and Buhl was good for ten to twelve victories as well. Both would stabilize the Phillies rotation, which already consisted of three solid pitchers in Bunning, Short, and Culp. On the other hand, the only pitching the Phils gave up was Mahaffey, who could manage only a 2–5 record and an inflated 6.21 ERA because of a chronically sore arm, and an unproven rookie in Jenkins. Amaro was not much of a loss, having been demoted to Bobby Wine's backup at shortstop, and his three seasons in New York would be marred by injuries. Linz, on the other hand, able to play second, short, third, and the outfield, brought postseason experience as well as versatility. White, Groat, and Uecker were also seasoned veterans with postseason experience, which made them more valuable to the Phillies in their quest for a pennant than Johnson, Herrnstein, Corrales, and Phillips, who were all young, unproven talent. As it turned out, the Phillies' decision to trade youth for veteran talent cost them longer-term success.[47] Johnson and Jenkins, in particular, blossomed into stellar performers elsewhere.

Johnson hit .298 in 140 games in his two years in Philadelphia. But within the Phillies organization the black ballplayer was considered "moody" and a "loner," and there was no place to put him in the outfield with Callison, Gonzalez, and Briggs, who showed signs of superstardom. However, Johnson went on to compile a respectable .288 batting average and .953 fielding percentage in a thirteen-year major league career that included stints with the pennant-contending Cardinals, Reds, and Yankees.[48] Jenkins did even better, becoming a Cy Young Award winner and a consistent twenty-game winner for the Cubs. At the end of his Hall of Fame career, he had collected 286 victories, 3,192 strikeouts, and an impressive 3.34 ERA.[49] Some believe that Jenkins never showed any sign of that remarkable talent when he was with the Phillies.[50] In his eight appearances, the young black hurler compiled a 2–1 record, 10 strikeouts, and a 2.51 ERA.[51]

Clay Dalrymple, who caught Jenkins, thought otherwise. "Fergie had tremendous potential because he kept the ball down," he recalled. "He didn't walk many hitters, and he had a great attitude. But Mauch believed that black pitchers buckled under pressure. In fact, Fergie had problems picking up his signs. Gene always had complicated signs. In one game, Ferguson crossed me up a couple of times simply because he was guessing. Instead of coming to me, or to anybody on the team, to review the signs, he just kept quiet and tried to pitch. I'll tell you one thing. That kid had great ability, and Mauch traded away one of the best pitchers in the game."[52]

Dalrymple's remark suggests that the Jenkins trade was racially motivated. But when asked if Mauch harbored ill feelings toward the team's African American players, the veteran catcher quickly rejected the notion, stating that it was a prevailing belief among many managers that black pitchers cracked under pressure. The Phillies' other white and Hispanic players also discounted racial prejudice as the reason for the trade. The fact that the Phils obtained thirty-two-year-old veteran first baseman Bill White, an African American, from the Cardinals reinforces their belief. In fact, White, having experienced segregation as a young player, was an outspoken critic of major league baseball's refusal to employ blacks in coaching, management, and broadcasting positions.[53]

Raised in Warren, Ohio, in the late 1930s and early 1940s, William DeKova White briefly attended Hiram College before signing with the New York Giants in 1953. The Giants assigned him to their Danville, Virginia, farm team, where he was among the first black players in the Carolina League. Playing in the tobacco-belt towns of Raleigh, Greensboro, Durham, and Winston-Salem gave the nineteen-year-old Buckeye an education in the realities of the Jim Crow South, where legal segregation was a valued way of life. On the field, White was called "nigger" and "black cat." Off the field, he was barred from hotels, movie theaters, and drugstore lunch counters. By 1960, his second year with the St. Louis Cardinals, he had had enough. During spring training in St. Petersburg, he leaked stories to the liberal northern press of Florida's segregationist treatment of black ballplayers. Soon after, other black major leaguers began to speak out. Working together with the Cardinals general manager, Bing Devine, White convinced owner August A. Busch Jr. to put pressure on the owners for integration of some of the best motels in St. Petersburg, or see the

Fig. 32   First baseman Bill White came to the Phillies in 1966, but his career was cut short by an injured Achilles tendon. He went on to become a broadcaster and, later, president of the National League. (National Baseball Hall of Fame and Library)

Cardinals move out of Florida altogether. Realizing the financial implications of the threat, the motel owners agreed.[54]

White, who helped St. Louis to a world championship in 1964, immediately became an impact player in Philadelphia. During the first two months of the 1966 campaign, the veteran first baseman's defense saved many games for the Phillies, who moved within one and a half games of first place on June 8. After Memorial Day, White went on a hitting tear that carried through mid-July. At the All-Star break, he was hitting at a .350 clip with 9 homers, 10 doubles, 4 triples, and 29 RBIs.[55]

"With Bill over there at first, I don't have a thing to worry about," said Allen, who quickly endeared himself to the veteran infielder.[56] White, a consummate professional with a remarkable work ethic, proved to be a positive influence. Like Allen, he had experienced racial discrimination firsthand and could sympathize with the young slugger's plight. But unlike Allen, White had been around the majors longer and knew how to fight for change within the system. When, for example, black professional athletes from football, basketball, and baseball made plans to organize a union "for the purpose of gaining greater shares of the income generated by their respective teams," White proved to be a voice of reason. "Maybe I'm old-fashioned," he said, "but I feel we have all channels open to us, regardless of color, to make as much money as we can with our ability to play matched against the club's ability to pay. If the Negro professional were to be separated from the main body of players, we'd not only be losing twenty hard years of progress since Jackie Robinson's entrance into the game, but we'd also be removed from the free market of bargaining for top money. This would be a giant step backward."[57] His counsel was taken to heart, and the movement folded.

Bob Uecker also endeared himself to Allen. The two players developed a hilarious routine that included singing as well as a series of self-deprecating skits that kept their teammates in stitches, both in the clubhouse and on the road. One of Allen's favorites was a slow-motion imitation of Bill White bailing out of the way of a blazing Sandy Koufax fastball.[58] "Richie Allen was a real cashew," joked Uecker, years later when he was a comic entertainer. "He liked everything about a ballpark except getting there on time. He also liked to sip the cooking sherry. We would get in the back of the plane, glowing slightly, and sing harmony, all the old barber shop songs. We were a happy pair."[59] Uecker helped Allen rediscover his fun-loving side, which he had stifled in the wake of the Thomas fight. The budding superstar began to loosen up, and, as long as the Phillies were winning, the fans as well as the press left him alone. But when the bullpen collapsed in mid-June and Callison suffered a prolonged hitting slump, the Phillies went into a tailspin, losing eleven of the next sixteen games, and the season took a turn for the worse. The Boo-Birds returned with a vengeance, and Allen was their primary target.

Allen was having a career year at the plate, but the fans were booing him every night. Even when Mauch moved him into the outfield in an attempt to spare his young star from the hecklers who sat along the third-base line, it only made matters worse. Fans sitting in the outfield bleachers threw pennies, bolts, or beer bottles at Allen, who began wearing a batting helmet just to protect himself from the projectiles. His only salvation came, it seemed, in a bottle. Matters came to a head on July 21t in San Francisco, when Allen missed curfew and Mauch slapped him with a $500 fine. The following day, when Bill Conlin of the *Philadelphia Daily News* asked the Little General if Allen was having trouble hitting the high fastball, Mauch, with a jaded sense of humor, replied: "No, he's having trouble with the fast highball."[60]

Frustrated by his team's losing ways, Mauch tried to turn things around by antagonizing his own players. Clubhouse tirades became more common, focusing on individuals who had an especially bad game. Once, after Dalrymple went hitless in three straight contests, Mauch exploded at his catcher, telling him he was "going to put a postage stamp on [his] head and send [him] so fuckin' far to Alaska that no one would ever find [him]."[61] No one was immune from the barbs, not even Mauch's personal favorite, Johnny Callison. During a weekend series against the Giants at Candlestick Park, the slumping Phillies right-fielder misplayed a routine fly ball, and three runs scored. When Callison returned to the dugout, Mauch berated him for "dogging it."

"That's bullshit!" exploded Callison, insulted by the remark. "You can go fuck yourself!"

"That'll cost you a thousand, Callison," snapped the Little General.

Callison, his pride bruised, told Mauch that he wanted "out of Philadelphia." He eventually paid $250 of the fine, and Mauch never bothered to collect the balance. Allthough the incident was soon forgotten by the two men, the Philadelphia sportswriters kept dredging it up.[62] In the absence of winning, confrontation was the best topic.

Frank Dolson of the *Inquirer* was one of the writers in the Philadelphia manager's doghouse. "Mauch was a fascinating character," said Dolson, recalling the Little General's tempestuous behavior. "He once told me, 'I'm sick of writing your God-damned column for you. You're going to have to do it on your own, because I'm not going to talk to you!' Then he stormed out. He wouldn't talk with me for a while after that. After two months had passed and I'd served my probation, he'd act like nothing happened and provide some quotable responses. That was Mauch. In his mind, I had served my sentence."[63]

The Phillies finished fourth in 1966, eight games behind the pennant-winning Dodgers. There were plenty of reasons for the disappointing season. Callison had an off-year, dropping to just 11 homers and 55 RBIs. At age thirty-seven, Bob Buhl was too old to contribute much, as reflected by his 6–8 record and 4.77 ERA. The bullpen was horrendous. Darold Knowles, Roger Craig, Ray Herbert, Gary Wagner, Grant Jackson, Ed Roebuck, Terry Fox, and Steve Ridzik had a combined ERA of 6.19 and just twenty-one saves between them. Allen, Bunning, and Short provided the few highlights in an otherwise dismal season. Allen enjoyed his biggest year in a Phillies uniform with an impressive .317 average, 40 home runs, and 110 RBIs. Bunning won nineteen games for the third straight season, and Short won twenty.[64]

The year 1966 was also a turning point for both the Phillies and major league baseball. Labor relations would soon begin to dominate the game, with the player union's hiring of a new executive director, Marvin Miller, a labor economist for the United States Steel Workers. Before 1966, Judge Robert Cannon served as part-time legal counsel for the players' union and acted in the interests of the owners and Commissioner Ford C. Frick. He made sure that salaries remained low by refusing even to consider arbitration, which would, in his estimation, destroy the reserve clause binding a player to one club. The average player salary was $16,000 a season, and the total payroll for all major league clubs was $8,225,000.[65] While a player might augment his salary with off-the-field endorsements, such an arrangement only went to the best players. Even then, star performers, like all the rest of the major leaguers, had to negotiate their salaries individually with the general manager, whose main objective was to cut the club's payroll.

John Quinn, general manager of the Phillies, was adept at the bargaining process. With young prospects recently called up to the majors, he refused to pay the minimum bonus of $2,500.[66] Players who had an off-year could predict a pay cut, along with the disparaging remark "You're lucky that we're even keeping you on the roster." Bob Uecker, a veteran of many off-years, knew what to expect. In 1966 he went into Quinn's office to negotiate a raise. When the Phils general manager told him he was lucky to be with any major league club, the future comedian said, "That's okay, I'll settle for the money you collected on Richie Allen's last fine and I'll still come out ahead."[67] Veterans who objected to Quinn's offer would be scorned, or pressured into signing by the silent treatment. Jack Baldschun recalls holding out for $500 in 1965. "Quinn called me six times from spring training in Clearwater," he said. "The last time he phoned he went silent for five minutes. I knew he wanted me to stick my foot in my mouth. But I didn't. Finally, he asked, 'Are you still there?' I said I was and that he should just give me the money he was spending on all these phone calls. 'Okay,' he said. 'I'll give you $50. C'mon down.'"[68]

Even those who had successful seasons had to fight for a minimal raise. Tony Gonzalez, for example, asked for a $1,000 raise after the 1967 season in which he hit .339 and finished second to Roberto Clemente of Pittsburgh for the National League's batting title. When Quinn offered to raise him just $300, Gonzalez, dumbfounded, asked: "Are you kidding me?" "No, I'm not kidding," Quinn replied. "You players have to put people in the ballpark. We're losing money because the gate has dropped. How on earth do you expect me to pay you more?" When Gonzalez refused to sign for such an insignificant amount, Quinn said: "All right, see if you can make more money cutting sugar cane down in Cuba!" The centerfielder sat out until late March when Quinn, who realized that he could not replace a player of Gonzalez's abilities, grudgingly gave him the $1,000 raise.[69]

"Management owned you in those days," said Clay Dalrymple, who experienced his own share of Quinn's curmudgeonly negotiating tactics. "Quinn could do whatever the hell he felt like doing with you. Most of us didn't want to argue about money. We just wanted to play ball. The only guy Quinn never challenged was Jim Bunning. Jim wrote everything down—his statistics, his worth compared to pitchers on other teams. So when he went in to talk contract, he knew his facts. Quinn never gave him any trouble."[70]

Bunning had been the player representative for the Detroit Tigers before coming to Philadelphia. He had earned the reputation of a "briefcase ballplayer," one who paid more attention to union business than to his pitching. Many suspected that Detroit traded Bunning for that reason alone. Quinn realized what he was getting, but he believed that Bunning's pitching ability was worth whatever problems he might create as a diehard union man.[71]

To be sure, Bunning wasted no time creating problems for Quinn. When he arrived in Philadelphia in 1964 and learned that the Phillies made the players pay for parking at the ballpark, he challenged the policy, forcing ownership to rescind it.[72] Over the next few years, the Phillies' ace proved to be a successful negotiator as well. He met Quinn with the facts and figures of his previous season's performance. If Quinn, who drank a lot, became belligerent, Bunning would suspend negotiations and meet another time. He also learned to go over the general manager's head. "In dealing with John Quinn I had no luck," admitted Bunning. "But if I went to Bob Carpenter and said, 'Here's what I'd like, Bob,' he never would fight with me. Never would argue."[73]

Before the 1966 campaign, Bunning approached Chris Short, the team's number-two pitcher, with the idea of staging a joint holdout, as Sandy Koufax and Don Drysdale of the Dodgers had done the year before. "Shorty was the worst negotiator," recalled Bunning. "He always signed the first contract Quinn sent him, and it was terrible. I said, 'Shorty, you won twenty games last year. Don't you think you deserve a raise? But he didn't have the stomach to hold out."[74] Bunning didn't have to stage a holdout. After his third straight nineteen-win season, he signed for $70,000, the biggest contract awarded by the club to that date.[75]

Bunning also assumed the role of Phillies player representative and became a relentless fighter for players' rights. Complaining that pensions were too small, the Phillies' ace pushed to create a more effective union and was instrumental in the hiring of Marvin Miller as a full-time, paid executive director of the Players' Association in the spring of 1966. Immediately Miller addressed salaries and a more favorable basic agreement. He forced the owners to accept an outside arbitrator to solve any dispute in the basic agreement, a concession that eventually led to the elimination of the reserve clause in 1975.[76] Miller also fought for a substantial increase in player salaries. Within a year of his hiring, the average major league contract jumped from $16,000 to $21,000.[77]

Bunning eventually fell out of favor with owner Bob Carpenter because of his active role in the Players' Association. "I can remember being harassed and harangued by John Quinn," he said, years later. "Bob Carpenter came to me and said, 'You don't need Marvin Miller.' I said, 'No, Bob, if you were the owner and I was the player representative we wouldn't need Marvin Miller. But you don't own all the other teams, and I'm not the player representative on all the other teams. We're getting a lot of corporate ownership in here, and we don't have a clue who's responsible and you don't have a clue who's responsible. So we need to be as firm as we can on what our rights are. If I had a dispute with you, I wouldn't worry. We'd solve it. Not everybody has that kind of relationship, though."[78]

Bunning pitched just one more year in red pinstripes after that discussion, and it would be the most frustrating season of all. In 1967 the Phillies began to pay the price for trading their young prospects for other clubs' veterans. Bill White, who tore his Achilles tendon in the off-season, reinjured it in spring training.[79] When he returned to the lineup in May, he was still hampered by the tendon and managed to hit only eight home runs in 308 at-bats. Dick Groat faded even faster, hitting only .115 in twenty-six at-bats that season. Veteran pitchers Larry Jackson (13–15) and Dick Ellsworth (6–7), who was acquired in the off-season from the Cubs for Ray Culp, lost more games than they won.[80] By the end of May, the Fightin's were, in the words of *Bulletin* sportswriter Sandy Grady, "twenty-five guys wandering in the second division wasteland without any direction from the manager."[81]

Even the team's stars struggled. Bunning, who went 17–15, should have coasted to a twenty-win season. He led the National League with 253 strikeouts in a league-high 302 innings, and his earned run average dropped to 2.29. But he got little offensive support, losing five 1–0 games.[82] Short also pitched well, but still slipped to 9–11. Allen, who was named the starting third baseman for the National League All-Stars for the second straight season, should have had another tremendous year, but his numbers dropped to .307, with 23 homers and 77 RBIs. This time, he was not entirely without blame.

Once again, the Phillies, in what had become a curious pattern, traded away Allen's closest friend on the team, Bob Uecker. Without Uecker's comedic diversion, all the anger and resentment Allen had been feeling toward the fans and the press took control of him. "I'd been hearing that I was a bum for so long that I began to think maybe that's just what I was," he admitted, years later.[83] Allen rebelled. He repeatedly requested a trade from owner Bob Carpenter. Each time the request was denied, the black slugger responded with curfew violations and excessive lateness to games.[84]

By mid-season, Allen's drinking was also a serious problem. "Before ball games, instead of going straight to the ballpark, I started making regular stops at watering holes along the way," he admitted. "I had a regular route from my home in Northwest Philadelphia to the ballpark in the inner city. Whenever Mauch would smell booze on my breath, he'd throw a tantrum and then fine me. I told 'em, I expect to pay when I mess up. Let him put an envelope in my box, but don't call me in for no lectures."[85] On Saturday evening, July 8, 1967, the sixth-place Phillies were scheduled to play the league-leading St. Louis Cardinals. Allen, who was hitting .328 with 11 homers and 40 RBIs, arrived at Connie Mack Stadium unable to walk a straight line or talk without slurring his words. He was told to go home by veteran coach George Myatt. But Allen stayed and was benched by Mauch, who slapped him with a late fine.[86] Allen pinch-hit in the eighth and was called out on strikes as the Phils dropped the game, 6–4. Afterward, Mauch covered for his superstar, telling the press that he'd decided to give Allen "a rest."[87] When asked about the wisdom of benching his best player in a pennant race against the league-leading Cardinals, Mauch snapped: "Whatever goes on between Allen and myself stays that way!"[88]

Allen refuted his manager's story two days later, though. "Yes, I was late," he admitted, responding to sportswriters' questions about Saturday's benching. "Yes, I expected to be fined," he added. "No, there aren't two sets of rules on this ball club. I wear the same uniform as others. I expect the same treatment." He should have stopped there. Instead, Allen incriminated himself by confessing that he "finds it difficult to live within rules." "I can never be a nine-to-five worker," he said. "I can't stand having a hammer held over my head."[89] Whatever else he said in his attempt to resolve the issue was lost on his inquisitors. On July 19, Allen made matters worse by arriving late at the ballpark for a game against the Los Angeles Dodgers, this time because his "car broke down." Again, Mauch slapped his star third baseman with a late fine.[90] It was becoming a joke among the writers, who knew that fines were no deterrent for Allen. He simply paid them, realizing that his $82,000 contract would more than make up the cost.

Sandy Grady of the *Bulletin* questioned whether Allen's irresponsible behavior warranted such an exorbitant salary. "Instead of fining him, maybe the Phillies should have given Allen a $10 raise for a new alarm clock," he joked. "Traditionalists shook their heads when Allen signed for an estimated $82,000, a moon-shot into the fiscal unknown for a fourth-year player." Using Allen's own words against him, Grady wrote: "Rich argued firmly, 'Remember that I should be paid for what I'm doing now, not what I might do someday,'" and then added, "What he has done in July doesn't count for much."[91] Stan Hochman of the *Daily News* was more caustic. "Allen marches to a mournful tune that only he hears, moving with an insolent grace," he wrote, dismissing Mauch's explanation that Allen needed a "mental rest" when he benched him against the first-place Cardinals. "It wasn't that he was late or anything, was it?" Hochman asked patronizingly. "There aren't two sets of rules for the twenty-four other guys and for Allen, are there?"[92]

Bill Conlin, Hochman's colleague at the *Daily News*, was more forgiving.

"I like Rich Allen," he wrote. "Behind that sleepy-eyed facade there's one hell of a man submerged. It is a man's man. Wild, to be sure, but it is a man you would want to hunt with, play games with, or just be with." Conlin was surprised by Allen's admission that he "never wanted to be a superstar" and that the only way he would be happy playing the game was "if they kept the fans and the press out of the ballpark." He called the remark "childlike naiveté," observing that Allen, "when cornered, invariably panics, then overreacts with the petulance of a black Billy Budd." "The hang-up in the life of Rich Allen," concluded the young beat writer, "is that he hasn't discovered who he is."[93]

For the next few years, Conlin would vacillate between harsh criticism and his own childlike admiration for the black Phillies superstar. He even admitted the inconsistency. "Writing about Richie Allen in the 1960s, I kept veering from one point of view to another: awe, empathy, and finally disgust," Conlin wrote, years later. "The awe was for his huge talent, the empathy for his rebellious streak and his endurance of needless racial hassles—many inflicted by his own ball club. The disgust was for his self-regard and indifference to the team."[94]

But even when Conlin was lauding Allen, his writing continued to stir up the specter of racial discord. In one especially poignant column, the *Daily News* scribe painted a sympathetic portrait of the brooding Phillies slugger against the ugly treatment of racist fans. "It should have been a happy night to Rich Allen," began the piece. "He should have been grinning and content in the knowledge that his three-run homer in the twelfth inning won a game for the Phillies. But it is tough to grin when you come to the ballpark and there are letters calling you 'Dirty, Black Nigger.'"

"It is tough to be happy when they start booing you during infield practice and from there the night is a steady escalation of abuse. So instead of being happy and grinning, like the stereotype we all expect a great ballplayer to be, Rich Allen said he would like very much to be traded to another team, any other team. It doesn't make any difference."

Conlin went on to point out that there had been 25,780 fans at Connie Mack Stadium to see the Phils defeat the Chicago Cubs, 5–2, on Allen's home run. "All night that loud minority of bigots, self-styled professional critics, had booed him unmercifully," he wrote. "It was as if he were a piece of garbage who had no business wearing a big league uniform. So he won the game for them, and when he did it they all cheered for him in a classic of hypocrisy." After the game, Allen admitted that he "just wanted one thing, and that is to get out of Philadelphia."[95]

There were exceptions to all the negative press. Both the *Inquirer's* Allen Lewis and the *Bulletin's* Ray Kelly continued to operate on the old school philosophy of writing about the game and not about the personal lives of the players. Their accounts were much more objective, concentrating on Allen's on-the-field performance while offering nothing more than a brief acknowledgment of his off-the-field problems. Predictably, Claude Harrison of the *Tribune* also suspended his judgment of Allen's escapades, insisting, amid all the scandalous reports: "Allen is the third baseman most National League managers would want in their lineup."[96]

All the negative press was temporarily suspended on August 24 when Allen's season came to an abrupt end. While trying to push his stalled car up the driveway of his Mount Airy home in the rain, Allen's right hand slipped and went through the headlight. Two tendons were cut, and the ulna nerve was completely severed. Rushed to Temple University Hospital, the young Phillies star underwent a five-hour operation to repair the damage. Two five-inch pins were placed in the wrist to keep the rejoined tendons in place until they healed. The arm was then encased in a cast from shoulder to fingertips. Doctors gave him a fifty-fifty chance of making a comeback.[97] Immediately rumors spread among the press that Allen's story of an accident was a cover-up, that he had actually b en knifed in a bar fight or had jumped through a window after being caught sleeping with a team-mate's wife. Fortunately for Allen, none of the stories made it into print.[98]

With their most prodigious hitter lost for the rest of the season, the Phillies found themselves juggling the lineup. Fringe players like Gary Sutherland, Billy Cowan, and Gene Oliver saw more playing time than they would have otherwise. Other regulars were forced to play out of position in order to make up for the lost offense. Tony Taylor moved to third base, Bobby Wine played first, and Cookie Rojas set a team record by becoming the first Phillie ever to play all nine positions.[99] Considering all the incon-sistency, the Phillies were lucky to finish the season in fifth place with an 82–80 record.

What had happened to this once-promising team of young black, white, and Hispanic players? Just three years earlier they had come within three games of clinching a pennant. Now, they were struggling to stay out of the second division. Ownership blamed the changing dynamics of baseball. Bob Carpenter cited the beginnings of the amateur draft in 1965 when the Phillies, like every other major league team, had to take a number and wait their turn to pick a prospect. No longer could Carpenter outspend the other clubs, which was how he had secured the services of such talented

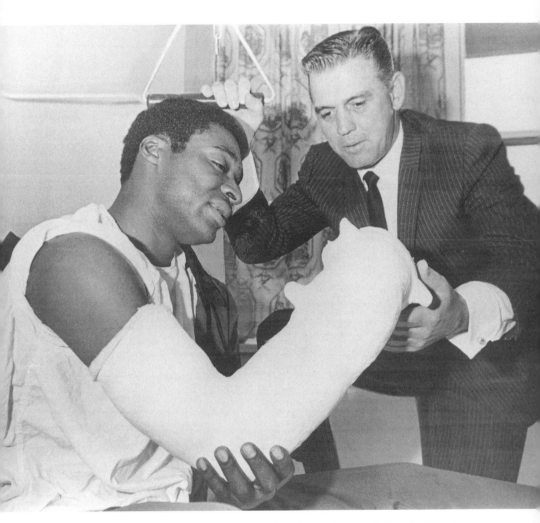

Fig. 33 Manager Gene Mauch visits Richie Allen at Temple University Hospital on August 27, 1967, after the slugger severed tendons in his hand trying to push his stalled car up the driveway of his Mount Airy home. (Temple University Urban Archives)

pitchers as Robin Roberts, Curt Simmons, and Chris Short. "We were lost souls after they implemented the draft," said Carpenter's son Ruly, in a recent interview. "All of a sudden we couldn't go and sign the guys we wanted. Instead, the draft forced us to choose in the reverse order of where we finished. Since the Phillies finished near the top in '64, we were among the last to pick. We tried to group the prospects by talent and then decide who to take in the second or third rounds, but it was absolute chaos."[100]

In the first year of the amateur draft, the Phillies selected near the bottom and got pitcher John Adamson. In 1966 they selected another pitcher, Mike Biko, and in 1967 they chose yet another hurler, Larry Keener. All three were busts, not one making it beyond Double A ball.[101] Consequently, the Phillies were forced to trade for pitching talent.

Mauch blamed himself for the decline. "What happened after 1964?" he asked, trying to explain the inexplicable in a 1991 interview. "Let me put it in real simple terms. The Phillies had a manager who was so cocky, thought his players were so good that he thought he could beat anyone at any time. But the chemistry we had after '64 just wasn't the same. That's baseball. It's a difficult thing to repeat."[102] But Ruly Carpenter believes that Mauch did "a hell of a job with what he had." "If you stop and look at the those teams in the mid-sixties, you've got to admit that they were good, but not *championship* caliber," he insisted. "The '64 club, in particular, accomplished a lot for their abilities, but they weren't a *great* team because they couldn't reproduce the same performance in subsequent years. The fact that that team contended is a testimony to Gene Mauch's genius as a manager."[103]

The players, on the other hand, believe that the team's downfall was the result of trading away talented but inexperienced prospects for proven veterans in a desperate attempt to clinch a pennant. In the process, management mortgaged the club's future. "I thought we took a turn for the worse in '65, trying to make up for '64," said Dick Allen recently. "Poor trades took us down the wrong road, especially losing Fergie Jenkins, who went on to become a consistent twenty-game winner with the Cubs."[104] Johnny Briggs agreed. "We never had any real chance after '64 because we didn't have the pitching you need to win close ball games," he said. Briggs cited the trading of Ferguson Jenkins as a major reason for the team's inability to regroup after the collapse. Together with the sporadic playing time that he and another black outfielder, Larry Hisle, received, the Jenkins trade underscored Briggs's belief that the Phillies "just didn't give blacks much of a chance."[105] White players like Rick Wise and Clay Dalrymple, and Hispanic players like Cookie Rojas and Tony Taylor, also agreed that the Phillies might have contended after 1964 "if there had been some changes in the right direction," noting that age as well as injury eventually took its toll on the club.[106]

Contributing to these problems was the negative press the Phillies and their superstar Richie Allen received after Frank Thomas was waived in July 1965. Mauch later admitted that both he and the Phillies had mishandled the situation. "Thomas was going to go anyway," he conceded. "I should have shipped him sooner. Instead the press came down on Richie's head. If he did one little thing wrong, they would see it as so much worse because, in their heads, he was a bad guy."[107] According to Tony Taylor, the press "never knew Dick Allen." "They made a much bigger thing out of the fight than it really was. They knew that Thomas liked to intimidate young players, but he was also a popular veteran who was brought over here to Philadelphia to help win the pennant. Dick, on the other hand, was still a young player making his name. Everybody on the team liked him. But the press blamed Dick for Thomas's release. Since Dick was black and Thomas was white, they made it into a racial thing and gave Dick the label of a 'trouble-maker.' It wasn't fair."[108]

Johnny Briggs was also quick to dismiss the racial rhetoric surrounding the incident. The sportswriters "never knew the details behind the fight," he insisted, "because Mauch ordered Richie to keep quiet. Thomas agitated everybody on the team. He was just as abusive to the white guys. But the press turned that fight into a racial issue and refused to let up."[109] Bob Uecker, on the other hand, saw the problem stemming from the unrealistic expectations of the press and the fans, both of which he characterized as "smart and mean." Allen became a lightning rod for their frustration with the Phillies' losing ways. "No matter how much Richie accomplished," said Uecker, "it was never good enough to satisfy his critics. Some just didn't like him, his color, his style, or his habits. Others simply felt he didn't get the most out of his huge gifts. But more often than not, he came through for us."[110]

Sandy Grady, Larry Merchant, Stan Hochman, and Bill Conlin, in particular, led the media's assault on the Phillies. They belonged to a new breed of sportswriters, inspired by the pull-no-punches style of Dick Young of the *New York Post*. Young and these "chipmunk writers" believed that they had a responsibility to tell athletes, coaches, and owners that "they're full of shit, and then go out and face them the very next day."[111] Their inherent combativeness allowed them to stand their ground against an angry player and still manage to cull some insightful remarks from him. But it also created an adversarial relationship. No longer would the writers and the players spend their days together on the road trading barbs or drinking in bars together. No longer would the writers shield the players from the public by refusing to print the nasty little secrets of their private lives. In the 1960s, players and managers began to distance themselves from the writers because of their jaded coverage, which celebrated controversy and discouraged the fair play, heroism, and grace that the national pastime once represented.

"I despised the *Daily News*," admitted Clay Dalrymple. "Their writers didn't cover the game. They were simply spouting off their opinions about how the players *should* be. For me, their opinions weren't worth shit. None of those guys ever wore a major league uniform. What gave them the right to pass judgment on me or my teammates? Ray Kelly of the *Bulletin* and Allen Lewis of the *Inquirer* were fine sportswriters. I could always be frank with them because I trusted them to quote me accurately. If I told them my remarks were 'off the record,' they'd honor it. None of us could do that with the *Daily News* writers, though. They had to get a lot of their material through hearsay. They're the guys who invented the story that race was dividing our club. None of us saw it that way."[112]

Dallas Green, who would have his own share of problems with the media as manager of the 1980 World Champion Phillies, underscored the confrontational style of the Philadelphia media. "The press doesn't like to talk positively about sports in this town," he said. "I wasn't an ostrich, but I can't say there was the kind of racism within the Phillies organization they were seeing in the mid-sixties. I just didn't see it in the decision-making process, the scouting, or the handling of the players."[113] Ruly Carpenter echoed those sentiments. "Sure we had run-ins with the press," he admitted. "But we certainly didn't make any decisions based on what the press wrote, and certainly not on the basis of a player's skin color. My father, when he owned the Phillies, and later, when I assumed control of the club, made our decisions based on what the manager, coaches, and scouts thought were in the best interests of the organization. Any time you allow the press to run your organization, you're in trouble. I'm not going to say we didn't read the papers. But generally, we didn't pay attention to the press unless they wrote something outrageous or blatantly inaccurate."[114]

Whether or not they consciously stirred controversy, the Philadelphia press was partially responsible for the negative attitude and behavior of the fans after 1964. The chipmunk writers' constant emphasis on racial division within the Phillies clubhouse became a self-fulfilling prophecy by 1968, as Allen's rebellious behavior to force a trade fragmented the team.

7

BREAKUP

Shortly after the 1967 season ended, Richie Allen, sporting a stylish Afro, pork-chop sideburns, and mustache and wearing a brand-new Edwardian suit, walked into Bob Carpenter's office to do business. Refusing to negotiate with General Manager John Quinn, who insisted on signing the Phillies star to a conditional contract because of the severe injury to his hand, Allen was taking his case directly to the owner.

He wasted no time in stating his demand. Reminding Carpenter that he had hit .307 with 23 home runs and 77 RBIs in an abbreviated season, Allen said he wanted $100,000 to play for the Phillies in 1968.

Carpenter was not like most of the owners. He was first and foremost a fan of the game, a player's owner who spent considerable time in the clubhouse and on the field with his employees. But he also did not know how to treat black players, and he struggled in the effort. Realizing the sensitivity of the situation with his most prized athlete, Carpenter resorted to the role he knew best with young players, that of "father figure." After citing a litany of offenses Allen had committed over the last year, the Phillies owner began with: "Richie, you've just got to grow up!"

"I did grow up," snapped Allen. "Black and poor. You grew up white and rich!"

Carpenter was dumbfounded. Not knowing how to respond, the two men sat in an awkward silence until Allen, after collecting himself, admitted, "But we're both grown-ups now. So let's settle the issue."

Realizing that Allen was the key to his club's success and wouldn't think twice about holding out, Carpenter listened attentively to his superstar's case. After presenting his own, the two men agreed on an $85,000 contract and parted on friendly terms. It was still the highest salary in the game for a fourth-year player.[1]

Richie Allen's sole objective entering the 1968 campaign was to "get the hell out of Philadelphia" by using the "double standard to work in my favor."[2] With free-agency not yet a viable option, Allen launched a campaign of minor transgressions, often exploiting the issue of race hoping to force a trade. Allen's rebelliousness mirrored the social and moral conventions of the time period, which stressed individuality, personal expression, and open defiance at the expense of conformity and deference to authority. Philadelphia, like the rest of urban America, found itself caught in the crosscurrents of social unrest spawned by the Vietnam War and the civil rights and youth movements of the 1960s.

Philadelphia's growing racial conflict, in particular, heightened the social awareness of a young generation that was coming of age. Members of the largest generation in the history of the United States, the baby-boom generation—the first babies born after World War II—enjoyed the opportunity of going to college before finding employment. Unlike their parents, whose outlook was tempered by the experiences of the Great Depression and war, baby-boomers did not have to make the same sacrifices. And neither could they relate to the day-to-day struggles of the more conservative white working class, who felt threatened by the movement for better housing, employment, and educational opportunities for African Americans. Instead, the baby-boomers rewrote the old rules of political action, social behavior, and moral convention.[3]

Inspired by President John F. Kennedy's call to action, students at Temple, Penn, and Drexel became more politically active than the previous generation. For them, the "political" was "personal." From the race struggle at home to the war in Vietnam, they set out to change the world by taking action against social and political injustice.[4] They did not believe that racism would quietly disappear once the institutional barriers to racial equality were eliminated. For them, racism did not end with the passage of the Civil Rights Act of 1964; it only seemed to worsen. The bloody riot-ing during August of that year reinforced their belief that integration was not the solution. Vietnam only added to their frustration, as it drained bil-lions of dollars in federal funding once earmarked for Lyndon Johnson's Great Society programs.

By 1968 the greatest casualty of the Vietnam conflict was the War on Poverty at home. Student protests and civil rights demonstrations intensi-fied as the white liberals of an earlier generation shifted their concern from building a "Great Society" to maintaining an orderly one.[5] Mayor James Tate appointed Frank Rizzo, the tough-minded assistant police commis-sioner, to the top post, trying to curry favor with white ethnic voters for his own reelection in 1967. Rizzo wasted no time staging raids against the militant Black Panthers and other black gangs that controlled the drug traffic in the city's ghettos.[6]

The neighborhood surrounding Connie Mack Stadium was a popular target, being 97 percent African American. Exide Battery, Baldwin Loco-motive, Budd, and Philco, the factories that once were the lifeblood of the community, had left the area. Small but vital businesses like Acme super-markets, theaters, banks, bakeries, pharmacies, and small convenience stores were also closing down.[7] "Car fleecing" by the neighborhood kids—the practice of directing drivers to empty spots and offering to "watch" their car for a fee—was the smallest of concerns. Blacks' frustration with un-employment and poor housing turned to anger and resentment toward the white baseball fans who came into the neighborhood from the suburbs to see a game. Vandalism, drugs, assaults, and muggings by black gangs who laid claim to the neighborhood as their turf kept white fans away from the ballpark. Police referred to the area as the "Black Belt" or, worse, the "Jungle."[8]

The growing crime rate in the stadium neighborhood drove down not only property values, but also the Phillies attendance. In 1964 the team attracted 1.4 million fans, but after the August riots there was a steady decline in ballpark attendance. In 1965 the Phillies drew 1.2 million; in 1966, 1.1 million; in 1967, 800,000; 1968, in 660,000; and in 1969, just 500,000. "Connie Mack Stadium represented white baseball, white Philadelphia," according to Bruce Kuklick, author of *To Every Thing a Season: Shibe Park and Urban Philadelphia, 1909–1976*. "Black residents saw white people com-ing into their neighborhood to do their 'white thing' and resented it."[9]

Increased crime provoked more unchecked police brutality, and that combination only became a vicious cycle that mobilized more responsible groups committed to nonviolence. Membership in Philadelphia's chapter of the NAACP ballooned to 60,000 in 1967, the largest in the nation. Led by President Cecil B. Moore, the organization staged protests throughout the city to win concessions on hiring, promotion, and equal educational opportunity. NAACP members could be found picketing post offices, bus terminals, department stores, drug stores, and the Board of Education building on the Ben Franklin Parkway.[10] Relations between the city's African Americans and whites had become so strained that on April 4, 1968, when Dr. Martin Luther King Jr. was assassinated in Memphis, Tennessee, Philadelphians braced themselves for an explosion.

Rioting broke out across the nation. For three full days, bands of angry African Americans burned buildings, looted, and clashed with police in a dozen cities. The National Guard took to the streets in Nashville and Memphis, Tennessee; and in Raleigh and Greensboro, North Carolina. Rioting also erupted in Detroit; Birmingham; Jackson, Mississippi; Tampa, Florida; Hartford, Connecticut; and Winston-Salem, Charlotte, and Wilmington, North Carolina. But Harlem, New York; Washington, D.C.; and Tallahassee, Florida, witnessed the worst violence. Hundreds were arrested, dozens were injured, and at least twenty-seven were killed by the outbursts. Just a few miles to the south of Philadelphia, in Wilmington, Delaware, rioters also took to the streets, burning buildings and looting businesses.[11]

In Philadelphia, though, there was no violence. Mayor Tate declared a state of emergency and directed the city police to monitor two large public gatherings held in memory of Dr. King. More than 5,000 Philadelphians—both white and black—gathered at Independence Hall and at City Hall. Rizzo ordered seventeen busloads of police officers to fan out among the crowds, their sheer presence discouraging any trouble. At City Hall, Tate denounced the assassination as "a terrible and cruel act" and declared a day of mourning with the city's flags to be flown at half-mast. When Philip Savage of the NAACP addressed the audience asking them "not to desecrate Dr. King's memory" by resorting to violence, a small minority of young black militants began shouting, "Less moralizing and more organizing!" But cooler heads prevailed as African American religious and civic leaders pleaded for restraint and calmness.[12]

Baseball's traditional opening games at Washington and Cincinnati were postponed out of respect for Dr. King, as were other opening days.[13] Ironically, the Dodgers, the team that broke the color barrier, announced their intention to play their opener against the Phillies and received the support of National League President Warren Giles, who threatened the Phils with a forfeit and penalty if they refused to take the field. Still, owner Bob Carpenter refused to play, as the opener was scheduled for the day of Dr. King's funeral. Gene Mauch asked his team, which was en route to Los Angeles, to take a vote. The players decided to open the season with an 0–1 record before they would put a team on the field the day of King's funeral.[14] When told of Dodger President Walter O'Malley's decision to play, Jackie Robinson said, "Mr. O'Malley is a man with tremendous ability, but also a man with a total lack of knowledge of the frustrations of the Negro community. It grieves me that he did not understand the importance of this issue."[15] In the end, the Dodgers agreed to postpone their opener, and the season began a day later.[16]

The spring of 1968 was in many respects the beginning of the end for Gene Mauch's Phillies. Jim Bunning, who at the age of thirty-six had already seen the best years of his career, was traded to Pittsburgh for a twenty-eight-year-old veteran pitcher Woodie Fryman and Don Money, a young infielder whom Quinn projected as the team's next shortstop.[17] There were other new young faces in camp as well, including outfielders Larry Hisle and Rick Joseph, pitchers Steve Arlin and Billy Champion, and catcher Mike Ryan. But that did not mean Mauch was in the throes of a youth movement. On the contrary, the Little General had a year remaining on his contract. He had to win sooner rather than later. Accordingly, Mauch stayed with his veteran players. Bill White was slated to start at first, Cookie Rojas at second, Bobby Wine at short, Tony Taylor at third, Clay Dalrymple behind the plate, and Gonzalez, Callison, and Allen in the outfield. Moving Allen into the outfield allowed Mauch to stabilize the infield defense by moving Taylor to third and improving his offense by making Wine and Rojas regulars.[18] To be sure, Allen was the key to the team's success. If he could rebound from his hand injury to hit for both power and average, the Phils would have another crack at the pennant. But Allen's commitment to winning was secondary to forcing a trade, and he made that clear almost from the start of spring training.

On March 8, Allen, who never liked spring training, left the Phillies' Clearwater camp for his Philadelphia home without permission. He left to see his wife, Barbara, who was expecting the couple's third child, and to have his injured hand checked by physicians at Temple University Hospital. When he returned to Clearwater, two days later, Allen was slapped with another $500 fine. While Mauch initially told the press that his star was "very worried about his injured hand" and had gone to see a doctor in Philadelphia, he later admitted that Allen went AWOL.[19]

Fig. 34 By 1968, Dick "Don't Call Me Richie" Allen wanted to be traded. When his repeated requests were denied, he adopted the behavior and look of a rebel. (Philadelphia Phillies)

Allen, on the other hand, began to manipulate the press to force a trade. Stan Hochman of the *Daily News* became a willing—if not unwitting—accomplice. "Rich Allen didn't think it was strange that he didn't let anybody know he was coming north for medical advice," wrote Hochman. Then, using Allen's own words against him, the chipmunk writer quoted the slugger as saying, "Why should I tell anybody? Let 'em fine me. They gave me a contract that had a clause in it saying I'd be fined $500 for every day of spring training I miss without authorization. Well, for everybody else its $100. Let 'em take the $500, I've been fined before, including times I wasn't guilty. I know that if I went to another club, I'd be a different guy. I wouldn't do any of the things I'm doing now."[20] Four days later, Hochman interviewed Clem Cappozoli, Allen's self-styled "manager" and president of the American Baking Company. Although the tone of Cappozoli's remarks was largely supportive of Allen, Hochman chose to highlight the negative quotes. "There have been other players who've given their clubs more trouble than this kid," insisted Cappozoli. "But as long as he gives them a good game of baseball, they ought to put up with him a little longer." More damning was Cappozoli's admission that Allen "needs to grow up," which, of course, became the headline of Hochman's column.[21]

Bill Conlin also aided Allen's cause, whether he realized it or not. "Rich Allen has deceived the Phillies, the public, the press, and himself for four years," he wrote in a March 9 column. "Now he's run out of rope. Has he hung himself? Probably not. Allen's AWOL caper will surely be met with a whopping fine, perhaps as much as $5,000. But what happens after that?" Conlin predicted that Allen "will probably continue to be the most pampered baseball player in captivity." To reinforce his case, the *Daily News* scribe pointed out that the Phillies permitted their star player to "miss batting practice on Sundays after Saturday night games when the rest of the team had to report," and that the team did nothing to punish Allen whenever he missed the team plane or showed up for games "not in the best condition to play." Even though the Phillies have "bent over backwards to keep him in baseball," Allen, according to Conlin, made "wild claims about [the club's] cruel and inhuman treatment" of him and "refused to be interviewed by that segment of the press who has tried to tell it like it is."[22]

Conlin's diatribe was instigated, in part, by Allen's threat to inflict "bodily harm" when he tried to reach the slugger by telephoning his mother, Era. Not knowing when to quit, Conlin pursued the matter in his column, reprimanding Allen: "Twenty-six-year-old super athletes just don't go around threatening to 'get' sportswriters."[23]

Writers like Conlin and Hochman were redefining the rules of engagement between sportswriters and athletes. Nothing, not even the personal life, or a mother, of a star performer was "off limits" anymore. Instead off-the-field lives were considered "good copy" that sold more papers. Even writers who made an earnest effort to cover Allen objectively had difficulty with him. "I didn't like some of the things Dick Allen did," admitted Frank Dolson, years after he retired as sports editor at the *Inquirer.* "I thought he was taking advantage of the situation: the injuries, the repeated lateness. He carried himself like a prima donna, a guy who wanted to play by his own rules. I guess my major complaint with him in those days was that he'd tell one thing to one writer and another thing to another."[24] To be sure, Allen was adept at pitting one writer against another by giving misinformation to some and half-truths to others. It was part of his manipulation. But the Phillies star also obliged the writers by giving them what they wanted—controversial subject matter.

On April 30, Allen had another run-in with Mauch. Driving his own car from Philadelphia for an afternoon game against the Mets at New York's Shea Stadium, Allen arrived twenty minutes before game time, insisting that he had been "stuck in a traffic jam" on the Long Island Expressway. Mauch exploded at him for refusing to ask permission to drive to the game. Scratching his star player from the lineup, the Little General slapped him with another fine while also revoking permission for players who want to drive to New York in the future. The Phillies went on to drop the game, 1–0. Afterward, the press asked how he planned to handle Allen's violation, Mauch again protected his star. "If the rest of my players produced the way he does, they can be late too. Besides, whatever's going to be done has been done."[25] But the conflict only continued to escalate.

On May 26, Mauch fined Allen for his failure to hustle on the base paths, and the following night Allen reported to the ballpark drunk. Mauch sent him home, telling the press that his slugger was out with a groin injury. In fact, Allen was hit with a two-week suspension. "Hell, how can they suspend me until they hear my side of the story?" he asked the Philadelphia press. Shortly after, he was given that opportunity by sportscaster Al Meltzer in a candid television interview. Registering his "deep disappointment with the behavior of the fans," Allen insisted that he be "left alone off the field" and be "judged solely on his playing abilities." Owner Bob Carpenter had heard enough. In a closed-door meeting, Allen agreed to a truce, telling the owner that he had been "ready to play all along." When Mauch was informed of the response, he supposedly gave Carpenter a "me-or-him" ultimatum.[26] Finally, on June 15, the Phillies owner chose Allen and fired Mauch. Allen's plan had backfired.

To be sure, Allen wasn't the only reason for Mauch's firing. The Phillies were going nowhere in 1968. Having traded Bunning, the club pinned their hopes on a new ace, Chris Short, and on Larry Jackson, a thirty-seven-year-old veteran acquired from the Cubs.[27] But Short missed several stretches early in the season because of a knee injury, and Jackson was ineffective. Youngsters Rick Wise and Grant Jackson were too inexperienced to pick up the slack, and the pitching staff collapsed, ending the season with the third worst earned run average in the National League at 3.36. Worse, the team's top two hitters were trying to recover from serious injuries. Allen was still hampered by the damaged nerves in his right hand, and aging first baseman Bill White was struggling with a bad leg.[28] As long as the Phils fielded a contender, Mauch's job was safe. The Little General did not have the patience to wait for younger players to develop. But as the Phils dropped lower in the standings, it became clear that a change had to be made.

While Quinn admitted that the "Allen problem was a factor" in the decision to fire Mauch, he insisted that it was not the "entire reason."[29] Mauch's wife had recently been hospitalized with a serious illness, and the Phillies questioned whether he would be able to manage with the added pressure. Four days after his firing, Mauch absolved Carpenter and Quinn for the decision. "Something had to be done," he admitted. "They made the best decision under the circumstances. They couldn't foresee Nina Lee getting sick. It was a terribly tough situation for them. Besides, if someone had told me I'd be here nine years, I'd have said they were nuts. I didn't get a raw deal." When asked about the difficulty of managing Allen, Mauch refused to go into any detail. "I'm not going to knock Richie Allen," he replied, dismissing the question. "That son-of-a-gun gave me many a thrill. There was nothing personal in my handling of Allen. It was objective. When I jump on a player, it is to make him better."[30]

Mauch's response was a calculated one. He knew that major league baseball was expanding to Montreal the next season and that he would be the most eligible candidate for a managerial post there, as long as he took the moral high ground. The press would do the rest, and they did. Hochman made Mauch into a martyr. "Richie Allen did not tell the Phillies it was 'he or me,' which is why Gene Mauch got fired." "If anything," Hochman speculated, "Gene Mauch might have told the Phillies it was 'he or me' before he got fired" and that the Phillies "conducted a frantic all-night auction, trying to get rid of Richie Allen." Unable to trade Allen to the Giants for Jim Ray Hart, or to Houston for Jimmy Wynn, asserted Hochman, the Phils "fired Mauch, whose only concern was winning the next game."[31]

Arthur Daley of the *New York Times* also defended the Little General, attributing his dismissal almost solely to "disciplinary problems with Richie Allen, a superstar with a built-in distaste for discipline." Daley registered his admiration for Mauch's repeated public defense of Allen whenever he broke team policy. "But no manager can permit an athlete to erode the morale of an entire ball club by disregarding the rules that others faithfully observe," he added. Comparing the Mauch-Allen situation to Yankee manager Miller Huggins' ongoing conflict with Babe Ruth, Daley pointed out that Huggins "was deemed a joke manager until he finally brought Ruth into line. That's when he gained the respect of all his players, including a contrite Babe. Through it all, Ruth was a joyous character, the pet of his teammates. Allen is not. Whereas the Babe's shenanigans were known only to a few insiders, if that, Richie has done the damnedest things. Yet Gene might have survived if he had bowed his neck ever so slightly to Allen, another guy with an unbowable neck."[32]

Allen didn't see it that way, though. "Hell, I didn't want Mauch fired," he said, in his autobiography, years later. "I liked him. He was tough, but mostly he was fair. I wanted to get myself traded instead. I'd gone to Bob Carpenter four or five times and asked to be traded. He refused. He kept telling me that things would turn around. I didn't believe it. The fans were no longer just booing, it was open warfare. My family was scared and unhappy. And the Phillies were a lousy team. I had my mind on only one thing: getting the hell out of Philadelphia. That's when I began to act the role that Philadelphia had carved out for me. I'd been hearing that I was a bum for so long that I began to think maybe that's just what I was. By May, Mauch and I were no longer communicating. By that time he was fining me every week: $1,000 for drinking, $500 for missing batting practice, $1,500 for showing up late for a game. My weekly fines were the equal of some player's pay checks. We were coming to a showdown."[33]

Only Claude Harrison of the *Philadelphia Tribune* saw Mauch's firing as a victory for Allen. Comparing the embattled Phillies star with Jackie Robinson's struggle to break the color barrier, Harrison suggested that Mauch too told Allen to "be submissive" and to "turn the other cheek at times when he wanted to knock someone's teeth down their throat." Allen's every move, "especially the bad ones, have been aired in public with the backing of the free press." Accordingly, Harrison viewed the slugger's rebellious behavior as nothing more than Allen "demanding his due, both on and off the field."[34]

Whether they defended or excoriated him in the press, the sportswriters all agreed on one thing: baseball itself was changing, and Allen was a catalyst for that change. Before Mauch's firing, a manager could threaten a player with a demotion, no matter how talented he was. But Allen was a high-priced superstar, and one who was coveted by the owner. Mauch could demean him, fine him, and suspend him. Carpenter, however, certainly would not allow Allen to be demoted or traded. Like other owners with big-name players, Carpenter knew that Allen generated revenue for his club. Television contracts, expansion, and the 162-game schedule meant greater national exposure, which in turn translated into greater profits, especially if the Phillies did well. Allen was the key to their success. Carpenter had no choice. Ultimately, the black superstar's differences with Mauch determined the forty-year-old manager's employment.

The nature of the players themselves was changing too. They were bigger, younger, more numerous, and more savvy than their predecessors of an earlier era. Their sophistication was representative of the larger baby-boom generation to which they belonged. In their determination to live out what their parents had repressed or abandoned, the "sixties generation" tended to equate freedom with bigger and better thrills. Too often, the tendency manifested itself in a narcissistic focus on sex, drugs, and rock music. Millions of those in their teens and twenties abandoned the old strictures against premarital intercourse, oral sex, and candid public discussion of the sensual. The erotic was celebrated, if not openly flaunted. They experimented with marijuana, LSD, and other drugs that varied from the hallucinogenic to the mildly intoxicating.[35] Their music alternatively reflected either the hedonistic desires of the baby-boomers or their concern for social justice. On one hand, there were musicians like the Beatles and Janis Joplin, who distrusted politics of any kind and refused to be manipulated by the protesters of their generation. "My music isn't supposed to make you riot," Joplin explained. "It's supposed to make you fuck."[36] On the other hand, there were socially conscious artists like Marvin Gaye and Bob Dylan, whose folk song "Blowin' in the Wind" evoked the demands of black insurgency with lyrics like "How many years can some people exist, before they're allowed to be free?"[37] Challenging authority was universal in the 1960s. Antiauthoritarianism was celebrated in music, writing, and personal behavior, and it was no different for baseball players.

On and off the field, the new breed of players questioned established practices and traditions. Pitcher Bo Belinsky of the Angels, for example, flaunted his relationship with Hollywood sex symbol Mamie Van Doren, in open defiance of the expectations for a baseball hero. Embarrassed by his promiscuous behavior, the Angels first demoted him to the minors and later traded him to the Phillies. Some players resorted to writing "kiss and tell" accounts of their teammates, including Jim Brosnan's *Pennant Race*, about the irreverent clubhouse antics of the 1962 Cincinnati Reds, and Jim Bouton's more famous *Ball Four*, chronicling the sexual escapades of some of the Yankees' greatest stars.[38] Others began to challenge ownership's control of salaries after Sandy Koufax and Don Drysdale of the Dodgers staged a successful joint holdout in 1965. Increasingly, veterans from other teams followed their lead, refusing to report to spring training until their salary demands were met. In the spring of 1968, the Phillies found themselves locked in contentious battles with no less than four players: Rick Wise, Johnny Callison, Johnny Briggs, and Cookie Rojas.[39]

While excessive drinking and reporting to the ballpark with a hangover were nothing new in baseball, the use of amphetamines was, and it became a popular practice among players during the 1960s. Trainers dispensed so-called "greenies" or "pep pills" to any player who needed a lift in order to get through the second game of a doubleheader, or during the dog days of August when the season took an especially hard toll. The drug, which could be addictive, elevated a player's heart rate, giving him at least the illusion of more energy. Some teams even made large jars accessible to their players in the clubhouse, seeing nothing wrong with the practice because doctors prescribed them to millions of patients for the purpose of losing weight or getting a quick energy boost. Often, a club's biggest drinkers were also those who used the drug most.[40]

In the past, all these controversial issues were handled in a discreet manner by the press. But in the 1960s, when television made on-stage celebrities of baseball players, and the chipmunk writers were rewriting the rules of player coverage, drinking, drugs, promiscuity, and deviant behavior in general gave the game greater appeal among a baby-boom generation that indulged in the same vices itself. In that kind of atmosphere, Richie Allen became a hero for a generation of rebellious youth. His insistence on being called "Dick" instead of "Richie" was a part of that independent-mindedness. "People who call me 'Richie,'" he explained, "are people who don't want to see me as anything but a baseball player. They don't want to see me as a complex man, to take me seriously."[41] Out of spite, the Philadelphia press began to refer to him as Dick "Don't Call Me Richie" Allen.

It is interesting that Mauch's firing seemed to improve Allen's situation with management, at least in the short run. Bob Skinner, a soft-spoken
thirty-six-year-old who managed San Diego of the Pacific Coast League,
was the Phils' new skipper. When asked about the possibility of having one
set of rules for Allen and another set for the twenty-four other players,
Skinner told the press, "Rich Allen is a tremendous player" and that "many
managers in the league would love to have him, and I am one of them." He
added that he "anticipated no trouble" with Allen and that there would
be "one set of rules" for all the players.[42] Allen responded to Skinner's
hiring by going on a tear. After the All-Star Game, he led the Phils to
a seven-game winning streak. Using a 42-ounce bat, the heaviest in the
majors, Allen banged out fifteen hits in thirty trips to the plate, including
five homers and 15 RBIs. By mid-July he was hitting at a .314 clip. In an
especially impressive performance, Allen, whose wife Barbara had just given
birth to a son, celebrated by hitting two home runs, a double, and two singles, leading the Phillies to a doubleheader sweep against the San Francisco
Giants, 10–2 and 9–1.[43]

But even Allen's prodigious hitting could not help his team climb out of
the second division. By August, Bill White, who had struggled at the plate
all season, was replaced at first base by Johnny Briggs, who had seen limited
playing time in the outfield.[44] With retirement near, White pondered a
new career in sportscasting, or managing, though he believed that the first
"Negro who's hired to be a manager will be nothing more than a showcase."[45] Briggs did not hit for power or average, though, and with Callison
mired in another off-year, the Phillies' team offense was an anemic .233.
Nor was the pitching much better. With the exception of Chris Short, who
went 19–13, all the other starters posted losing records.

As the Phillies dropped lower in the standings, the fans became more
abusive of the team's only real star. "The fans were brutal to Richie," said
Howie Bedell, a former Milwaukee Brave who was playing outfield in
Reading before being called up in June. "I remember watching him shag
fly balls during batting practice and wearing a batting helmet out there to
protect himself from the batteries and coins the fans would throw at him.
One day he said to me, C'mon, Howie, let's go shag some flies. You're a
white guy. If you go out there, they won't throw anything at me!'"[46] Throwing projectiles at Allen from the outfield bleachers had become such a popular pastime among the Boo-Birds that the slugger was given the nickname
"Crash" by teammates because of the trademark batting helmet he routinely wore in the outfield to protect himself. Allen never knocked the fans

and even accepted some of the blame for their negative behavior. "It was sad," said Bedell. "Richie really was a genuinely good person. My eight-year-old son, Greg, adored him. One night we got home from the game and Greg was crying. When I asked him what was wrong, he said, 'I don't like it when they boo Mr. Allen, Dad. I want you to go back to Reading.' I was very moved by that. My son, as young as he was, was sensitive to Richie's feelings, and he was also expressing his concern that he didn't want to see me treated the same way."[47] Bedell's son got his wish. Three weeks after his father had been promoted to the Phils, Bedell was sent back down to Reading, but not before ending Don Drysdale's record string of scoreless innings at 58⅔ with a long sacrifice fly that knocked in teammate Tony Taylor in a 5–3 loss to the Dodgers.[48]

Although Allen completed the season with a .263 average, he was among the National League's leaders in home runs (33) and RBIs (90) for a Phillies squad that finished in seventh place, twenty-one games behind the pennant-winning Cardinals.[49] It was their worst performance since 1961, and it showed at the gate. Only 664,546 turned out to see the Phillies that season, when it took about 950,000 to break even.[50]

"One way or another, you'll see a new team on the field in 1969," vowed Bob Carpenter, who planned to rebuild. "I feel we'll bounce back next year with four or five kids to excite people. Even Allen's not untouchable. I'm disappointed in his production. I think he should give us a .300 average and 120 RBIs."[51] Skinner was more candid about his desire to rebuild the team. "I think we've got to go into a youth program," he told the press. "This club has been going downhill since 1964, no question about it. If things stay the same, it's going to keep going down. We're going to have to rebuild."[52] The new Phillies manager had reason to be optimistic when he looked at the organization's Triple A club at San Diego. Shortstop Don Money was the key prospect. In 1968 he hit .303 and played outstanding defense in the Pacific Coast League. Larry Hisle also impressed management, hitting over .300 in San Diego. He was projected as the Phils' starting centerfielder for 1969. Pitchers Billy Champion, Barry Lersch, Lowell Palmer, and Billy Wilson also appeared to be ready for the big leagues.[53] Comfortable with his manager's decision to build a team around this youthful core, Carpenter directed John Quinn to explore possibilities to trade Allen, Callison, and Rojas to the New York Mets and the Cleveland Indians during the off-season. But the Phillies' asking price proved to be too high in both cases.[54]

Allen grudgingly returned to the Phillies in 1969 as a full-time first baseman, but he was more intent than ever on forcing a trade. In early May he missed a flight to St. Louis, then missed the same flight the next morning. As a result, he missed one complete game and part of another against the Cardinals. Skinner was furious and fined him $1,000. "I definitely need to get out of Philadelphia," Allen told the press. "Bob Carpenter has been real good to me, but I've got to play somewhere else." When asked to explain the reasons for his frustration with Philadelphia, Allen pointed to the press. "I have no trouble with the other players," he insisted. "I get along great with my teammates. But you fellas have created an atmosphere where people who have never met me, hate me. You knock me and say I'm a 'no good black so and so' and I can still be your friend. But if you don't ask me about something and take someone else's word for it and write it as fact, then I got to cut you loose. Sometimes I get so disgusted. I really do love to play the game, but the writers take all the fun out of it."[55] Again, Allen brought the issue of race into the conflict. His choice of the words— "I'm a no-good black so and so"—suggested that the press was treating him poorly because of the color of his skin. It was part of his own manipulation, and it was beginning to wear on his teammates as well, whether he realized it or not.

In late June, reserve infielder Cookie Rojas called a clubhouse meeting and tore into Allen. Rojas told him that the team "resented his coming and going as he pleased" as well as his "lack of hustle on the field." The team, which had previously been supportive, was now divided in its opinion toward Allen. "When Carpenter gave him that $85,000 contract, everybody lost authority over him," said one disgruntled white veteran. "Nobody that age deserves that kind of money. He doesn't hustle all the time and he has his own set of rules. He's letting us down." But another white player suggested that it "might just look like he doesn't care, the way he never changes his expression when he strikes out. Maybe we're jealous of his talent and expect too much of him."

Allen's manipulation had caught up with him. "It hurt me," he said of his teammates. "I just started to say 'The hell with it.'"[56] Clay Dalrymple tried to offer support. "I sat down with Richie after that meeting," he recalled, "and I told him that he had the ability to be the leader of the ball club, if he'd only let himself. Sure, there was jealousy on the team because of the money Richie was making, and I don't know if he handled his success too well. But I told him that he was a smart guy and that he had some great leadership qualities. I guess he didn't appreciate all the talent he had at that time, though."[57]

On June 24 Allen missed a twi-night doubleheader at Shea Stadium, choosing to stay at a horse race in New Jersey. The Phillies, stalled in fifth place, sixteen games out, dropped the twin bill, 2–1 and 5–0. Allen claimed he had tried to telephone Skinner when he realized that he would be late. On his way to the stadium, he learned over the radio that Skinner had suspended him. Instead of going to the game, Allen went to his hotel room. "I sat there all night and got madder and madder. I really thought Skinner had been treating me fairly. He said he'd never take any action until he heard my side of the story." Though the suspension was indefinite and Allen could have returned at any time, he chose to stay away from the game for twenty-six days, claiming that he would "never again play for the Phillies."[58]

Once again, Allen manipulated the press in the hope of being traded. When asked how he felt about the suspension, he told the sportswriters, "Good. I need a vacation." "Besides," he added, "how important can the games be? [The Phillies] aren't trying [to win]. They could be bringing guys up to find out what they could do here, guys like my brother, Ron, who's hitting home runs in Reading this summer."[59] During a thirty-minute television interview with Channel 17's sports director, Al Meltzer, Allen said he'd "play somewhere, maybe in Japan," but refused to say whether he planned to stay out of baseball until the Phillies traded him or whether he would return to the club. "I won't be tricked into saying I'll play with the Phillies or that I will not put on a Phillies uniform again," he told Meltzer. Allen insisted he had done nothing wrong and that the Phillies had made the first move "by suspending me without hearing my side of the story," and that he had "made the second move by leaving the team." He ended the interview by admitting that he was "in no hurry to rejoin the Phillies."[60] Despite the antagonistic treatment he received from Stan Hochman, who in a recent *Daily News* column told Allen to "grow up," the Phillies slugger agreed to take part in a thirty-minute television program about his career written and produced by the columnist. At the end of the program, he thanked Hochman for the opportunity and shook his hand.[61]

At the urging of owner Bob Carpenter and his personal manager, Clem Cappozoli, Allen agreed to be reinstated on the condition that the Phillies would trade him at the end of the year.[62] Now the fans registered their disapproval even more forcefully. They not only refused to vote Allen to the 1969 All-Star Game, even though he was among the National League leaders in home runs and batting average, but also refused to name the slugger to the organization's all-time team as part of baseball's centennial celebration. Instead, they named Eddie Waitkus, a popular Whiz Kid of the 1950 pennant-winning Phillies, as their first baseman. When Willie Mays, the San Francisco Giants' future Hall of Famer, learned of the choice he was incredulous: "It's stupid! How could Richie Allen not be on that team? He's the best hitter they've had since I've been around. None of those Whiz Kids could carry his bat."[63]

By now Allen's behavior was a regular topic of discussion throughout the nation. At a White House press reception before the All-Star Game, President Richard Nixon, an avid baseball fan, approached the Phillies' lone representative on the team, pitcher Grant Jackson, and said, "You tell Richie Allen to get back on the job. You tell him he's not going to get as good a job if he quits baseball. You tell Richie it's not for the good of the Phillies, or the good of the fans, but for the good of Richie Allen that he get back."

"You tell him, Mr. President," replied Jackson with a smile. "He's making more money than the both of us!"[64]

A week before he was to play his first postsuspension game, Allen removed his belongings from the clubhouse and set up his own private dressing room in a storage area near the manager's office at Connie Mack Stadium. When the press asked why he had moved his belongings, Allen said, only half in jest: "To keep the writers away."[65] In fact, Allen had told Skinner that "he just wanted to be left alone" and that "something might happen" if he remained in the clubhouse.

"I don't want any trouble," he insisted. "I really don't care if my teammates dislike me. I've got some friends on this team, and there really isn't anyone I dislike. But baseball is an individual game. What I do doesn't hurt them. When I've done wrong, I've paid for it, and the only one who is hurt is Dick Allen himself."[66] Years later, Allen would admit that his action was taken to "keep my teammates from getting into trouble." He recognized that his reputation as "baseball's bad boy, the bad ass of the National League" could have a negative effect on his closest friends, such as Johnny Briggs and Grant Jackson.[67] Allen had mentored these young players, both on and off the field, when they were promoted to the Phillies. He gave them pointers on how to play the game at the major league level, shared his house and his car with them, and offered his unconditional friendship.[68]

Allen's self-imposed exile infuriated Skinner, who ordered his belongings returned to the clubhouse. "I don't care if he sits in that closet," Skinner told the press, "but he'll dress with everyone else!" Nevertheless, Allen continued to dress in his private locker room for the next two weeks, and Skinner kept ordering the clubhouse attendants to return his things to the locker room. "He'll play under my ground rules," Skinner muttered to the press, "or he won't put on a uniform for the rest of the year."[69] But when the Phillies manager complained to Bob Carpenter about Allen's antics, the owner turned a deaf ear, preferring to compare his prized slugger's moodiness to Ted Williams's temperament. Carpenter pointed out that Williams's "contemptuous gestures enraged people, but he always showed up in the end."[70]

Finally, the Phillies skipper gave up. On August 7, in a conference room at Reading Municipal Stadium, where the Phillies were scheduled to play their Double A club that night, he announced his resignation. According to Skinner, the "straw that broke the camel's back" occurred earlier in the day, when Allen came to him and said he refused to play at Reading because his "deal with Mr. Carpenter didn't include playing in exhibition games." When Skinner confronted both Carpenter and Quinn on the issue, they defended Allen's position. "I have too much pride to stay without support from the front office, particularly in my handling of Richie Allen," Skinner told the press. "Everything Allen wants he gets. He's been spoiled to the point that a manager cannot handle him. Now I know what Gene Mauch went through. I feel like I've done a great job. I am a winner and I want to be a winner and you can't win this way. Not with Allen, who's been a big factor in our losing."[71] Skinner also intimated that Carpenter and Quinn had been returning fines to Allen, which only served to undermine his authority even more.[72]

Carpenter immediately rejected the notion. Expressing his regret at Skinner's decision to resign, the Phillies owner admitted that he "interceded on occasion to mediate problems with Allen." "Whatever I did," he said, "was, in my opinion, in the best interests of the team." At the same time, Carpenter insisted that he never "interfered with the operation of the team on the field" or returned fine money.[73]

After the resignation, Allen claimed that he was being made a scapegoat. Referring to his former manager, Allen stated: "He don't show me any guts by quitting like that and laying it in my lap. He's got a team that's twenty-one games under .500, and it's all my fault. Besides, I never told him I could go over his head. What did I ever do to him? I resent being made a scapegoat in another managerial move. If it boiled down to him or me, he didn't have to go. He can't put all the blame on me. He can't blame me for a 44–64 record. Nor have I ever seen a cent of the money Skinner said was returned to me by the front office. They say I call my own shots. How can they say that when all I want to do is get the hell out of Philadelphia."[74]

There was some truth to Allen's statement. He had already missed forty-four games at that point in the season, but in spite of that he still led the team in batting average, home runs, and RBIs. With the exception of prospects like centerfielder Larry Hisle and infielder Don Money, the team was a collection of journeyman players and aging veterans. There wasn't much talent left, and what little there was struggled. Chris Short, the one-time ace of the team, suffered a lower-back ailment early in the season that forced him to miss all but two games. Callison hit just sixteen homers and 64 RBIs. Johnny Briggs and Cookie Rojas labored to hit .230. But Skinner was correct in his belief that Allen's divisive behavior put the Phillies in almost constant turmoil. *The Sporting News* registered that point in a stinging editorial on August 23: "If ever a young man needed some counseling and guidance, that man is Richie Allen," began the piece. "The Phillies slugger has $1,000,000 worth of talent and ten cents worth of ability to understand what his role is with a team that has twenty-four other players besides himself. Unless a firm hand is taken with Allen, he'll go through more managers than Bluebeard does wives." The editorial placed the blame with owner Bob Carpenter for failing to "take a firm hand" with his superstar and "refunding the fines" Allen pays whenever he "shows up late for games or not at all." "Skinner underwent the same harassment as his predecessor, Gene Mauch," according to the editorial. "But Skinner brought to light something that many had suggested but didn't know for sure—that Allen's rebellious attitude had caused disharmony on the club, creating an intolerable situation. It might pay Carpenter to realize that he has a team to consider—and it isn't composed of one man."[75]

When Quinn handed over the interim manager's position to George Myatt, the press asked Myatt how he would handle Allen. "I believe God Almighty hisself would have trouble handling Richie Allen," remarked the Phillies' longtime coach.[76] When he heard about his new manager's remark, Allen said: "I don't think I do such bad things. It all just gets blown up. All I want to do is play ball and be left alone. I wish they'd shut the gates and let us just play ball with no press and no fans. Like it was in Wampum when I was a kid. It was fun them."[77]

To his credit, Allen played his heart out for Myatt, who was hired as a coach in 1964 for the specific purpose of grooming him. "I want Myatt to win so they'll let him keep the job next year," admitted the controversial star. "He's a good man. He deserves to win."[78] Refusing to become embroiled in more controversy, Myatt suspended most of the club's rules for the remaining games and humored Allen's behavior, which now included scratching messages to the fans in the dirt around first base.[79]

On August 9, Allen scratched "Oct. 2"—the last day of the regular season and his date of liberation from the Phillies. Quinn telephoned National League President Warren Giles for a ruling on the action, and Giles told him it was "inappropriate." Quinn had the grounds crew erase the message. But Allen would not be deterred. The following night he scratched "COKE" onto the first-base cutout, later explaining that the fans were "getting on me and I wanted to hit a home run over the Coca-Cola sign to shut them up." The next night he wrote "BOO"—and the fans happily obliged him.

Allen continued scratching messages over the next six days, a span in which he hit five home runs. "I kept it up 'cause everyone made such a fuss over it," he admitted. Shortly after, Commissioner Bowie Kuhn attended a doubleheader, witnessed Allen's artwork, and ordered him to stop. Allen responded to Kuhn's edict during the second game by writing "NO" and "WHY?" Finally, the home plate umpire called time out, went over to Allen, and told him that Quinn had called to complain. Grudgingly, Allen erased the words. His final message came the next night when he scratched "MOM" into the dirt. It was a reference to his mother, who Allen claimed was "the only one who can tell me what to do."[80]

In 1969 the Phillies sputtered to a fifth-place finish in the National League's newly organized Eastern Division, thirty-seven games behind the "Miracle Mets" of New York, who went on to shock the Baltimore Orioles in the World Series.[81] Shortly after, Allen was traded to the St. Louis Cardinals in a seven-player deal that would later go down in the annals of baseball history. The Phillies sent Allen, Cookie Rojas, and pitcher Jerry Johnson to St. Louis, for Curt Flood, a Gold Glove centerfielder; Byron Browne, a young outfield prospect; catcher Tim McCarver; and reliever Joe Hoerner.[82] Allen was overjoyed by news of the trade. "You don't know how good it feels to get out of Philadelphia," he said. "They treat you like cattle. It was like a form of slavery. Once you step out of bounds they'll do everything possible to destroy your soul."[83]

It is interesting that Allen's comparison of playing baseball to "slavery" was echoed by Curt Flood, the black St. Louis centerfielder who was also involved in the trade. After the Cardinals informed him of the trade, Flood, a thirty-one-year-old veteran who did not want to relocate his family or business interests, decided to challenge the reserve clause. He wrote to Commissioner Bowie Kuhn, informing him that he "did not feel ... he was a piece of property to be bought or sold irrespective of [his] wishes," Adding, "I believe that any system which produces that result violates my basic rights as a citizen and is inconsistent to the laws of the United States."

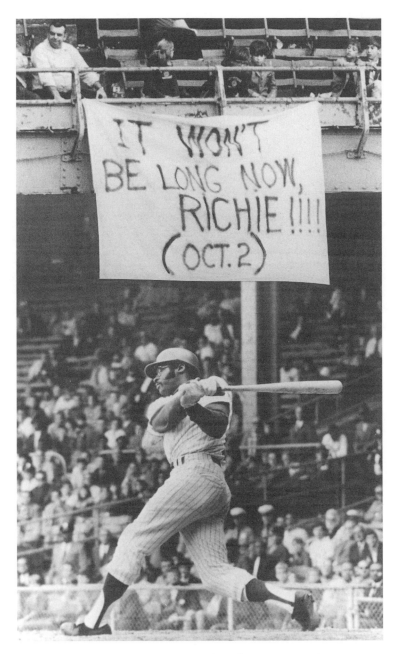

Fig. 35 At his last game at Connie Mack Stadium, on September 29, 1969, a homemade banner reminds Richie Allen that his days with the Phillies are numbered. (Temple University Urban Archives)

Flood closed the letter by declaring his "desire to play baseball in 1970" but added that he wanted to "consider offers from other clubs before making any decision" to accept Philadelphia's contract offer.[84] Kuhn feigned ignorance, insisting he did not understand how Flood's "rights as a human being" applied to the reserve clause and stating further that if the former Cardinal refused to report to Philadelphia, he could not play at all.[85]

Flood regarded Philadelphia as the "scene of Richie Allen's ordeals" and "the nation's northernmost southern city" because of the Phillies' poor history of race relations.[86] Some believed that Flood's decision was based on monetary considerations, a notion that Tim McCarver quickly dismisses. According to McCarver, who had been a teammate of Flood's for eleven years in St. Louis and was also part of the trade, "Curt was a man of conviction, and nobody was going to talk him out of his decision to challenge the reserve clause." Phillies General Manager John Quinn offered Flood a salary "in the area of $110,000," said McCarver. "That was a considerable amount of money at that time, but Curt still turned it down out of principle."[87]

Refusing to report to Philadelphia, Flood filed a $3.1 million damage suit against his old team and took his case all the way to the Supreme Court. Although he eventually lost the battle, Flood's action set in motion a chain of events that led to the 1975 arbitration ruling that granted players the right to free-agency.[88]

Richie Allen's turbulent career in Philadelphia had come to an end with a legal explosion that would rock the baseball world for years to come. It also brought a painful end to a once promising team of young black, white, and Hispanic players who, at least for 150 games in 1964, inspired Philadelphians, allowing them to dream of a pennant, a perennial contender, and a city of brotherly love.

CONCLUSION

"For all sad words of tongue and pen," wrote nineteenth-century Quaker poet John Greenleaf Whittier, "the saddest are these—'it might have been.'"[1] Although Whittier died three-quarters of a century before the 1964 Phillies blew the pennant, he certainly would have sympathized with their frustrations. To have played for a team that is remembered only for suffering the greatest collapse in major league history is a tragedy, especially when that team had the potential to contend throughout the mid-to-late 1960s. That tragedy also had a painful influence on the professional sports culture of an entire city. After 1964, Philadelphia struggled with an inferiority complex of epic proportions until the 1980s, when its football, hockey, basketball, and baseball teams routinely made the playoffs and the Phillies won their first and only world championship.[2]

Poor decision-making by the front office, incompetent coaching, and bad trades were some of the reasons for the lackluster performances of the Phillies. But the city's contentious sportswriters and a minority of boorish fans also have to accept part of the responsibility for the failure to field a winning team. In their ongoing attempt to control Philadelphia baseball, the chipmunk writers only prevented pennant-winning performances. They did it by baiting and bashing players, by writing sensationalist stories, and, ultimately, by driving Richie Allen, the city's first black superstar, out of town. The self-styled Boo-Birds were just as bad. At best, they were "unreasonably demanding," at worst they were "obnoxiously self-indulgent." They constantly provoked Allen, both on and off the field, until he left. When the issue of race was added to such a volatile combination, the result could only have been explosive. Allen was caught in the middle of the storm.

Whether or not he intended to, Allen forced Philadelphia's sportswriters and fans to come to terms with the racism that existed in the city during the turbulent 1960s. He may not have done it with the self-discipline or tact of a Jackie Robinson, but he exemplified the emerging independence of major league players as well as the growing African American consciousness. While his unexcused absences, candid opinions, and pregame beer-drinking earned him some of the harshest press in Philadelphia's sports history, his tape-measure home runs and exceptional speed gained for him the tremendous admiration of fellow players—both black and white.

Allen became eligible for induction into the National Baseball Hall of Fame in 1982, but his candidacy has been tainted by the scathing opinions of baseball writers like Bill James, who claim that the Phillies superstar "used racism as an explosive to blow his own teams apart." James dismisses Allen's eligibility for the Hall of Fame on the ground that he "did more to *keep* his teams from winning than anybody else who ever played major league baseball."[3] In so doing, James has committed the same fundamental error that colored the sensationalist sports writing and negative fan treatment of Allen and the Phillies back in the 1960s: the failure to understand the important distinction between *racism* and *prejudice*.

Racial prejudice refers to individual beliefs and attitudes that frequently manifest themselves in psychologically or physically abusive actions toward people of color. Racism, on the other hand, cannot be fully explained as an expression of prejudice alone. It is a much broader, cultural phenomenon, encompassing institutional policies as well as the beliefs and actions of individuals. Thus, racism is best understood as a "system of advantage based on race."[4] Whites are uncomfortable with such a *systematic* definition because it contradicts traditional notions of American meritocracy, individual enterprise, and the mainstream belief that "success comes to those who earn it." It is easier to think of racism as a particular form of prejudice, because notions of power or privilege can quickly be dismissed. This has too often been the case in major league baseball, where "color-blindness" has become the convenient excuse for not promoting African Americans, whether in the ranks of the players or of management.[5] Perhaps more unsettling for the white baseball establishment is that this definition exonerates people of color from the charge of racism, simply because they do not *systematically* benefit from it. In other words, people of color can and do have racial prejudices. Because of their minority status, however, they cannot benefit from institutional or cultural practices that favor whites, who intentionally or unintentionally benefit from racism.[6]

Yet the charge of "racism" has often been leveled against Richie Allen. Allen might have benefited from a double standard the Phillies created, but he certainly cannot be accused of "using racism as an explosive to blow [the Phillies] apart." If anything, the Phillies, during the 1960s, can be accused of naiveté in their understanding and practice of race relations. The organization was hypersensitive about race and tried to distance itself from an infamous history of race relations. Accordingly, Owner Bob Carpenter and Manager Gene Mauch created a double standard for their African American players. Consciously at times, and unwittingly at others, the Phillies management indulged Richie Allen and his personal irresponsibility because he was an *African American* player with tremendous talent. Johnny Briggs, Wes Covington, and Alex Johnson, on the other hand, were not given as much playing time or latitude. Nor were they always judged by merit, or treated the same as a white player of similar ability, although the organization claimed that they were.

Allen, Briggs, and Johnson, in particular, were *young* black ballplayers. They were at a point in their lives when they were struggling to establish an identity, not only as professional athletes but also as African American men in a white mainstream society. The process of resolving the dilemma was especially difficult for them because of the high visibility a professional athlete receives. They were not only encountering racism for the first time, but also were immersed in an environment where they were forced to grapple with what it means to be a member of a group targeted by racism. Having internalized the stereotypes of a white world, they struggled, often painfully, to come to terms with their own identities as members of the African American race.[7] For Allen, the Phillies' first black superstar, the resolution of this process resulted in the adoption of an oppositional identity. If Allen manipulated racism to divide the Phillies, it was only because the chipmunk writers and a minority of contentious fans had already made racism an issue. Allen was their target, a victim of racial prejudice.

In 1963, when the twenty-one-year-old prospect was sent to Little Rock, he became the first African American ballplayer in Arkansas history. That season was a nightmare for him. He received threatening telephone calls, had the windshield of his car painted with "Nigger, Go Home" signs, and could not be served in a restaurant unless accompanied by a white player. After the infamous brawl with Frank Thomas in 1965, fans never forgave him for the Phillies' decision to trade the popular white veteran. They provoked Allen with racial epithets from the stands, threw pennies, bolts, or beer bottles at him when he played in the outfield, sent hate mail, and threw garbage on the front lawn of his Mount Airy residence. At the same time, the chipmunk writers launched their own character assault, painting the beleaguered star as a malcontent or "prima donna" who expected special treatment. While Allen somehow managed to hit .300 and average 30 homers and 90 RBIs for the next five seasons, he also began to internalize the negative treatment of the fans and the media.

By 1968, Allen wanted out of Philadelphia, and he did not have the luxury of free-agency to achieve that goal. Having asked repeatedly for a trade—and being denied repeatedly by owner Bob Carpenter—Allen, as a last resort, forced his own departure. He did it by manipulating the double standard the Phillies had created and the negative press the chipmunk writers relished. Nor were his tactics "racist." Unexcused absences, arriving late to games, and scrawling letters in the dirt around first base are acts of a player desperate to escape the kind of nightmarish psychological and emotional abuse that no player—black, white, or Hispanic—should have to endure. But in the process, Allen's rebellious behavior reinforced the negative stereotype that the fans and media had imposed on him in the first place. Perhaps that explains, in part, Allen's sensitivity as well as his fierce independence. There is, however, more to his story than those early years in Philadelphia.

Most Valuable Players are men who not only compile impressive statistics but also contribute to a team effort. Often they are players who do the most off the field as well as on it to help their team win. In 1972, Allen earned the MVP award for his performance with the Chicago White Sox, hitting .308 with 37 homers and 113 RBIs. Manager Chuck Tanner underscored his first baseman's intangible value to the team, crediting him for "taking care of the young kids" and "playing every game as if it was his last day on earth." Tanner also credited Allen with turning a mediocre White Sox squad into a "first division team" during his three years in Chicago.[8] Again, when Allen returned to Philadelphia in 1975, he provided the inspiration for a young group of Phillies who were struggling to compete with the likes of Cincinnati's "Big Red Machine." He took Mike Schmidt, a future Hall of Famer, under his wing, teaching the introverted young third baseman how to cope with the fickleness of Philadelphia sportswriters and fans. "I admired Dick," said Schmidt, recently. "The baseball writers used to claim that he divided the clubhouse along racial lines. That was a lie. The truth is that Dick never divided any clubhouse. He just got guys thinking, and I, for one, learned a lot from him."[9] It is not surprising that the Phillies captured an Eastern Division title in 1976, Allen's final season in Philadelphia.

Today, Allen is the Phillies' most popular community relations representative. He makes appearances throughout the city, promoting the positive attributes of baseball among its most vital resource—youngsters who are just learning to play the game. Instead of being bitter, Allen has chosen to forgive and forget. "At the time, I thought of myself as a victim of racism," he admitted recently. "I was also something of a jerk. There were others who had to deal with racism, and some of them handled it better than I did. But that's all in the past. I'm at peace with my career, and grateful that the Lord gave me the opportunity."[10]

Does Dick Allen deserve a place in Cooperstown? A lifetime batting average of .292, some 351 career home runs, 1,119 RBIs, six All-Star Game appearances, a Rookie of the Year Award, and an American League MVP say that he does. Those numbers place him in the same company as Yogi Berra, Roy Campanella, Orlando Cepeda, Roberto Clemente, and Harmon Killebrew. But then, again, the numbers were never the issue—character was. Perhaps it is high time to reconsider that factor too.

DICK ALLEN was the 1964 National League Rookie of the Year playing third base, a new position for him. He played another five years for the Phillies before being traded to the St. Louis Cardinals in 1969 for Curt Flood, who, in a challenge to the reserve clause, refused to report to Philadelphia. Allen's reputation as an unruly player haunted him for the next three years. St. Louis traded him to the Dodgers after just one year, and Los Angeles traded him to the Chicago White Sox the following year. In 1972, Allen led the American League in home runs (37), RBIs (113), walks (99), and slugging percentage (.603) and was named Most Valuable Player. Despite retiring with a month left to play in the 1974 season, his thirty-two homers were good enough to lead the American League in that category. Allen returned to baseball, again with the Phillies, in 1975, but his power production had left him, and after two unproductive seasons in Philadelphia and a third with Oakland, Allen retired for good. His career totals include a .292 average, 351 home runs, and 1,119 RBIs. During the 1980s, he resolved his long-standing differences with Frank Thomas stemming from their July 1965 fight. Allen resides in Los Angeles, California, and works as a part-time coach and community relations representative for the Phillies. He is especially involved in the team's "RBI" program ("Reviving Baseball in the Inner City" program) for disadvantaged youth.

RUBEN AMARO won a Gold Glove at shortstop in 1964. Traded to the New York Yankees for Phil Linz after the 1965 season, he played for the Yanks for three years and for the California Angels for one year before retiring in 1969. Turning his attention to scouting and coaching in the minor leagues, Amaro returned to the Phillies organization and headed the club's Latin

American scouting department. He also served as first-base coach for the 1980 World Champion Phillies before taking positions in the Chicago Cubs and Detroit Tigers organizations. Amaro resides in Miami, Florida, and currently works as a roving instructor in the Phillies farm system. His son, Ruben Jr., who also played for the Phillies, is the club's assistant general manager.

JACK BALDSCHUN was the workhorse of the Phillies bullpen from 1961 through 1965. During that period he registered fifty-nine saves in sixty-five or more appearances each year. After baseball, he joined his brother in a carpentry business and later became a salesman for a lumber company. Retired, he lives in Green Bay, Wisconsin.

DENNIS BENNETT posted a 12–14 record in 1964. A chronically sore left shoulder, the result of a 1961 automobile accident, prevented him from contributing down the stretch. Traded to the Boston Red Sox in 1965, Bennett never regained his earlier form. After spending parts of the next three seasons with Boston, the New York Mets, and the California Angels, he retired and went to work for a plywood company in Klamath Falls, Oregon. He now owns and operates a tavern in the same town.

JOHN BOOZER posted a 3–4 record and two saves for the 1964 Phillies. Never able to secure a spot in the starting rotation, the tall right-hander bounced between the minors and Philadelphia for the next four years before retiring in 1969. He died in Lexington, South Carolina, on January 24, 1986.

JOHNNY BRIGGS, a fast, muscular rookie outfielder, hit .258 in sixty-one games with the 1964 Phillies. He went on to play a total of twelve seasons in the majors with the Phils, the Brewers, and the Twins. After he retired in 1975, Briggs returned to his hometown of Paterson, New Jersey, where he works for the Passaic County Sheriff's Office and the City of Paterson's Recreation Department.

JIM BUNNING was the ace of the Phillies staff in 1964, posting a 19–8 record that included a perfect game. During the next three seasons, he averaged more than 300 innings pitched and won a total of fifty-five games. Traded to the Pittsburgh Pirates after the 1967 season, Bunning slipped to 4–14, then to 10–9. Late in the 1969 season he was traded to Los Angeles, where he posted a 3–1 record. The Dodgers released him after the season, but Bunning, still convinced he could pitch, re-signed with the Phillies in 1970 and went 10–15. When he finally retired in 1971, he was the first pitcher since Cy Young to win more than 100 games or to strike out more than 100 in each league, and was second only to Walter Johnson, with 2,885 strikeouts. After managing in the Phillies farm system for five years, he turned his attentions to Republican politics in his native Kentucky, where he was elected to the U.S. House of Representatives. Elected by the Veterans Committee to the Hall of Fame in 1996, Bunning's Number 14 was retired by the Phillies that same year. Today, he is a U.S. Senator.

JOHNNY CALLISON, the all-star outfielder with movie-star good looks, was runner-up to Cardinal Ken Boyer for the National League's Most Valuable Player award in 1964. Had the Phillies clinched the pennant, he would have won it outright. Callison hit .274 that year, with 31 homers and 104 RBIs, and he won the mid-summer classic with a dramatic three-run homer. Although his average dropped to .262 the following year, he hit 32 homers and knocked in 101 runs. After that his power disappeared. Traded to the Chicago Cubs after the 1969 campaign, Callison completed his sixteen-year career with the New York Yankees in 1973. After retiring from baseball, he tried to land a coaching job in professional baseball. When that failed, he became a car salesman and, later, a bartender in suburban Philadelphia. Retired, he lives in Glenside, Pennsylvania.

DANNY CATER hit .296 in sixty games for the 1964 Phils. He was traded to the Chicago White Sox the following year and became a regular in the outfield. He was traded five times in his twelve-year major league career, playing for the A's, the Yankees, the Red Sox, and the Cardinals before retiring in 1975. He became an accounts examiner for the Texas State Comptroller's Office.

PAT CORRALES played in only two games with the 1964 Phillies, but he made sixty-two appearances behind the plate the following year. The weak-hitting catcher was traded to St. Louis in 1966 and then to Cincinnati, where he spent most of his career as a backup to Hall of Famer Johnny Bench. After retiring, Corrales turned to managing. He first piloted the Texas Rangers and later the Phillies, who fired him in mid-season 1983 while his team was in first place. Within the next week, the Cleveland Indians named him manager. Today, Corrales is a bench coach with the Atlanta Braves.

WES COVINGTON played 108 games in the outfield and hit .280 for the 1964 Phillies. Notorious for wasting time at the plate and for his candid interviews, he was traded to the Chicago Cubs by the Phillies after the 1965 campaign and retired after the following season. Today, he works in advertising for the *Edmonton Sun*, a Canadian newspaper.

RAY CULP went 8–7 with a 4.13 ERA for the 1964 Phillies, his second season in the big leagues. In 1965 he posted a fourteen-victory season, but arm troubles put him in a slump the following season and the Phillies traded him to the Cubs. Traded to the Boston Red Sox in 1968, Culp discovered the palm ball and resurrected his career. He won seventy-one games for the Red Sox over the next five years, retiring in 1973. Today he works as a real-estate agent in Austin, Texas.

CLAY DALRYMPLE, the popular Phillies catcher, hit only .238 in 1964 but led the National League in sacrifice flies. In 1968, his last season with the Phils, Dalrymple platooned with Mike Ryan. The next season, he was traded to the Baltimore Orioles and finally got to the World Series. After his first wife, Celia, died of cancer, Dalrymple retired from the game and dedicated himself to raising his three small daughters. He remarried and moved to Baltimore, where he did play-by-play for the Orioles and worked for a plumbing wholesaler. Now retired, he lives in Gold Beach, Oregon, where he coaches the high school baseball team.

RYNE DUREN, nicknamed "Blind Ryne" because of the coke-bottle eyeglasses he wore, had already seen the best days of his pitching career with the Yankees by the time he arrived in Philadelphia in 1963. Appearing in thirty-three games for the Fightin's that season, Duren posted a 6–2 record and a 3.33 ERA. An ongoing battle with alcoholism finally cost him his effectiveness in 1964, and he was traded to Cincinnati. He retired after the 1965 season with fifty-seven career saves. A retired substance-abuse counselor, Duren lives in Waunkee, Wisconsin.

TONY GONZALEZ, a mainstay of the 1964 Phillies, was the first regular centerfielder ever to field 1.000. His career-high .339 batting average in 1967 was second in the majors. Taken by the San Diego Padres in the 1969 expansion draft, Gonzalez was traded to the Atlanta Braves in June of that year, where he helped the team clinch the Western Division title with a .294 average. Sold to the California Angels in 1970, he slumped to a career-low .245 average and retired after the 1971 campaign. Unable to secure regular employment in pro baseball as a coach, Gonzalez worked as a security guard in Miami, Florida, where he still lives today.

DALLAS GREEN saw limited use with the 1964 Phillies, posting a 2–1 record in only twenty-five appearances. Traded to the Washington Senators in 1965, he retired after the 1967 season, and turned to managing in the Phillies farm system. Climbing up through the ranks, Green served as assistant director and then director of the farm system until 1979, when he was made manager of the Phillies. The following year, he guided the team to their first and only world championship. Green left the Phils after the 1981 season to become general manager for the Chicago Cubs. Three years later, the Cubs won the National League Eastern Division, their first title in almost forty years. Green's rebuilding process resulted in a pennant in 1989, but by that time he was serving as manager of the New York Yankees. Fired before the end of the season, Green managed the New York Mets from 1993 until late in the 1996 season, then returned to the Phillies brain trust. Today he serves as a special assistant to the general manager.

JOHN HERRNSTEIN split time between the outfield and first base in 1964, his third season with the Phillies. Hitting just .234, he saw little action in the last month of the season. After he slumped to .200 in 1965, the Phils traded him to the Cubs. He completed his major league career with the Atlanta Braves in 1966. After baseball, Herrnstein became vice president of a bank. Now retired, he lives in Chillicothe, Ohio.

DON HOAK lost his third-base position to rookie Richie Allen in spring training of 1964, and after just six games in the regular season he was released by the Phillies and retired as an active player. Known for his outspokenness and aggressive nature, Hoak, who had been a leader on the 1960 World Champion Pittsburgh Pirates, returned to that organization as a minor league manager. He died of a heart attack on October 9, 1969.

ALEX JOHNSON, an introverted but talented hitter, batted .303 in forty-three games for the 1964 Phillies. Traded to the Cardinals after the 1965 campaign, Johnson was criticized for a lackadaisical attitude. Over the next decade, he would play for six more teams, including the Cincinnati Reds, the California Angels, the Cleveland Indians, the New York Yankees, and the Detroit Tigers. Best remembered for beating out Carl Yastrzemski for the 1970 American League batting title with a .328 average. Johnson never achieved popularity despite his tremendous ability. He lives in Detroit, Michigan.

JOHN KLIPPSTEIN, a journeyman pitcher near the end of his career in 1964, went 2–1 in eleven appearances before being traded to the Minnesota Twins. The following season, his nine wins and five saves helped the Twins to their first pennant. He lives in Palatine, Illinois.

GARY KROLL, a 6-foot-7-inch fireballer, pitched in two games with no decision for the Phillies before being traded to the Mets in 1964, his rookie year. He also pitched for the Houston Astros and the Cleveland Indians before retiring after the 1969 season. He lives in Tulsa, Oklahoma.

HARRY LEE "PEANUTS" LOWREY was the team's colorful outfield coach in 1964. He enjoyed a twelve-year major-league-playing career with the Cubs, the Reds, the Cardinals, and the Phillies. He died on July 2, 1986, at Inglewood, California.

ART MAHAFFEY posted a 12–9 record with a 4.52 ERA in 1964. Having lost his fastball to an arm injury, he was traded to the St. Louis Cardinals in 1965 and retired from baseball after the following season. He is an insurance agent in West Chester, Pennsylvania.

GENE MAUCH managed the Phillies to a 92–70 record and a second-place finish in 1964. When he left Philadelphia to manage the Montreal Expos in 1969, he had collected 645 wins, the second most in franchise history. In Montreal he oversaw another rebuilding process and earned a second National League Manager of the Year Award in 1973 (the first came with the Phillies in 1962), but he never finished higher than fourth place. Mauch managed the Minnesota Twins from 1976 until he resigned in 1980, insisting that he would only manage a contender in the future. That opportunity came with the California Angels in 1982 when he guided his team to the Western Division title, only to lose in the best-of-five playoffs to Milwaukee. The pennant eluded Mauch a third time in 1986, when his Angels blew a 3–1 lead in the best-of-seven playoffs against the Boston Red Sox. When he retired from major league baseball in 1988, he had managed more games for more years (twenty-six) than anyone but Connie Mack, John McGraw, and Bucky Harris, and yet he never won a pennant. He lives in Rancho Mirage, California.

CAL McLISH, a lifelong friend of Gene Mauch, came to Philadelphia in 1962 and pitched until arm trouble forced him to retire in 1964. Mauch made him his pitching coach the following year, and he followed the Little General to Montreal, where he again served as pitching coach from 1969 to 1975. Retired, McLish lives in Edmond, Oklahoma.

GEORGE MYATT was the hitting instructor for the 1964 Phillies, his first season with the team. He had a sixteen-year career in professional baseball, including major league stints with the New York Giants and the Washington Senators. Before coming to Philadelphia, Myatt managed two years in the minors. A veteran coach since 1950 with the Senators, the Cubs, the White Sox, the Braves, and the Tigers, Myatt was expected to groom the Phils' young stars, such as Richie Allen. Retired, he lives in Orlando, Florida.

BOB OLDIS was the bullpen coach in 1964. He had a seven-year major league career with the Senators, the Pirates, and the Phillies. A scout for the Montreal Expos, he lives in Iowa City, Iowa.

ADOLFO PHILLIPS hit .231 in thirteen games in 1964, his first year in the majors. When he was traded to the Chicago Cubs in 1966, Manager Leo Durocher made him a regular outfielder and tabbed him "another Willie Mays." But after two disappointing seasons, Phillips was traded again, this time to Montreal, where he was made a part-time player. He completed his major league career with the Cleveland Indians in 1972 and returned to his native Panama, where he lives today.

VIC POWER, a showboating first baseman, was acquired from the Los Angeles Angels in mid-season to help the Phillies down the stretch in 1964, but he hit only .208 in eighteen games. Traded to California the following year, Power retired at the end of the season. He is now fully retired and living in Puerto Rico.

ED ROEBUCK, a former Dodger reliever, joined the Phillies in mid-season in 1964 and posted a 5–3 record in sixty appearances. He spent two more seasons in the Phils' bullpen before retiring at the end of the 1966 campaign to become a scout. Roebuck lives in Lakewood, California.

COOKIE ROJAS was a key utility man for the 1964 Phils, playing six positions and hitting .291 in 109 games that year. The Cuban-born infielder led all National League second basemen with a .987 fielding percentage in 1968. Traded to the Cardinals in 1970, he played only twenty-three games in St. Louis before the Kansas City Royals acquired him to be their regular second baseman. The most productive year of his major league career came in 1973, when he helped set a Royal record 192 double plays, drove in 69 runs and scored 78. After he retired in 1977, Rojas briefly managed the California Angels and has served as a coach for several clubs, including the New York Mets and the Florida Marlins. He lives in Miami, Florida.

BOBBY SHANTZ posted a 1–1 record as a reliever in 1964, the final season of a very respectable fifteen-year major league career. The peak of his career was in 1952, when he posted a 24–7 record for the Philadelphia Athletics and won the American league MVP Award. He lives in Ambler, Pennsylvania, where he is active in the Philadelphia Athletics Historical Society.

CHRIS SHORT was the Phillies' top left-handed pitcher in 1964. Between 1964 and 1968 he won seventeen or more games each season. Back trouble curtailed his career. Released by the Phillies in 1972, Short spent a year with the Milwaukee Brewers before retiring. After baseball, he worked for a Wilmington, Delaware, insurance company. In October 1988, Short suffered a brain aneurysm and slipped into a coma. He never regained consciousness and died almost three years later on August 1, 1991.

ROY SIEVERS was a part-time first baseman for the Phillies in 1964, the last of his three years in Philadelphia. Hitting only .183 with 4 home runs and 16 RBIs, Sievers was sold to the expansion Washington Senators in August. He was released during the following season, and retired from the game. He lives in Spanish Lake, Missouri.

TONY TAYLOR was the Phillies' regular second baseman and lead-off hitter in 1964. He played a total of nineteen years in the majors with the Cubs, the Phillies, and the Tigers. Taylor compiled a lifetime average of .261 in 2,195 games, collecting 2,007 hits and 234 stolen bases. One of Philadelphia's most popular athletes, he played more games in Phillies history (1,003) than any other second baseman. After he retired in 1975, Taylor returned to the Phillies organization as a coach at both the minor and the major league levels. He also coached and now scouts for the Florida Marlins. He lives in Palm Harbor, Florida.

FRANK THOMAS was acquired from the New York Mets in August 1964 to provide some offensive production down the stretch. In thirty-nine games, he hit .294 and collected 7 homers and 26 RBIs before breaking his thumb in early September. After getting into a fight with Richie Allen on July 3, 1965, Thomas was placed on waivers. Claimed by the Houston Colt 45s, he finished his career with the Chicago Cubs the following year. Retired, he lives now in Pittsburgh, Pennsylvania.

GUS TRIANDOS came to the Phillies from the Detroit Tigers along with Jim Bunning in 1964. On June 21 he caught Bunning's perfect game against the New York Mets at Shea Stadium. Traded to the Colt 45s the following season, Triandos completed his thirteen-year career in Houston. Now retired, he lives in San Jose, California.

AL WIDMAR was the pitching coach for the 1964 Phillies. Under his direction, the Phils' pitching staff was rated the third best in the National League in 1963. An active professional pitcher from 1942 through 1958, Widmar had major league stints with the Boston Red Sox, the St. Louis Browns, and the Chicago White Sox. Over the winter, Widmar managed Phillies players in the Dominican League. After leaving the Phillies organization, he served as a pitching coach for the Toronto Blue Jays. Retired, he lives in Tulsa, Oklahoma.

BOBBY WINE played shortstop and hit .212 for the Phillies in 1964. He played for thirteen years in the majors for the Phillies and the Expos. After he retired as an active player, he turned to coaching, first with the Phillies and later with the Atlanta Braves. Wine also managed Atlanta for part of the 1985 season. Today, he is a Braves scout and lives in Norristown, Pennsylvania.

RICK WISE went 6–3 with a 4.04 ERA for the Phillies in 1964, his rookie year. Considered the ace of the Phillies pitching staff beginning in 1968, Wise pitched a no-hitter against the Cincinnati Reds in 1971 and hit two homers to aid his cause. After the 1971 season, he was traded to the St. Louis Cardinals for Steve Carlton, who would become a Hall of Famer and the greatest left-hander in Phillies history. Wise pitched eighteen years in the majors for the Phillies, the St. Louis Cardinals, the Boston Red Sox, the Cleveland Indians, and the San Diego Padres. He posted a 188–181 career record with a 3.69 ERA. After Wise retired, he became a minor league pitching coach for the Houston Astros. Today he coaches in the Independent League and lives in Beaverton, Oregon.

INDIVIDUAL STATISTICS FOR THE 1964 PHILLIES

	Age	Throws	G	GS	CG	IP	H	BB	SO	W	L	PCT	ShO	SV	ERA
Pitchers															
Baldschun, Jack	27	R	71	0	0	118	111	40	96	6	9	.400	0	21	3.13
Bennett, Dave	18	R	1	0	0	1	2	0	1	0	0	.000	0	0	9.00
Bennett, Dennis	24	L	41	32	7	208	222	58	125	12	14	.462	2	1	3.68
Boozer, John	24	R	22	3	0	60	64	18	51	3	4	.429	0	2	5.10
Bunning, Jim	32	R	41	39	13	284	248	46	219	19	8	.704	5	2	2.63
Culp, Ray	22	R	30	19	3	135	139	56	96	8	7	.533	1	0	4.13
Duren, Ryne	35	R	2	0	0	3	5	1	5	0	0	.000	0	0	6.00
Green, Dallas	29	R	25	0	0	42	63	14	21	2	1	.667	0	0	5.79
Klippstein, John	36	R	11	0	0	22	22	8	13	2	1	.667	0	1	4.09
Kroll, Gary	22	R	2	0	0	3	3	2	2	0	0	.000	0	0	3.00
Locke, Bobby	30	R	8	0	0	19	21	6	11	0	0	.000	0	0	2.84
Mahaffey, Art	26	R	34	29	2	157	161	82	80	12	9	.571	2	0	4.53
McLish, Cal	38	R	2	1	0	5	6	1	6	0	1	.000	0	0	3.60
Roebuck, Ed	32	R	60	0	0	77	55	25	42	5	3	.625	0	12	2.22
Shantz, Bobby	38	L	14	0	0	32	23	6	18	1	1	.500	0	0	2.25
Short, Chris	26	L	42	31	12	221	174	51	181	17	9	.654	4	2	2.20
Steevens, Morrie	23	L	4	0	0	3	5	1	3	0	0	.000	0	0	3.00
Wise, Rick	18	R	25	8	0	69	78	25	39	6	3	.667	0	0	4.04
Totals:	26	—	162	162	37	1460	1402	440	1009	92	70	.568	17	41	3.37

Appendix B *(continued)*

	Age	Bats	G	AB	R	H	2B	3B	HR	RBI	BB	SO	SB	BA	PO	A	E	FA
Catchers																		
Dalrymple, Clay	27	L	127	382	36	91	16	3	6	46	39	40	0	.238	737	61	7	.991
Triandos, Gus	33	R	73	188	17	47	9	0	8	33	26	41	0	.250	371	24	6	.985
Infielders																		
Allen, Richie	22	R	162	632	125	201	38	13	29	91	67	138	3	.318	154	325	41	.921
Amaro, Ruben	28	R	129	299	31	79	11	0	4	34	16	37	1	.264	295	200	10	.980
Herrnstein, John	26	L	125	303	38	71	12	4	6	25	22	67	1	.234	488	22	5	.990
Hoak, Don	36	R	6	4	0	0	0	0	0	0	0	2	0	.000	0	0	0	—
Power, Vic	32	R	18	48	1	10	4	0	0	3	2	3	0	.208	—	—	—	—
Rojas, Cookie	25	R	109	340	58	99	19	5	2	31	22	17	1	.291	164	76	7	.972
Shockley, Costen	22	L	11	35	4	8	0	0	1	2	2	8	0	.229	57	4	2	.968
Sievers, Roy	37	R	49	120	7	22	3	1	4	16	13	20	0	.183	—	—	—	—
Taylor, Tony	28	R	154	570	62	143	13	6	4	46	46	74	13	.251	325	358	16	.977
Thomas, Frank	35	R	39	143	20	42	11	0	7	26	5	12	0	.294	297	28	8	.976
Wine, Bobby	25	R	126	283	28	60	8	3	4	34	25	37	1	.212	153	257	15	.965

Outfielders

Player			G	AB	R	H	2B	3B	HR	RBI	BB	SO	SB	BA	PO	A	E	FA
Briggs, Johnny	20	L	61	66	16	17	2	0	1	6	9	12	1	.258	22	1	1	.958
Callison, Johnny	25	L	162	654	101	179	30	10	31	104	36	95	6	.274	319	**19**	4	.988
Cater, Danny	24	R	60	152	13	45	9	1	1	13	7	15	1	.296	110	7	3	.975
Covington, Wes	32	L	129	339	37	95	18	0	13	58	38	50	0	.280	99	4	3	.972
Gonzalez, Tony	27	L	131	421	55	117	25	3	4	40	44	74	0	.278	243	5	1	**.996**
Johnson, Alex	21	R	43	109	18	33	7	1	4	18	6	26	1	.303	47	1	1	.980
Phillips, Adolfo	22	R	13	13	4	3	0	0	0	0	3	3	0	.231	5	1	0	1.000
Totals:	27	—	162	5493	693	1415	241	51	130	649	440	924	30	.258			30	

Note: Bold statistics denote National League leader in that category.

Key to column headings:

G	Games	GS	Games Started	CG	Complete Games
BB	Walks	SO	Strikeouts	W	Wins
ShO	Shutouts	SV	Saves	ERA	Earned Run Avg
2B	Doubles	3B	Triples	HR	Home runs
BA	Batting Avg	PO	Put Outs	A	Assists

P	Innings Pitched	H	Hits
L	Losses	PCT	Winning Pct
AB	At Bats	R	Runs
RBI	Runs Batted	SB	Stolen Bases
E	Errors	FA	Fielding Avg

APPENDIX C:

THE 1964 NATIONAL LEAGUE RACE

April 21, 1964

Team	W	L	Pct	GB
Philadelphia	4	1	.800	—
San Francisco	5	2	.714	—
Pittsburgh	3	2	.600	1
St. Louis	4	3	.571	1
Milwaukee	4	3	.571	1
Cincinnati	3	3	.500	1½
Houston	3	3	.500	1½
Chicago	2	3	.400	2
New York	1	4	.200	3
Los Angeles	1	6	.143	4

May 27, 1964

Team	W	L	Pct	GB
Philadelphia	21	14	.600	—
San Francisco	22	15	.595	—
St. Louis	22	17	.564	1
Pittsburgh	22	17	.564	1
Milwaukee	21	17	.553	1½
Cincinnati	19	18	.514	3
Houston	20	22	.476	4½
Los Angeles	19	22	.463	5½
Chicago	14	21	.400	7
New York	12	28	.300	11½

June 15, 1964

Team	W	L	Pct	GB
Philadelphia	32	21	.604	—
San Francisco	33	23	.589	½
Cincinnati	30	25	.545	3
Pittsburgh	29	27	.518	4½
Milwaukee	30	28	.517	4½
Chicago	27	27	.500	5½
Los Angeles	28	30	.483	6½
St. Louis	28	39	.483	6½
Houston	27	32	.458	8
New York	19	40	.322	16

June 16, 1964

Team	W	L	Pct	GB
San Francisco	52	35	.598	—
Philadelphia	49	34	.590	1
Cincinnati	47	39	.547	4½
Pittsburgh	44	39	.530	6
St. Louis	44	42	.512	7½
Milwaukee	44	42	.512	7½
Los Angeles	42	43	.494	9
Chicago	41	43	.488	9½
Houston	39	49	.443	13½
New York	26	62	.295	26½

August 25, 1964

Team	W	L	Pct	GB
Philadelphia	76	48	.613	—
San Francisco	79	55	.560	6½
Cincinnati	69	55	.557	7
St. Louis	66	58	.532	10
Pittsburgh	64	61	.512	12½
Milwaukee	63	60	.512	12½
Los Angeles	60	63	.488	15½
Chicago	57	68	.456	19½
Houston	55	71	.437	22
New York	42	83	.336	34½

September 21, 1964

Team	W	L	Pct	GB
Philadelphia	90	60	.600	—
St. Louis	83	66	.557	6½
Cincinnati	83	66	.557	6½
San Francisco	83	67	.553	7
Milwaukee	77	72	.517	12½
Pittsburgh	76	72	.514	13
Los Angeles	75	75	.500	15
Chicago	67	82	.450	22½
Houston	63	87	.417	27½
New York	50	99	.336	39½

September 27, 1964 (top four teams)

Team	W	L	Pct	GB
Cincinnati	91	66	.580	—
Philadelphia	90	67	.573	1
St. Louis	89	67	.571	1½
San Francisco	86	70	.551	4½

October 1, 1964 (top four teams)

Team	W	L	Pct	GB
St. Louis	92	67	.578	—
Cincinnati	91	68	.573	1
Philadelphia	90	70	.563	2½
San Francisco	88	70	.557	3½

October 4, 1964 (top four teams)

Team	W	L	Pct	GB
Cincinnati	92	69	.571	—
St. Louis	92	69	.571	—
Philadelphia	91	70	.565	1
San Francisco	90	71	.560	2

Final Standings (top four teams)

Team	W	L	Pct	GB
St. Louis	93	69	.574	—
Cincinnati	92	70	.568	1
Philadelphia	92	70	.568	1
San Francisco	90	72	.556	3

Key to column headings: W = Wins, L = Losses, Pct = Winning percentage, GB = Games behind.

NOTES

Introduction

1. Dick Allen, interview with author, Wampum, Pa., September 15, 2002.
2. Frank Thomas, quoted in Dave Anderson, *Pennant Races* (New York: Doubleday, 1994), 285.
3. Ruben Amaro, interview with author, August 11, 1999, Lackawanna County Stadium, Scranton, Pa.
4. Gene Mauch, quoted in Anderson, *Pennant Races*, 288.
5. Ibid.
6. Rich Westcott and Frank Bilovsky, *The Phillies Encyclopedia* (Philadelphia: Temple University Press, 1993), 172–73.
7. Ibid., 194–95.
8. Ibid., 192–93, 340–41.
9. Ibid., 121–23.
10. Jackie Robinson, *I Never Had It Made* (New York: Putnam, 1972), 71–76; David Falkner, *Great Time Coming: The Life of Jackie Robinson from Baseball to Birmingham* (New York: Simon & Schuster, 1995), 163–64.
11. Tom McGrath, "Color Me Badd," *The Fan* 11 (September 1996): 39; and Michael Sokolove, "Nice Is Not Enough," *Philadelphia Inquirer Magazine*, March 30, 1997, 21.

Chapter 1: A Shameful Past

1. W. E. B. Du Bois, *The Philadelphia Negro: A Social Study* (1899; reprint, Philadelphia: University of Pennsylvania Press, 1996).
2. Nathaniel Burt and Wallace E. Davies, "The Iron Age, 1876–1905," in *Philadelphia: A 300-Year History*, ed. Russell F. Weigley (New York: W. W. Norton, 1982), 492–93; and Theodore Hershberg, ed., *Philadelphia: Work Space, Family, and Group Experience in the Nineteenth Century* (New York: Oxford University Press, 1981), 461–91.
3. Robert Gregg, *Sparks from the Anvil of Oppression: Philadelphia's African Methodists and Southern Migrants, 1890–1940* (Philadelphia: Temple University Press, 1993). Gregg offers an important corrective to the "ghettoization thesis," which attributes racial discrimination and, in particular, the segregation of blacks into impoverished areas as the primary reason for poor employment, poor educational opportunities, and poor health care. Instead, he argues that ghettoization must be seen in the larger context of northbound migration and

the African American church. Class divisions within the black community, and the proactive efforts of African Americans at socioeconomic uplift, are just as important in understanding the black assimilation process in Philadelphia.

4. David Craft, *The Negro Leagues* (New York: Crescent Books, 1993), 108.

5. Linn Washington Jr., "Philadelphia Part of Negro League Baseball History," *Philadelphia Tribune*, supp., April 8, 1997, 27F.

6. Roger Lane, *William Dorsey's Philadelphia and Ours: On the Past and Future of the Black City in America* (New York: Oxford University Press, 1991), 18–19.

7. Neil Lanctot, *Fair Dealing and Clean Playing: The Hilldale Club and the Development of Black Professional Baseball* (Jefferson, N.C.: McFarland, 1994).

8. Judy Johnson, quoted in James Bankes, *The Pittsburgh Crawfords: The Lives and Times of Black Baseball's Most Exciting Team* (Dubuque, Iowa: William C. Brown, 1991), 63.

9. Bankes, *Pittsburgh Crawfords*, 87.

10. Judy Johnson, quoted in Robert Peterson, *Only the Ball Was White: A History of Legendary Black Players and All-Black Professional Teams* (New York: Oxford University Press, 1970), 173.

11. Napoleon Cummings, quoted in ibid., 173.

12. Ibid., 174.

13. *Philadelphia Record*, November 22 and 29, 1923.

14. Eddie Joost, Philadelphia A's manager in 1954, interview with author, West Chester, Pa., April 14, 2000.

15. David Jordan, *The Athletics of Philadelphia: Connie Mack's White Elephants, 1901–1954* (Jefferson, N.C.: McFarland, 1999), 184–85.

16. Peterson, *Only the Ball was White*, 88–89; and Craft, *Negro Leagues*, 29–30.

17. *Philadelphia Tribune*, August 1, 1929.

18. *Philadelphia Tribune*, April 24, 1930.

19. Lanctot, *Fair Dealing and Clean Playing*, 66.

20. Bolden, quoted in the *Baltimore Afro-American*, April 11, 1925.

21. John Holway, "Black Star of Philadelphia: Gene Benson," in *Black Diamonds* (Westport, Conn.: Meckler Books, 1989), 70–88.

22. Gene Benson, interview with author, Philadelphia, December 9, 1998.

23. Stanley Glenn, interview with author, West Chester, Pa., December 7, 1998.

24. Mahlon Duckett, interview with author, West Chester, Pa., May 12, 1999.

25. Stanley Glenn, interview with author, West Chester, Pa., April 22, 1999.

26. Ibid.

27. Ibid.

28. Gene Benson, interview with author, Philadelphia, January 10, 1999.

29. Ibid.

30. Duckett, interview with author.

31. Bill Veeck and Ed Linn, *Veeck—As in Wreck: The Chaotic Career of Baseball's Incorrigible Maverick* (New York: G. P. Putnam's Sons, 1962), 171–72. According to David M. Jordan, Larry R. Gerlach, and John P. Rossi, Veeck "falsified the historical record" in order to "polish his own place in baseball history," among other reasons. In fact, Veeck "did not have a deal to buy the Phillies. He did not work to stock any team with Negro League stars. No such deal was quashed by Landis or Frick." (See Jordan et al., "The Truth About Bill Veeck and the '43 Phillies," *The National Pastime: A Review of Baseball History* 6 [1995]: 3–13.)

32. Judge Kenesaw Mountain Landis, quoted in Geoffrey C. Ward and Ken Burns, *Baseball: An Illustrated History* (New York: Alfred A. Knopf, 1994), 287.

33. Albert Chandler, quoted in John Holway, *Voices from the Great Black Baseball Leagues* (New York: Dodd & Mead, 1976), 14.

34. Donn Rogosin, *Invisible Men: Life in Baseball's Negro Leagues* (New York: Atheneum, 1987), 198–99.

35. Robert R. M. Carpenter Jr., quoted in Westcott and Bilovsky, *Phillies Encyclopedia*, 482.

36. Herb Pennock, quoted in *Philadelphia Inquirer*, July 1, 1947.

37. Westcott and Bilovsky, *Phillies Encyclopedia*, 487, 443.

38. Ibid., 443–44.

39. Roy Campanella, *It's Good To Be Alive* (Boston: Little, Brown, 1959), 94–98.

40. Peterson, *Only the Ball Was White*, 187.

41. Marvin Williams, interview with author, Conroe, Tex., August 4, 1999.

42. Ibid.

43. Ibid. Just before his death in 1972, Robinson confirmed the impressive performances of all three Negro Leaguers. "In my view, nobody put on an exhibition like we did," he wrote in his autobiography. "Everything we did, it looked like the Lord was guiding us. Every ball the pitcher threw up became a line drive someplace. We tatooed that short left field fence, that is, Marv and I did—and Jethroe was doing extremely well from the left side too." (See Jackie Robinson as told to Alfred Duckett, *I Never Had It Made* [New York: G. P. Putnam's Sons, 1972], 41–42).

44. Jackie Robinson, *I Never Had It Made*, 41–42.

45. Williams, interview with author.

46. Benson, interview with author, December 9, 1998.

47. Ibid.

48. Merl Kleinknecht, "Gene Benson," *The Ballplayers: Baseball's Ultimate Biographical Reference*, ed. Mike Shatzkin (New York: William Morrow, 1990), 69.

49. David Falkner, *Great Time Coming: The Life of Jackie Robinson from Baseball to Birmingham* (New York: Simon & Schuster, 1995), 121.

50. For historians who concentrate on the negative treatment Robinson received in Philadelphia, see Jules Tygiel, *Baseball's Great Experiment: Jackie Robinson and His Legacy*, expanded edition (New York: Oxford University Press, 1997), 182–87; Arnold Rampersad, *Jackie Robinson: A Biography* (New York: Alfred A. Knopf, 1997), 172–76; and Bruce Kuklick, *To Every Thing a Season: Shibe Park and Urban Philadelphia, 1909–1976* (Princeton: Princeton University Press, 1991), 145–47.

51. Tygiel, *Baseball's Great Experiment*, 182; and William Ecenbarger, "First Among Equals," *Philadelphia Inquirer Magazine*, February 19, 1995, 14.

52. Harold Parrott, *The Lords of Baseball* (New York: Praeger, 1976), 194.

53. Jackie Robinson, *I Never Had It Made*, 71–72.

54. Ecenbarger, "First Among Equals," 14.

55. Tygiel, *Baseball's Great Experiment*, 182–83.

56. Chapman, quoted in *The Sporting News*, May 14, 1947.

57. Ibid.

58. Jackie Robinson, quoted in *Pittsburgh Courier*, May 3 and 10, 1947.

59. Ward and Burns, *Baseball*, 291.

60. Ecenbarger, "First Among Equals," 14.

61. Branch Rickey, quoted in Carl T. Rowan with Jackie Robinson, *Wait Till Next Year* (New York: Random House, 1960), 181–84.

62. Parrott, *Lords of Baseball*, 192.

63. In 1998, Pennock's home town of Kennett Square, Pennsylvania, tried to raise money to construct and erect a statue of the Hall of Fame pitcher. The effort was thwarted by local minority groups who pointed to Pennock's alleged racist remarks against Robinson as an indication that he was undeserving of such an honor. Supporters of the statue raised doubts about the validity of Pennock's racial epithet and pointed to his family's distinguished history

as Quaker stationmasters on the Underground Railroad to refute any claims of racism. (See Chris Barber, "Allegations of Racism Won't Block Monument to Kennett Hall-of-Famer," *West Chester Daily Local News*, July 7, 1998; John Manasso, "Racial Issues Tarnish Hall of Famer Tribute," *Philadelphia Inquirer*, July 8, 1998; Mary Skrzat Hutchins and David Yeats-Thomas, "Support Wavers for Pennock Statue," *The Kennett Paper*, July 16–22, 1998; "Let's Build a More Lasting Memorial to Herb Pennock," *The Kennett Paper*, editorials, July 16–22, 1998; and Angela Galloway, "Borough Still Set to Honor Pennock," *Philadelphia Inquirer*, August 21, 1998.)

64. Tygiel, *Baseball's Great Experiment*, 373. Tygiel cites Parrott as the only source for the controversial phone conversation between Rickey and Pennock. Since then, the conversation has been cited repeatedly as fact by several writers, including Ecenbarger, "First Among Equals," 14; Mark Kram, "The Nightmare That Was Philly," *Philadelphia Daily News* (special supplement on Jackie Robinson, April 9, 1997): 10; Kuklick, *To Every Thing a Season*, 147; and Rampersad, *Jackie Robinson*, 175.

65. Pennock died of a cerebral hemorrhage on January 30, 1948, at the relatively young age of fifty-four. Rickey passed away, at the age of eighty-four, on December 9, 1965.

66. Jackie Robinson, *I Never Had It Made*, 74.

67. Rachel Robinson, quoted in John Manasso, "Racial Issues Tarnish Hall of Famer Tribute," *Philadelphia Inquirer*, July 8, 1998.

68. Westcott and Bilovsky, *Phillies Encyclopedia*, 89.

69. Andy Seminick, interview with author, West Chester, Pa., April 14, 2000.

70. Parrott, *Lords of Baseball*, 192.

71. Chapman, quoted in Wayne Martin, "'Sure, We Rode Jackie,' Says Chapman," *The Sporting News*, March 24, 1973.

72. Jackie Robinson in Rowan, *Wait Till Next Year*, 184.

73. Harry Walker, interview with author, Leeds, Ala., May 20, 1997.

74. Ken Raffensberger, interview with author, York, Pa., April 25, 2000.

75. Howie Schultz, interview with author, West Stillwater, Minn., April 26, 2000.

76. Glenn, interview with author, December 7, 1998.

77. Bill "Ready" Cash, interview with author, Philadelphia, April 18, 1999; Wilmer Harris, interview with author, Philadelphia, December 9, 1998; and Mahlon Duckett, interview with author, West Chester, Pa., May 12, 1999.

78. *Philadelphia Inquirer*, May 9 and 10, 1947; *Philadelphia Daily News*, May 9, 10, 1947.

79. Ben Chapman, quoted in the *Pittsburgh Courier*, May 10, 1947.

80. Chapman, quoted in "'Sure, We Rode Jackie.'"

81. Ibid. Time may have changed Chapman's perspective. Shortly before his death in 1993 he seemed to have come to terms with the explosiveness and inner tempests of his youth, admitting that he "went too far with the jockeying" and that he was "sorry for many of the things [he] said." (Chapman, quoted in Ray Robinson, "The Life and Death of an Enemy Within," *The Sporting News*, October 31, 1994.)

82. Robin Roberts, interview with author, West Chester, Pa., April 14, 2000.

83. Ibid.

84. Rich Ashburn, interview with author, Veterans Stadium, Philadelphia, June 11, 1996.

85. Rich Ashburn, "Honoring Jackie Robinson," *Philadelphia Bulletin*, April 21, 1973.

86. Ashburn, interview with author.

87. Tygiel, *Baseball's Great Experiment*, 185–89.

88. Ecenbarger, "First Among Equals," 15.

89. Glenn, interview with author, April 22, 1999.

90. For Jackie Robinson's career statistics, see Rick Wolff, *The Baseball Encyclopedia*, 8th ed. (New York: Macmillan, 1990), 1389.

91. Benson, interview with author, January 10, 1999.

92. See Robin Roberts and C. Paul Rogers III, *The Whiz Kids and the 1950 Pennant* (Philadelphia: Temple University Press, 1996).

93. Ed Linn, "The Tragedy of the Phillies," *Sport Magazine* 36 (March 1965): 23–26; and "Obituary of John Kennedy, Former Phillies Shortstop, 71," *Philadelphia Inquirer*, April 30, 1998. Among the early black prospects who signed with the Phillies but never made it to the majors with the team were pitcher Jim Mason and shortstop Teddy Washington.

94. See Ray Kelley, "Fine Work of Kennedy Acclaimed in Phillies Exhibition," *Philadelphia Bulletin*, March 23, 1957.

95. Mayo Smith, quoted in Ed Pollock. "Playing the Game, Kennedy Proves Ability to Phils," *Philadelphia Bulletin*, March 27, 1957.

96. Roy Hammey, quoted in Kelley, "Fine Work of Kennedy Acclaimed."

97. Ray Kelly, "Phils Deal for Hernandez Shapes Up as a Wise Move, Baseball Experts Say," *Philadelphia Bulletin*, April 6, 1957.

98. Ray Kelly, "Fernandez Has Jittery Debut with Phillies," *Philadelphia Bulletin*, April 8, 1957.

99. Claude Harrison, "Phillies Have Major League Material in John Kennedy," *Philadelphia Tribune*, April 13, 1957.

100. Ed Pollock, "Trading Edge in Phillies' Infield Wealthy," *Philadelphia Bulletin*, March 17, 1959; and Westcott and Bilovsky, *Phillies Encyclopedia*, 110.

101. "Phils Option Kennedy to High Point Club," *Philadelphia Inquirer*, May 6, 1957.

102. Dallas Green, interview with author, West Chester, Pa., October 13, 1999.

103. Curt Simmons, interview with author, Prospectville, Pa., April 22, 2000. See also David Halberstam, *October 1964* (New York: Villard, 1994). Halberstam argues that the Cardinals' willingness to sign black players allowed them to replace the all-white New York Yankees as the toast of major league baseball.

104. Westcott and Bilovsky, *Phillies Encyclopedia*, 479–83.

Chapter 2: Integrating the Phillies

1. Dick Allen and Tim Whitaker, *Crash: The Life and Times of Dick Allen* (New York: Ticknor & Fields, 1989), 47–48.

2. Craig Carter, *Daguerreotypes: The Complete Major and Minor League Records of Baseball's Greats*, 8th ed. (St. Louis: Sporting News, 1990), 10.

3. Allen, *Crash*, 14; and Carl Nesfield, "New Team. New Town. New Richie?" *Black Sports* 16 (July 1971): 31.

4. Ibid.

5. See Walter Bingham, "The Dalton Gang Rides Again," *Sports Illustrated*, June 13, 1960.

6. Donald Honig, *The Philadelphia Phillies: An Illustrated History* (New York: Simon & Schuster, 1992), 167.

7. See Mark Ribowsky, *A Complete History of the Negro Leagues, 1884–1955* (1995); and John Holway, *Voices from the Great Black Baseball Leagues* (New York: DeCappo Press, 1993). Both Ribowsky and Holway examine the higher profile stars, such as Jackie Robinson, Willie Mays, Hank Aaron, and Satchel Paige, and their experience with integration in professional baseball. They argue that economics outweighed the moral imperatives as the driving force of integration. Initially, integration was a delicate issue for the owners, who sought to improve their product without driving away white fans. But as black players entered the majors, they brought with them a more exciting style of play. Their success on the field also resulted in more revenue for the owners.

8. Westcott and Bilovsky, *Phillies Encyclopedia*, 490–91.

9. Norman Macht, "Gene Mauch," in *The Ballplayers Biographical Reference*, ed. Shatzkin 686.

10. Westcott and Bilovsky, *Phillies Encyclopedia*, 452–54.

11. Mauch, quoted in Ray Kelly, "Mauch Cracks Down on Phillies," *Philadelphia Evening Bulletin*, May 12, 1960.

12. See "Robert M. Carpenter Papers, Philadelphia Baseball Club / National League," Manuscript Box 1, Player Development Papers, 1957–64, Manuscript Collection, Hagley Library, Wilmington, Del. (hereafter, "Carpenter Papers"). Approximately twenty players were on the roster of each team in the Phillies minor league system during the period 1957–64. Those teams were Buffalo (AAA), Indianapolis (AAA), Chattanooga (AA), Asheville (A), Williamsport (A), Des Moines (B), Bakersfield (C), Tampa (D), Elmira (D), and Johnson City (D).

13. See "Player Signings, 1958–1964," Carpenter Papers.

14. Ibid.

15. See "Player Development Papers, 1957–62," Carpenter Papers.

16. Tatum, *Conversations About Race*, 133–36. The U.S. Bureau of the Census defines "Hispanic" as an ethnic label that includes Latinos who trace their family background to Mexico, Puerto Rico, Cuba, the Dominican Republic, Colombia, Ecuador, El Salvador, Guatemala, Peru, and Nicaragua.

17. Ford Frick, quoted in Ron Briley, "The Times Were A-Changin': Baseball as a Symbol of American Values in Transition, 1963–1964," *Baseball Research Journal* 17 (1988): 56.

18. *The Sporting News*, quoted in ibid.

19. Allen, *Crash*, 11.

20. Ibid., 14.

21. Frank Lucchesi, interview with author, Colleyville, Tex., January 6, 2002. See also Lucchesi, quoted in Bill Conlin, "Richie Is Beautiful, He Don't Give a Damn for Nobody," *Jock* 3 (January 1970): 94.

22. Allen, *Crash*, 47–52.

23. Ibid., 35–36.

24. Ibid., 37.

25. Ibid., 36.

26. Howie Bedell, interview with author, Pottstown, Pa., April 30, 2002.

27. Allen, *Crash*, 47–48.

28. Dick Allen, interview with author, West Chester, Pa., April 21, 2001.

29. Allen, *Crash*, 13–15, 21.

30. Ibid., 20.

31. Robert R. M. Carpenter Jr., interview with author, Monchanin, Del., June 13, 2002.

32. Allen quoted by Allen Lewis, "Phils May Transplant Speedy Gardener Allen at Hot Corner," *The Sporting News*, October 26, 1963.

33. See Bruce Adelson, *Brushing Back Jim Crow: The Integration of Minor League Baseball in the American South* (Charlottesville: University of Virginia, 2000). Adelson argues that many of the blacks and Latinos who played minor league ball in the South were buffered by supportive black fans and their white teammates. Despite taunts by white fans and opposing players, and southern legislators' refusal to change segregationist policies on the clubs, many of these minority ballplayers managed to succeed and go on to successful big league careers.

34. Johnny Briggs, interview with author, West Chester, Pa., April 21, 2001.

35. Grant Jackson, interview with author, Lackawanna County Stadium, Scranton, Pa., June 8, 2001.

36. Westcott and Bilovsky, *Phillies Encyclopedia*, 740–41.

37. Carpenter, interview with author.

38. See Peter C. Bjarkman, *Baseball with a Latin Beat: A History of the Latin American Game* (Jefferson, N.C.: McFarland, 1994); William B. Mead, *The Explosive Sixties: Baseball's Decade of Expansion* (Alexandria, Va.: Redefinition, 1989), 134–35; and David Q. Voigt, *American Baseball*, 3 vols. (University Park, Pa.: The Pennsylvania State University Press, 1983), 3:244–45. Light-skinned Latinos, easily mistaken for white players, had been in major league baseball since 1911. But after World War II, with the elimination of the color barrier, major league scouts turned to Cuba, Venezuela, Panama, Mexico, and Puerto Rico to recruit talent. By 1960 the Caribbean had become a vital source of new talent for American teams. Despite Fidel Castro's embargo of players from Cuba to the United States in 1961, the impact of Hispanic players continued throughout the decade. By 1968, thirty-nine Latinos—almost twice the number in 1960—were on the regular season rosters of the sixteen major league clubs that existed. By 1979, Latinos comprised 10 percent of the major league ranks and 40 percent of the minor league rosters. Most of these players came from poor households and played baseball year-round. The scouts knew they could sign them cheaply.

39. Sandy Grady, "Taylor Fills Need at 2nd, Phils Explain, After Cubs Get Cardwell, Bouchee," *Philadelphia Bulletin*, May 14, 1960.

40. Hugh Brown, "Difference? Phils Putting on a Show," *Philadelphia Bulletin*, June 26, 1960.

41. Westcott and Bilovsky, *Phillies Encyclopedia*, 115–17.

42. Tony Taylor, interview with author, Veterans Stadium, Philadelphia, July 27, 1999.

43. Ruben Amaro Sr., interview with author, Lackawanna County Stadium, Scranton, Pa., August 11, 1999.

44. Ibid.

45. Tony Gonzalez, interview with author, Burlington, N.J., April 14, 2001.

46. Westcott and Bilovsky, *Phillies Encyclopedia*, 116.

47. Bingham, "Dalton Gang Rides Again."

48. Westcott and Bilovsky, *Phillies Encyclopedia*, 287–88.

49. Bingham, "Dalton Gang Rides Again."

50. Westcott and Bilovsky, *Phillies Encyclopedia*, 298.

51. Art Mahaffey, interview with author, West Chester, Pa., April 21, 2001.

52. Clay Dalrymple, interview with author, Gold Beach, Ore., May 12, 2002. See also Westcott and Bilovsky, *Phillies Encyclopedia*, 215.

53. Johnny Callison with John Sletten, *The Johnny Callison Story* (New York: Vantage Press, 1991), 62–53.

54. Ibid., 70, 93–94.

55. Dallas Green, interview with author, West Chester, Pa., October 13, 1999.

56. Westcott and Bilovsky, *Phillies Encyclopedia*, 117–18.

57. Tom Jozwik, "Wes Covington," in *Ballplayers*, 229.

58. Honig, *Philadelphia Phillies: Illustrated History*, 170.

59. Westcott and Bilovsky, *Phillies Encyclopedia*, 287.

60. Jack Baldschun, interview with author, Veterans Stadium, Philadelphia, April 20, 2001.

61. Westcott and Bilovsky, *Phillies Encyclopedia*, 117.

62. For all the scores of the twenty-three-game losing streak, see ibid., 730.

63. Tony Gonzalez, interview with author.

64. Jack Baldschun, interview with author.

65. "Can Phils Keep Losing Forever?" *New York Herald Tribune*, August 17, 1961.

66. Callison, *Johnny Callison Story*, 177.

67. Ray Kelly, "Phils Also Win Back Their Good Humor," *Philadelphia Bulletin*, August 21, 1961.

68. Allen Lewis, *The Philadelphia Phillies: A Pictorial History* (Virginia Beach, Va.: JCP Corporation, 1981), 100.

69. Mauch, quoted in Ray Kelly, "Buzhardt Halts Phillies' Losses at 23," *Philadelphia Bulletin*, August 21, 1961; and Mauch, quoted in Si Burick, "What It Feels Like to Lose 23 in a Row," *Dayton Daily News*, August 22, 1961.

70. Rich Westcott, *Philadelphia's Old Ballparks* (Philadelphia: Temple University Press, 1996), 106, 113; and Lawrence Ritter, *Lost Ballparks: A Celebration of Baseball's Legendary Fields* (New York: Penguin, 1992), 178.

71. Westcott, *Philadelphia's Old Ballparks*, 167.

72. Larry Shenk, quoted in ibid., 168.

73. Allen Lewis, quoted in Westcott, *Philadelphia's Old Ballparks*, 177.

74. Linda Belsky Zamost, "The Year That Almost Was," *Philly Sport* 2 (June 1989): 17–20.

75. Ritter, *Lost Ballparks*, 185.

76. Johnny Callison, interview with author, Glenside, Pa., July 19, 2001.

77. Bobby Wine, quoted in Callison, *Johnny Callison Story*, 127.

78. Baldschun, interview with author; and Ed Richter, *View from the Dugout: A Season with Baseball's Amazing Gene Mauch* (Philadelphia: Chilton Books, 1964), 8.

79. Westcott and Bilovsky, *Phillies Encyclopedia*, 118–19.

80. Ibid.

81. Richter, *View from the Dugout*, 26.

82. Hugh Brown, "1963 Phils Resemble Whiz Kids of 1950," *Philadelphia Bulletin*, March 22, 1963.

83. Richter, *View from the Dugout*, 3–8.

84. Ibid., 29.

85. Westcott and Bilovsky, *Phillies Encyclopedia*, 119.

86. Tom Jozwik, "Ray Culp," in *Ballplayers*, 242.

87. Westcott and Bilovsky, *Phillies Encyclopedia*, 214.

88. Ibid., 119; and *1964 Philadelphia Phillies Yearbook* (1st ed.), 20–21.

89. Westcott and Bilovsky, *Phillies Encyclopedia*, 120.

90. Mauch, quoted in Richter, *View from the Dugout*, 36.

91. Westcott and Bilovsky, *Phillies Encyclopedia*, 120–21.

92. Mauch, quoted in Richter, *View from the Dugout*, 36.

93. Westcott and Bilovsky, *Phillies Encyclopedia*, 323–24.

94. Lewis, *Phillies History*, 105.

95. Mahaffey, interview with author, August 18, 1999.

96. Dalrymple, interview with author.

97. Lewis, *Phillies History*, 105.

98. Westcott and Bilovsky, *Phillies Encyclopedia*, 121.

Chapter 3: The Spring of '64

1. See William Leggett, "The Rise and Fall of the Phillies," *Sports Illustrated*, March 1, 1965, 57–58; and William A. Cook, *The Summer of '64: A Pennant Lost* (Jefferson, N.C.: McFarland, 2002), 17–18.

2. Frank Dolson, *Jim Bunning: Baseball and Beyond* (Philadelphia: Temple University Press, 1998), 1, 100.

3. Ray Robinson, "Jim Bunning: Daddy's Day Pitcher," in *The Phillies Reader*, ed. Richard Orodenker (Philadelphia: Temple University Press, 1996), 143–44.

4. Dolson, *Jim Bunning*, 102–3.

5. Ibid., 51–52.

6. Dalrymple, quoted in Stan Hochman, "Little Room for Three Catchers in Phils' Roster Jam," *Philadelphia Daily News*, March 12, 1964.

7. Amaro, quoted in Ray Kelly, "Amaro Bats .450 in Bid," *Philadelphia Bulletin*, April 3, 1964.

8. Gonzalez, quoted in Stan Hochman, "Tony's HR Motto: More Than 4 in '64," *Philadelphia Daily News*, March 24, 1964. See also Gonzalez, quoted in Claude Harrison, "Phillies Could Win Pennant If Covington and Gonzalez Click," *Philadelphia Tribune*, March 24, 1964.

9. Mauch, quoted in Ray Kelly, "Mauch Set to Deal at Winter Confab," *Philadelphia Bulletin*, November 26, 1963.

10. Mauch, quoted in Leggett, "Rise and Fall of the Phillies," 58.

11. Allen, quoted in Ray Kelly, "Phils Rich Allen 'Loves' Chance to Play Third Base," *Philadelphia Bulletin*, January 12, 1964.

12. Hoak, quoted in Larry Merchant, "Hoak's Vow: 'I'm Going to Play,'" *Philadelphia Daily News*, March 26, 1964.

13. Allen, quoted in Stan Hochman, "Hoak's Eyes Pinned on Allen," *Philadelphia Daily News*, March 9, 1964.

14. Hoak, quoted in Merchant, "Hoak's Vow."

15. *1964 Phillies Yearbook*, 25.

16. Ibid., 27.

17. Ibid. See also Merritt Clifton, "Adolfo Phillips," in *The Ballplayers*, ed. Shatzkin, 866.

18. Stan Hochman, "Sour Bat Spoiling Hermstein's Script," *Philadelphia Daily News*, March 28, 1964.

19. Stan Hochman, "Phillies After Mets' Thomas and Jackson?" *Philadelphia Daily News*, March 28, 1964.

20. Stan Hochman, "Mauch Gives Cater Quite a Chance," *Philadelphia Daily News*, April 1, 1964.

21. Stan Hochman, "New Rule Can Cost Phils Promising Pitchers," *Philadelphia Daily News*, March 9, 1964. The Phillies were not the only club with this problem. The Dodgers also had four first-year players, in whom they had invested bonus payments totaling $265,000.

22. *1964 Phillies Yearbook* (1st ed.), 21.

23. Stan Hochman, "Wise and Bennett Have Slight Edge with the Phillies," *Philadelphia Daily News*, March 10, 1964.

24. Ibid.

25. Allen Lewis, "John Briggs," in *Ballplayers*, 115. See also *1964 Phillies Yearbook* (1st ed.), 24.

26. Stan Hochman, "'Forgotten' Green Vows 'I'll Start,'" *Philadelphia Daily News*, March 10, 1964.

27. Stan Hochman, "Green: 18 Runs in 12 Innings," *Philadelphia Daily News*, April 2, 1964.

28. *1964 Phillies Yearbook* (1st ed.), 12.

29. Mauch, quoted in Leggett, "Rise and Fall of the Phillies," 58.

30. Ibid.

31. Dolson, *Jim Bunning*, 57.

32. Stan Hochman, "Bunning Starts a Brush Fire," *Philadelphia Daily News*, April 13, 1964.

33. Joseph S. Clark Jr., "Rally and Relapse, 1946–1968," in *Philadelphia: A 300-Year History*, ed. Weigley, 660–62.

34. Ibid., 668.

35. Bruce Kuklick, *To Every Thing a Season: Shibe Park and Urban Philadelphia, 1909–1976* (Princeton: Princeton University Press, 1991), 154; and B. G. Kelley, "And There Used to Be a Ballpark Right Here," *Philly Sport* 3 (April 1990): 47–48.

36. For urban history of Philadelphia, see Edwin Wold II, *Philadelphia: Portrait of an American City* (Philadelphia: Camino Books, 1990), 320–47; and Weigley, *Philadelphia: A 300-Year History* (New York: W. W. Norton, 1982), 704–27.

37. For an analysis of the social problems confronting Philadelphia in the 1960s, see James A. Michener, *The Quality of Life* (Philadelphia: Girard Company, 1970).

38. Bruce Biossat, "Philadelphia Acts Quietly, Positively on Racial Issues," *Philadelphia Daily News*, May 18, 1964.

39. See Weigley, *Philadelphia*, 661–63.

40. Ibid., 678–79.

41. S. A. Paolantonio, *Frank Rizzo: The Last Big Man in Big City America* (Philadelphia: Camino Books, 1993), 72–73.

42. Ibid., 74.

43. Bruce Kuklick, *To Every Thing a Season: Shibe Park and Urban Philadelphia, 1909–1976* (Princeton: Princeton University Press, 1991), 148–49; and author interview with Dick Perez, April 16, 2001, Wayne, Pa.

44. Allen, quoted in John Brogan, "Richie Allen: 2 Hits, 4 Slips, No Butterflies," *Philadelphia Bulletin*, April 15, 1964.

45. Stan Hochman, "Bunning Has the Stuff When It Counts," *Philadelphia Daily News*, April 16, 1964.

46. See Ray Kelly, "Rookies Keep Phillies in First," *Philadelphia Bulletin*, April 20, 1964. See also Callison, *Johnny Callison Story*, 103; and Cook, *Summer of '64*, 36.

47. Stan Hochman, "There's Only One Richie Allen," *Philadelphia Daily News*, April 20, 1964.

48. Dolson, *Jim Bunning*, 58–59.

49. Ibid., 59.

50. Bunning, quoted in Stan Hochman, "Bunning on the Ball in Real All-Star Performance," *Philadelphia Daily News*, April 25, 1964.

51. Cook, *Summer of '64*, 44–45.

52. Callison, *Johnny Callison Story*, 104.

53. Ibid.

54. Claude E. Harrison Jr., "Phils Have Pride and Richie Allen," *Philadelphia Tribune*, May 19, 1964.

55. Mauch quoted by Allen Lewis, "Phils Get Rich with Wampum Whiz," *The Sporting News*, May 23, 1964.

56. Claude E. Harrison Jr., "Phils' Allen To Be Cited in Pittsburgh," *Philadelphia Tribune*, May 16, 1964.

57. Cook, *Summer of '64*, 55.

58. Clark, "Rally and Relapse, 1946–1968," 690–91; and Orodenker, ed., *Phillies Reader*, 162.

59. Allen Lewis, interview with author, Clearwater, Fla., December 29, 2001.

60. "Stories from the Press Box," History Channel documentary, aired on May 10, 2001; and Bill Conlin, *Batting Cleanup, Bill Conlin*, ed. Kevin Kerrane (Philadelphia: Temple University Press, 1997), xi–xii. Sportswriters Dick Young of the *New York Post* and Stan Isaacs of *Newsday* set the precedent for the new breed of sportswriter. Young once observed that a

chipmunk "had to tell people they're full of shit and then go out and face them the next day." Isaacs is widely credited with popularizing the intrusive line of questioning. After the New York Yankees pitcher Ralph Terry defeated the San Francisco Giants in Game 5 of the 1962 World Series, Terry excused himself from a group of sportswriters to take a telephone call from his wife. When he returned, Terry mentioned that his wife was feeding their baby. From the back of the group, Isaacs asked, "Breast or bottle?" It was the kind of intrusive personal question that became a trademark of the chipmunks.

61. Stan Hochman, "Amaro's Golden Summer Turns to Lead," *Philadelphia Daily News*, March 11, 1964.

62. Bennett, interview with author.

63. Jack Baldschun, Dennis Bennett, Johnny Briggs, and John Herrnstein, interviews with author.

64. Larry Merchant, "Mahaffey Threw Like Hell-O Dolly," *Philadelphia Daily News*, June 10, 1964.

65. Larry Merchant, "Letters Bombard the Bomb Squad," *Philadelphia Daily News*, September 4, 1964.

66. Larry Merchant, "Break up the Phillies!" *Philadelphia Daily News*, June 18, 1964.

67. John Herrnstein, interview with author, Chillicothe, Ohio, May 20, 2001. Dick Allen, Jack Baldschun, Johnny Briggs, Johnny Callison, Clay Dalrymple, Dallas Green, Art Mahaffey, and Tony Taylor confirmed Herrnstein's opinion.

68. Claude E. Harrison Jr., "Richie Allen Is Ready for the Big Time?" *Philadelphia Tribune*, May 2, 1964.

69. Cook, *Summer of '64*, 67–68.

70. Ibid., 69–70.

71. Ibid., 78–86.

72. Callison, quoted in Stan Hochman, "What, Callison Worried? Not This Year!" *Philadelphia Daily News*, April 2, 1964.

73. Callison, *Johnny Callison Story*, 102. In the spring of 1964, Callison refused to sign his contract, believing that he deserved more of a raise. Mauch convinced General Manager John Quinn to boost the outfielder's pay from the $17,500 he received in 1963 to $26,500 for 1964.

74. Dennis Bennett, interview with author, Klamath Falls, Ore., January 15, 2002.

75. Mike Kern, "Born to Win: The Secrets of Our Legendary Coaches," *Philadelphia Daily News*, special supplement, November 14, 2002, C25.

76. Mauch, quoted in Claude E. Harrison Jr., "Phils Have Pride and Richie Allen," *Philadelphia Tribune*, May 19, 1964.

Chapter 4: On Top of the National League

1. Cook, *Summer of '64*, 87.

2. Stan Hochman, "Phils Find Relief in Bunning's Sunny Afternoon," *Philadelphia Daily News*, June 19, 1964.

3. Eldon F. Libby, "Young Bunnings Catch Dad's Act in Late Innings," *Philadelphia Inquirer*, June 22, 1964.

4. Dalrymple, interview with author.

5. See game summary in Dolson, *Jim Bunning*, 288–89.

6. Tony Taylor, quoted in Allen Lewis, "Jim Asks Phillies for Help," *Philadelphia Inquirer*, June 22, 1964.

7. Callison, quoted in Dolson, *Jim Bunning*, 62; and Callison, *Johnny Callison Story*, 105.

8. Anderson, *Pennant Races*, 258.
9. Bunning, quoted in Ray Robinson, *Baseball Stars of 1965* (New York: Pyramid Books, 1965), 139.
10. Dolson, *Jim Bunning*, 61.
11. Ibid.
12. Triandos, quoted in Frank Dolson, "Bunning Gabs His Way to a Perfect Game," *Philadelphia Inquirer*, June 22, 1964.
13. Allen Lewis, "Pitcher Retires 27 Men in Row in 2d No Hitter," *Philadelphia Inquirer*, June 22, 1964.
14. Maury Allen, quoted in Dolson, *Jim Bunning*, 66.
15. Ibid., 65.
16. Allen Lewis, "New Whiz Kids Briggs and Wise Earn Phil Spurs," *The Sporting News*, July 4, 1964.
17. Rick Wise, interview with author, Rivershark's Park, Camden, N.J., September 5, 2001.
18. Allen Lewis, "Briggs Does It All," *Philadelphia Inquirer*, June 15, 1964.
19. Mauch, quoted in Allen Lewis, "Briggs Powers Phillies over Cards," *Philadelphia Inquirer*, June 27, 1964.
20. Johnny Briggs, interview with author, West Chester, Pa., April 21, 2001.
21. Westcott and Bilovsky, *Phillies Encyclopedia*, 211.
22. Covington, quoted in Claude Harrison, "Wes Covington's Future Plans in Freihofer's Oven," *Philadelphia Tribune*, June 16, 1964.
23. Claude Harrison, "Phillies Fail for Bid to Obtain Mets' Al Jackson," *Philadelphia Tribune*, June 20, 1964.; and Stan Hochman, "Trade Deadline Passes: All Phillies Are Still on Top of the League," *Philadelphia Daily News*, June 16, 1964. Another deal Quinn explored was sending Dennis Bennett or Chris Short to Pittsburgh for Donn Clendenon.
24. Claude Harrison, "Another Allen, Ron, Signed by Phillies," *Philadelphia Tribune*, June 20, 1964. Ron Allen was a "bonus baby" who signed for $30,000. In June 1964 he was hitting .308 at Chattanooga.
25. Dalrymple, quoted in Callison, *Johnny Callison Story*, 88.
26. Johnny Callison, interview with author, West Chester, Pa., April 21, 2001.
27. Cook, *Summer of '64*, 105.
28. Ibid., 106–9.
29. Ibid., 107.
30. Ibid., 114–15.
31. Stengel, quoted in Arthur Daley, "Sport of the Times," *New York Times*, August 8, 1964.
32. Cook, *Summer of '64*, 117–18.
33. Dolson, *Jim Bunning*, 96.
34. Ibid.
35. Cook, *Summer of '64*, 119.
36. Callison, *Johnny Callison Story*, 106.
37. Cook, *Summer of '64*, 119.
38. Chris Short, quoted in Allen Lewis, "Callison and Phillies Star at the Mid-Summer Classic," *Philadelphia Inquirer*, July 8, 1964.
39. Cook, *Summer of '64*, 120–21.
40. Callison, *Johnny Callison Story*, 107.
41. Ibid., 108.
42. Cook, *Summer of '64*, 130–31, 135.
43. Larry Merchant, "Something Special," *Philadelphia Daily News*, July 13, 1964.

44. Era Allen, quoted in Sandy Grady, "Mom Had Quick Hands Too—On Son's Seat," *The Sporting News*, May 23, 1964.

45. Richie Allen, quoted in Ibid.

46. Cook, *Summer of '64*, 139–40.

47. Allen, quoted in Callison, *Johnny Callison Story*, 175.

48. Cook, *Summer of '64*, 141–42.

49. Ibid.

50. Dalrymple, interview with author.

51. Bennett, interview with author.

52. Tony Taylor, interview with author, Veterans Stadium, Philadelphia, July 27, 1999.

53. Cookie Rojas, interview with author, Bensalem, Pa., July 14, 2001.

54. Westcott and Bilovsky, *Phillies Encyclopedia*, 323.

55. Frank Dolson, interview with author, Merion, Pa., December 28, 2001.

56. Art Mahaffey, interview with author, Westtown, Pa., August 18, 1999.

57. Dallas Green, interview with author, West Chester, Pa., April 21, 2001.

58. Tony Gonzalez, interview with author, Burlington, N.J., April 14, 2001.

59. Dalrymple, interview with author.

60. Wise, interview with author.

61. Grant Jackson, interview with author, Lackawanna County Stadium, Scranton, Pa., June 8, 2001.

62. Briggs, interview with author; and David Wolf, "Let's Everybody Boo Rich Allen!" *Life*, August 15, 1969, 51.

63. Allen, *Crash*, 105–6.

64. Bennett, interview with author.

65. Dave Grote, ed., *1965 National League Green Book* (Cincinnati: National League Public Relations Department, 1965), 14–15.

66. Dallas Green, interview with author, October 13, 1999, Chester County Historical Society, West Chester, Pa.

67. Michael Fitts, quoted in Christopher K. Hepp, "Fans Fondly Recall Connie Mack Stadium," *Philadelphia Inquirer*, August 5, 1999.

68. Baldschun, interview with author, April 20, 2001.

69. Dalrymple, interview with author. See also Wulf, "Year of the Blue Snow," *Sports Illustrated*, September 25, 1989, 84.

70. Callison, *Johnny Callison Story*, 111.

71. Leggett, "Rise and Fall of the Phillies," 59.

72. Roy Sievers, interview with author, October 5, 2002, Bensalem, Pa.

73. Wolff, *Baseball Encyclopedia*, 1452.

74. Leggett, "Rise and Fall of the Phillies," 59.

75. Allen Lewis, "Frank Thomas," in *Ballplayers*, 1080–81.

76. Cook, *Summer of '64*, 167–69.

77. Dolson, *Jim Bunning*, 67.

78. Cook, *Summer of '64*, 173.

79. Allen, quoted in ibid., 150.

80. Bunning, quoted in ibid.

81. Ray Kelly, "Phils Obtain Cubs' Shantz on Waivers," *Philadelphia Bulletin*, August 16, 1964.

82. Cook, *Summer of '64*, 186–87.

83. Clark, "Rally and Relapse," 676.

84. Paolantonio, *Frank Rizzo*, 74–75.

85. Baldschun, interview with author, April 20, 2001.

86. Cook, *Summer of '64*, 191.

87. Clark, "Rally and Relapse," 676; Bruce Kuklick, *To Every Thing a Season: Shibe Park and Urban Philadelphia, 1909–1976* (Princeton: Princeton University Press, 1991), 155–56.

88. Kelly, "And There Used to be a Ballpark Right Here," 64.

89. Gerald Early, "Baseball and African American Life," in *Baseball: An Illustrated History*, ed. Ward and Burns, 417.

90. North Philadelphia resident, named "R," quoted in ibid.

91. Allen, interview with author.

92. Tim McCarver, interview with author, Gladwyne, Pa., December 21, 1999.

93. Alvin Dark, quoted in an Associated Press article by Joe Reichler published in the *Daily Home News*, August 5, 1954.

94. Ron Briley, "The Times Were A-Changin': Baseball as a Symbol of American Values in Transition, 1963–1964," *Baseball Research Journal* 17 (1988): 59–60.

95. Alou, quoted in ibid., 56.

96. Cook, *Summer of '64*, 195.

97. Arnold Hano, "A Week with the Phillies," in *Phillies Reader*, ed. Orodenker, 146.

98. Mauch, quoted in ibid., 147–48.

99. Hano, "A Week with the Phillies," 152–53.

100. Allen, quoted in Stan Hochman, "Boo Birds of Unhappiness Find Nest in Allen's Glove," *Philadelphia Daily News*, September 4, 1964.

101. Cook, *Summer of '64*, 202–3.

102. Hano, "A Week with the Phillies," 157.

103. Leggett, "Rise and Fall of the Phillies," 59.

104. Cook, *Summer of '64*, 206.

105. Dolson, *Jim Bunning*, 68.

106. Cook, *Summer of '64*, 208.

107. Larry Merchant, "The Old Vic: New Face in Town," *Philadelphia Daily News*, September 11, 1964.

108. Leggett, "Rise and Fall of the Phillies," 60.

109. Frank Dolson, "Bennett Backs Up Words with Deeds," *Philadelphia Inquirer*, September 13, 1964.

110. Allen Lewis, "Marichal Defeated by Amaro's Double," *Philadelphia Inquirer*, September 12, 1964.

111. Dalrymple, interview with author.

112. Baldschun, interview with author, April 20, 2001.

113. Ibid.

114. Cook, *Summer of '64*, 212–13.

115. Ibid., 215.

116. Vic Powers, quoted in George Kiseda, "Phillies Shoot Holes in Pressure Theory," *Philadelphia Bulletin*, September 17, 1964.

117. Cook, *Summer of '64*, 215.

118. Dolson, *Jim Bunning*, 69.

119. Mauch, quoted in Frank Dolson, "Mauch a Task Master Going into Stretch," *Philadelphia Inquirer*, September 18, 1964.

120. Cook, *Summer of '64*, 216–17.

121. Leggett, "Rise and Fall of the Phillies," 60.

122. Dalrymple, quoted in Dolson, *Jim Bunning*, 70.

123. Mauch, quoted in ibid.

124. Dolson, *Jim Bunning*, 71.

Chapter 5: September Swoon

1. Anderson, "Phillies Phlop," 257–58.
2. Amaro, interview with author, August 11, 1999.
3. Mauch, quoted in Anderson, "Phillies Phlop," 262.
4. Orodenker, ed., *Phillies Reader*, 151.
5. Anderson, "Phillies Phlop," 262.
6. B. G. Kelley, "The Boys of Bummer," *Inside Sports* (October 1994): 77.
7. Gordy Coleman, quoted in Michael Sokolove, "The Big Swoon," *Philly Sport* (June 1989): 56.
8. Leggett, "Rise and Fall of the Phillies," 61.
9. Mahaffey, interview with author, August 18, 1999.
10. Dalrymple, interview with author.
11. Kelley, "Boys of Bummer," 78.
12. Leggett, "Rise and Fall of the Phillies," 61.
13. Laurence Beck, "The 10-Game Collapse," *Philly Sport* (June 1989): 36.
14. Sokolove, "The Big Swoon," 59.
15. Leggett, "Rise and Fall of the Phillies," 61; and Anderson, "Phillies Phlop," 265.
16. Mauch, quoted in Beck, "10-Game Collapse," 36.
17. Allen, *Crash*, 56.
18. Bennett, interview with author .
19. Leggett, "Rise and Fall of the Phillies," 61; and Anderson, "Phillies Phlop," 266.
20. Leggett, "Rise and Fall of the Phillies," 62.
21. Mauch, quoted in Anderson, "Phillies Phlop," 267.
22. Leggett, "Rise and Fall of the Phillies," 62; and Anderson, "Phillies Phlop," 269.
23. Mauch, quoted in Beck, "10-Game Collapse," 39.
24. Mahaffey, quoted in Kelley, "Boys of Bummer," 77.
25. Anderson, "Phillies Phlop," 270.
26. Sokolove, "The Big Swoon," 42.
27. Allen Lewis, "Braves Win, Cut Phils' Lead to Half Game," *Philadelphia Inquirer*, September 27, 1964.
28. Callison, quoted in Kelley, "Boys of Bummer," 76.
29. Dalrymple, interview with author.
30. Anderson, "Phillies Phlop," 272.
31. Beck, "10-Game Collapse," 43.
32. Mauch, quoted in Sandy Grady, "Phillies: Tired, Tense, and Unlucky," *Philadelphia Evening Bulletin*, September 28, 1964.
33. Joe Torre, quoted in Dolson, *Jim Bunning*, 74.
34. Johnny Callison, *Callison Story*, 119–20.
35. Grady, "Phillies: Tired, Tense, and Unlucky."
36. Larry Merchant, "Mauch Needs to Let Loose," *Philadelphia Daily News*, September 28, 1964.
37. Baldschun, interview with author, April 20, 2001. Clay Dalrymple also believed that Mauch's "decision to remain quiet during the losing streak contributed to the collapse." (See Dalrymple, interview with author.)
38. Allen, *Crash*, 54–55.
39. Bunning, quoted in Dolson, *Jim Bunning*, 78–79.
40. Allen Lewis, interview with author, Clearwater, Fla., December 29, 2001.
41. Anderson, "Phillies Phlop," 273.
42. Bennett, quoted in ibid., 275.

43. Johnny Callison, *Callison Story*, 123–24; and Leggett, "Rise and Fall of the Phillies," 63.

44. Richie Allen, quoted in Johnny Callison, *Callison Story*, 157–58.

45. Anderson, "Phillies Phlop," 277.

46. Bill White, quoted in Beck, "10-Game Collapse," 44.

47. Curt Simmons, quoted in Sandy Grady, "Cards Beat Phils as Pirates Defeat Reds in 16," *Philadelphia Evening Bulletin*, September 31, 1964.

48. Anderson, "Phillies Phlop," 278.

49. Ibid., 281.

50. Ibid.

51. Ibid., 284.

52. Ibid., 287.

53. Honig, *Philadelphia Phillies: Illustrated History*, 177.

54. Bob Carpenter, quoted in Jack Fried, "Carpenter Wishes He'd Invested More," *Philadelphia Bulletin*, October 6, 1964.

55. Thomas and Powers statistics taken from David S. Neft et al., *The Sports Encyclopedia: Baseball* (New York: Grosset & Dunlap, 1974), 378.

56. See author interviews with Bennett, Dalrymple, and Mahaffey. See also Westcott and Bilovsky, *Phillies Encyclopedia*, 123.

57. Bunning, quoted in Kelley, "Boys of Bummer," 79.

58. Bunning, quoted in Dolson, *Jim Bunning*, 79.

59. Bunning, quoted in Kelley, "Boys of Bummer," 79.

60. Gene Mauch, quoted in Westcott and Bilovsky, *Phillies Encyclopedia*, 214.

61. Ray Culp, quoted in ibid.

62. Dalrymple, interview with author.

63. Bennett, interview with author.

64. Dalrymple, interview with author; and Dalrymple, quoted in Kelley, "Boys of Bummer," 78.

65. Herrnstein, interview with author.

66. Baldschun, interview with author, April 20, 2001.

67. Green, interview with author, April 21, 2001.

68. Frank Dolson, interview with author, Merion, Pa., December 28, 2001.

69. Gus Triandos, quoted in Wulf, "Year of the Blue Snow," 79.

70. Jim Bunning, quoted in Dolson, *Jim Bunning*, 77.

71. Callison, interview with author, April 21, 2001. See also Callison, *Johnny Callison Story*, 125.

72. Dalrymple, interview with author.

73. Wise, interview with author.

74. Mahaffey, interview with author, August 18, 1999.

75. Diane Callison, quoted in Wulf, "Year of the Blue Snow," 84.

76. Mauch, quoted in Callison, *Johnny Callison Story*, 151.

77. Rick Wolff, *The Baseball Encyclopedia*, 8th ed. (New York: Macmillan, 1990), 398.

78. Ruben Amaro Sr., interview with author, Lackawanna County Stadium, Scranton, Pa., August 11, 1999.

79. Cookie Rojas, interview with author, Bensalem, Pa., July 14, 2001.

80. See Jordan, *Athletics of Philadelphia*; and William C. Kashatus, *Connie Mack's '29 Triumph: The Rise and Fall of the Philadelphia Athletics Dynasty* (Jefferson, N.C.: McFarland, 1999).

81. Matt Wilson, quoted in Leggett, "Rise and Fall of the Phillies," 57.

82. Wulf, "Year of the Blue Snow," 79.

83. Dolson, interview with author.

84. Larry Merchant, *Philadelphia Daily News*, October 5, 1964.

Chapter 6: Seasons of Frustration

1. Dolson, interview with author.

2. Dave Grote, ed., *1965 National League Green Book* (Cincinnati: National League Public Relations Department, 1965), 36.

3. Westcott and Bilovsky, *Phillies Encyclopedia*, 124.

4. Neft, *Sports Encyclopedia:, Baseball*, 384.

5. Ray Kelly, "Mail Bag Critics Put Stamp on Phils," *Philadelphia Evening Bulletin*, May 7, 1965.

6. Westcott, *Philadelphia's Old Ballparks*, 160.

7. Allen, *Crash*, 4–7.

8. Allen Lewis, "Briggs Came to Play and Phils Are Glad They Gave Him a Break," *Philadelphia Inquirer*, July 31, 1965; and Lewis, "Phils Eye Briggs as Stu's Successor," *The Sporting News*, October 30, 1965.

9. Johnny Briggs, interview with author, West Chester, Pa., April 21, 2001.

10. Pat Corrales, quoted in Craig R. Wright, "Another View of Dick Allen," *SABR's Baseball Research Journal* 24 (1995): 4.

11. Callison, quoted in Allen, *Crash*, 7.

12. Amaro, interview with author.

13. Ray Kelly, "Reds Snap Phils' 6-Game Streak, 10–8, *Philadelphia Evening Bulletin*, July 4, 1965.

14. John Quinn, quoted in Allen Lewis, "Thomas Says He Regrets Fight, Calls Waiver Unfair," *Philadelphia Inquirer*, July 5, 1965.

15. Allen, *Crash*, 8. See also Allen, quoted in Claude E. Harrison Jr., "Angered by Comparison to Clay, Richie Allen Lives up to 'Insult,'" *Philadelphia Tribune*, July 6, 1965; and Allen, quoted in Chris J. Perry, "Richie Allen's Mother Says: Frank Thomas Called Dick, 'A Black B —— d'!" *Philadelphia Tribune*, July 10, 1965.

16. Ibid.; and Conlin, "Richie Is Beautiful," 91.

17. Mauch, quoted in Wolf, "Let's Everybody Boo Rich Allen!" 51; and Allen, *Crash*, 9.

18. Thomas, quoted by George Kiseda, "Phillies Waive Thomas," *Philadelphia Evening Bulletin*, July 5, 1965; and Thomas, quoted by Lewis, "Thomas Says He Regrets Fight...."

19. Sandy Grady, "Three 'Wrongs' Do Not Make a Pinch Hitter," *Philadelphia Evening Bulletin*, July 6, 1965.

20. George Kiseda, "Allen Ignores Fans' Catcalls," *Philadelphia Evening Bulletin*, July 8, 1965.

21. Larry Merchant, "Fighting Phil Waived Goodbye," *Philadelphia Daily News*, July 6, 1965. See also Merchant, "Two Games and an Apology at Richie Allen Dell," *Philadelphia Daily News*, July 8, 1965.

22. Merchant, "Allen vs. Thomas: Round 10," *Philadelphia Daily News*, July 12, 1965.

23. Merchant, "Psst, Larry ... I Heard a Story," *Philadelphia Daily News*, July 9, 1965.

24. See Claude E. Harrison Jr., "Angered by Comparison to Clay, Richie Allen Lives Up to 'Insult,'" *Philadelphia Tribune*, July 6, 1965; Perry, "Richie Allen's Mother Says ... "; and Claude E. Harrison Jr., "Phillies' Richie Allen's Story is Titled, 'For Real,'" *Philadelphia Tribune*, July 10, 1965.

25. Claude E. Harrison Jr., "Philadelphia Is Where Roy Was Barred; Rich Allen Booed," *Philadelphia Tribune*, July 13, 1965.

26. Claude E. Harrison Jr., "Allen is an Annoying Fellow," *Philadelphia Tribune*, July 17, 1965.

27. Dolson, interview with author.

28. Lois Wark, editor, *Millennium Philadelphia: The Last 100 Years* (Philadekphia: Camino, 1999), 219.

29. William McMacklin, "Top Job," *Philadelphia Inquirer*, September 28, 1995.

30. William Bennett, John J. DiIulio Jr., and John P. Walters, *Body Count: Moral Poverty . . . and How to Win America's War Against Crime and Drugs* (New York: Simon & Schuster, 1996), 41.

31. See Marvin E. Wolfgang et al., *Delinquency in a Birth Cohort* (Chicago: University of Chicago Press, 1972); and Wolfgang and Paul E. Tracy, "The 1945 and 1958 Birth Cohorts," in James Q. Wilson, *Thinking About Crime*, rev. ed. (New York: Basic Books, 1983), 223, 279.

32. Clark, "Rally and Relapse," 662, 679. See also Jack Markowitz, "900 Hear Dr. King; Cecil Moore Absent," *Philadelphia Daily News*, August 2, 1965. Black males were finally admitted to Girard College in 1968.

33. Allen, *Crash*, 58–59.

34. Ibid.; and Ray Kelly, "37,110 Watch Allen Slam Phils to a Split with Giants," *Philadelphia Evening Bulletin*, July 9, 1965.

35. Perry, "Richie Allen's Mother Says. . . ."

36. Kelly, "37,110 Watch Allen Slam Phils to Split with Giants."

37. Allen, *Crash*, 58.

38. Wright, "Another View of Allen," 4.

39. Bill Conlin, "Phillies Enter No-Man's Land," *Philadelphia Daily News*, August 16, 1965.

40. "Can Negro Major Leaguers Enroll in Rights Fight?" *Philadelphia Tribune*, April 20, 1964.

41. Carpenter, interview with author.

42. Wes Covington, quoted in Westcott and Bilovsky, *Phillies Encyclopedia*, 211.

43. Honig, *Philadelphia Phillies: Illustrated History*, 181.

44. Alice B. Belgray, "Ruben Amaro," in *The Ballplayers*, ed. Shatzkin, 19.

45. Allen Lewis, "Phillips, Jenkins Swapped to Cubs with Herrnstein in Bid for '66 Flag," *Philadelphia Inquirer*, April 22, 1966.

46. Pat Corrales, quoted in Conlin, *Batting Cleanup*, 31.

47. See Lewis, *Philadelphia Phillies*, 112; and Westcott and Bilovsky, *Phillies Encyclopedia*, 125–26.

48. Wolff, *Baseball Encyclopedia*, 1064.

49. Ibid., 1936.

50. Author interviews with Dolsonand with Lewis.

51. Stewart Wolpin, "Ferguson Jenkins," in *The Ballplayers*, ed. Shatzkin, 523–24.

52. Dalrymple, interview with author.

53. See Claude E. Harrison Jr., "Baseball Has No Place for Retired Negro, Says Cardinal First Baseman, Bill White," *Philadelphia Tribune*, May 26, 1964.

54. See Claire Smith, "Baseball's Bill White," *New York Times Magazine*, October 13, 1991, 53, 56.

55. Allen Lewis, "White's Bat Like Weather, It Heats Up in Mid-Summer," *The Sporting News*, July 23, 1966.

56. Richie Allen, quoted in Ray Kelly "White's Bat Silent, But Phils Hail Him as Glove Magician," *The Sporting News*, May 7, 1966.

57. Bill White, quoted in Paul MacFarlane, "White Firm Foe of Drive to Form Athlete Union," *The Sporting News*, June 10, 1967.

58. Conlin, *Batting Cleanup*, 30–31.
59. Bob Uecker and Mickey Herskowitz, *Catcher in the Wry* (New York: G. P. Putnam, 1982), 72–76.
60. Gene Mauch, quoted in Conlin, "Richie Is Beautiful," 91; and Conlin, *Batting Cleanup*, 33.
61. Dalrymple, interview with author.
62. Callison, *Johnny Callison Story*, 155–56.
63. Dolso, interview with author.
64. Neft, *Sports Encyclopedia: Baseball*, 388.
65. Ron Briley, "The Times Were A-Changin': Baseball as a Symbol of American Values in Transition, 1963–64," *Baseball Research Journal* 17 (1988): 55; and David Q. Voigt, *American Baseball: From Postwar Expansion to the Electronic Age*, 3 vols. (University Park, Pa.: The Pennsylvania State University Press, 1983), 3:222.
66. Mahaffey, interview with author, August 18, 1999.
67. Uecker and Herskowitz, *Catcher in the Wry*, 83.
68. Baldschun, interview with author, April 20, 1999.
69. Gonzalez, interview with author.
70. Dalrymple, interview with author.
71. Dolson, *Jim Bunning*, 100.
72. Ibid.
73. Ibid., 102.
74. Bunning, quoted in Dolson, *Jim Bunning*, 101–2.
75. Ibid., 126.
76. Ibid., 110.
77. Voigt, *American Baseball*, 222.
78. Bunning, quoted in Dolson, *Jim Bunning*, 110.
79. Allen Lewis, "Rosy White Chasing Phillies' Blues," *Philadelphia Inquirer*, March 18, 1967; and Allen Lewis, "White's Return Delayed Until June 1, Result of Re-Injury to Torn Tendon," *The Sporting News*, March 25, 1967.
80. Westcott and Bilovsky, *Phillies Encyclopedia*, 126–27.
81. Sandy Grady, "A Team in Trouble," *Philadelphia Bulletin*, May 24, 1967.
82. Dolson, *Jim Bunning*, 90.
83. Allen, *Crash*, 71. See also Ueker, *Catcher in the Wry*, 176.
84. Ibid., 71–72.
85. Conlin, "Richie Is Beautiful," 91; and Allen, *Crash*, 71–72.
86. Conlin, "Richie Is Beautiful," 91.
87. Mauch, quoted in Ray Kelly, "Rich Allen Is Benched for 'A Rest,'" *Philadelphia Bulletin*, July 9, 1967.
88. Mauch, quoted in Ray Kelly, "Allen Admits Being Late Saturday, Homers Over Center Field Fence," *Philadelphia Bulletin*, July 10, 1967.
89. Allen, quoted in ibid.
90. Conlin, "Richie Is Beautiful," 91.
91. Sandy Grady, "Allen's Super Paycheck May Be Slipping Away," *Philadelphia Bulletin*, July 11, 1967.
92. Stan Hochman, "Sleepy-time Superstar," *Philadelphia Daily News*, July 10, 1967.
93. Bill Conlin, "Amid His Ups and Downs, Rich Remains a Man's Man," *Philadelphia Daily News*, August 16, 1967. See also Conlin, "Richie Is Beautiful," 90.
94. Conlin, *Batting Cleanup*, 27.
95. Bill Conlin, "Allen Answered to Boos: 'I Think I Might Like to Be Traded,'" *Philadelphia Daily News*, August 18, 1967.

96. Claude E. Harrison Jr., "Despite High Rate of Errors, Strikeouts, Allen Is NL's Most Wanted Third Baseman," *Philadelphia Tribune*, August 22, 1967.

97. "Allen Cuts Right Hand, Lost to Phils for Season," *Philadelphia Bulletin*, August 25, 1967. See also "Allen Out for Season After Slashing Arm on Headlight of Car," *Philadelphia Inquirer*, August 25, 1967; Bill Conlin, "Phillies Lose Allen for Season with a Slashed Hand," *Philadelphia Daily News*, August 25, 1967; and Claude E. Harrison Jr., "Allen's Jet-Fast Flight to Super-Star Status Grounded by Injury," *Philadelphia Tribune*, August 29, 1967.

98. Allen, *Crash*, 65; and Wright, "Another View of Allen," 5.

99. Allen Lewis, "Taylor Replaces Allen for Rest of Season," *Philadelphia Inquirer*, August 26, 1967; Westcott, *Philadelphia's Old Ballparks*, 160. On June 30, 1967, Cookie Rojas pitched a scoreless ninth inning in a 12–3 Phillies loss to the San Francisco Giants. With that mound appearance, Rojas became the first Phillie to play all nine positions since joining the club in 1963.

100. Carpenter, interview with author.

101. Conlin, *Batting Cleanup*, 22.

102. Mauch, quoted in Callison, *Johnny Callison Story*, 151.

103. Carpenter, interview with author.

104. Allen, interview with author.

105. Briggs, interview with author.

106. See author interviews with Wise, Dalrymple, Rojas, and Taylor.

107. Mauch quoted by Conlin, "Richie Is Beautiful," 91.

108. Taylor, interview with author.

109. Briggs, interview with author.

110. Uecker, *Catcher in the Wry*, 88.

111. Dick Young, quoted in Conlin, *Batting Cleanup*, xii.

112. Dalrymple, interview with author.

113. Green, interview with author, October 13, 1999.

114. Carpenter, interview with author.

Chapter 7: Breakup

1. Allen, *Crash*, 62–63. See also Conlin, "Richie Is Beautiful," 92; Wolf, "Let's Everybody Boo Rich Allen," 51; and Allen, quoted in Allen Barra, "An Embarrassment of Richies," *Philadelphia Magazine* 24 (August 1995): 56. Allen had the negotiating process down to a science. In his 1989 biography, he wrote: "Baseball owners know that black players come from unstable backgrounds, and either consciously or not—and in the case of Bob Carpenter, I truly believe it was unconscious—they often use that insecurity against them at contract time. Their standard line was to 'pay your dues first and the real dust will come later.' It's a lie. In baseball, as in life, you've got to get what's coming to you while you're producing, because the day you stop—it's later baby. In my case, having grown up in western Pennsylvania among white people, I could walk that walk, talk that talk. Contract time I had my act together. A jacket and tie, always. I would state clearly what I had done the season before. Front-office types weren't use to dealing with black players who could talk their game. When I came in for meetings at contract time, the boss men would perspire right through their jackets." (See Allen, *Crash*, 62–63.)

2. Allen, *Crash*, 71–72.

3. See Terry H. Anderson, *The Movement and the Sixties: Protest in America from Greensboro to Wounded Knee* (New York: Oxford University Press, 1995), 43–130. Anderson describes the "baby boom" generation as the enormous postwar birthrate that lasted eighteen

NOTES

years, from 1946 to 1964, and resulted in a generation of more than 70 million members. The sixties generation was even larger because it included not only the baby boomers (i.e., those born in the late 1940s and early 1950s) but also their older siblings. Thus, the sixties generation includes anyone who turned eighteen years old during the era from 1960 to 1972. (See Anderson, *Movement and the Sixties*, 89–90.)

4. See Todd Gitlin, *The Sixties: Years of Hope, Days of Rage* (New York: Bantam Books, 1987). Gitlin focuses on the student movement of the 1960s and its political core, the New Left. He argues that, in their attempt to change the world, this politicized generation "oscillated between narcissism and self-disparagement." Their methods included music, drugs, universal love, and "putting their bodies on the line" against social injustice and war.

5. See Maurice Isserman and Michael Kazin, *America Divided: The Civil War of the 1960s* (New York: Oxford University Press, 2000), 177–88.

6. Bruce Kuklick, *To Every Thing a Season: Shibe Park and Urban Philadelphia, 1909–1976* (Princeton: Princeton University Press, 1991), 158; and Clark, "Rally and Relapse," 662–63.

7. Kuklick, *To Every Thing a Season*, 165–66.

8. Ibid., 155.

9. Ibid. For statistics on Phillies attendance, see Kelley, "And There Used To Be a Ballpark Right Here," 49.

10. Clark, "Rally and Relapse, 676; and Lois Wark, ed., *Millennium Philadelphia: The Last 100 Years* (Philadelphia: Camino Books, 1999), 189.

11. Joseph R. Daughen, "Identification of Dr. King's Slayer Close, Attorney General Clark Says in Memphis," *Philadelphia Bulletin*, April 5, 1968; "Dr. Martin Luther King Assassinated," *Philadelphia Tribune*, April 6, 1968; "Sniper Hunted in Slaying of Dr. King," *Philadelphia Daily News*, April 5, 1968; "Three Die in Violence After King Slaying," *Philadelphia Daily News*, April 5, 1968; and Art Peters and Chet Coleman, "Washington Property Damage Bill May Hit $50 Million," *Philadelphia Tribune*, April 9, 1968; and "Army Flies 5,000 Troops into Chicago; 10 are Slain in Illinois, Disorders Toll in Nation Put at 27," *Philadelphia Bulletin*, April 7, 1968.

12. "Negro, White Leaders Here Plead for Calm," *Philadelphia Bulletin*, April 5, 1968; "5,000 Honor Memory of Dr. King at City Hall," *Philadelphia Bulletin*, April 5, 1968; and Lawrence H. Geller, "5,000 at Independence Hall in Tribute to Dr. King," *Philadelphia Tribune*, April 9, 1968; and Paolantonio, *Rizzo*, 96–97.

13. "Senators, Reds Delay Openers," *Philadelphia Daily News*, April 6, 1968.

14. Bill Conlin, "Phils Stand Firm, Won't Play—Dodgers Meet to Reconsider," *Philadelphia Daily News*, April 8, 1968; "Phils Risk Forfeit, Won't Play Tuesday," *Philadelphia Bulletin*, April 7, 1968; and Ray Kelly, "Dodgers Put Off Phillies Opener," *Philadelphia Bulletin*, April 8, 1968; and author interview with Allen, September 20, 2002.

15. Jackie Robinson, quoted in Milton Richmond, "Robinson: 'Negroes Not Violent in Nature,'" *Philadelphia Daily News*, April 9, 1968.

16. Bill Conlin, "No Forfeit as Dodgers Relent," *Philadelphia Daily News*, April 9, 1968.

17. Westcott and Bilovsky, *Phillies Encyclopedia*, 192.

18. Allen Lewis, "Lots of 'Ifs' in Mauch's Sizing of Phils," *Philadelphia Inquirer*, February 17, 1968.

19. Bill Conlin, "Allen AWOL from Phillies' Training Camp," *Philadelphia Daily News*, March 8, 1968; Conlin, "Richie Is Beautiful," 91; and Dick Young, "Mauch's Firing Proves Players Call Shots," *New York Daily News*, June 20, 1968.

20. Richie Allen, quoted in Stan Hochman, "AWOL Allen: I'd Be Different on Another Club," *Philadelphia Daily News*, March 9, 1968.

21. Stan Hochman, "Even Allen's 'Manager' Wishes He'd Grow Up," *Philadelphia Daily News*, March 12, 1968.

243

22. Bill Conlin, "After the Big Fine, More Pampering?" *Philadelphia Daily News*, March 9, 1968.

23. Ibid.

24. Dolson, interview with author.

25. Allen Lewis, "'Traffic Jam' Late Arrive Richie Tells Grim Mauch," *The Sporting News*, May 18, 1968; and Young, "Mauch's Firing."

26. Conlin, "Richie Is Beautiful," 91–92.

27. Sandy Grady, "Phillies Too Impatient to Start Rebuilding Now," *Philadelphia Evening Bulletin*, December 31, 1967.

28. Allen Lewis, "Lots of 'Ifs' in Mauch Sizeup of Phils," *The Sporting News*, February 17, 1968.

29. Quinn, quoted in Allen Lewis, "Allen Rift Called 'Factor' in Mauch's Firing," *The Sporting News*, June 29, 1968.

30. Mauch, quoted in Allen Lewis, "Mauch Absolves Phillies in Firing Snafu," *Philadelphia Inquirer*, July 6, 1968; and Mauch, quoted in Dick Young, "Gene Takes Phillies Off Hook," *New York Daily News*, June 20, 1968.

31. Stan Hochman, "Mauch Fired, Phils Try to Trade Allen," *Philadelphia Daily News*, June 17, 1968.

32. Arthur Daley, "Sports of the Times," *New York Times*, June 25, 1968.

33. Allen, *Crash*, 70–73; Wolf, "Let's Boo Allen," 52.

34. Claude E. Harrison, "Richie Allen Wins Mauch Battle, Now He Must Produce For Fans," *Philadelphia Tribune*, June 18, 1968.

35. Usserman and Kazin, *America Divided*, 151–57.

36. Janis Joplin, quoted in Godfrey Hodgson, *America in Our Time* (New York: Random House, 1976), 341.

37. Isserman and Kazin, *America Divided*, 92.

38. Briley, "Times Were A'Changin'," 55.

39. Bill Conlin, "Phils Holdouts Stay That Way," *Philadelphia Daily News*, March 5, 1968.

40. Michael Sokolove, *Hustle: The Myth, Life, and Lies of Pete Rose* (New York: Simon & Schuster, 1990), 78–79.

41. Allen Barra, "An Embarrassment of Richies," *Philadelphia Magazine* 38(August 1995): 53. Allen was christened "Richard Anthony," but he was called "Dick" as a youngster because "Richard" sounded "too stuffy" and "Richie," which he allowed himself to be called during his earlier years with the Phillies, "sounded too childish."

42. Skinner, quoted in Allen Lewis, "'Many Pilots Would Like Rich—I'm One of 'Em'—Skinner," *The Sporting News*, June 29, 1968; and Bill Conlin, "Skinner 'Poor Loser,' But ..." *Philadelphia Daily News*, June 17, 1968.

43. Claude E. Harrison, "Allen Celebrates Being New Father by Getting on Base 9 Times," *Philadelphia Tribune*, June 22, 1968.

44. Allen Lewis, "Phils Look Ahead, Put Briggs on First; Vet White Slipping," *The Sporting News*, July 20, 1968.

45. Allen Lewis, "White Open to Pilot Offers," *The Sporting News*, August 31, 1968.

46. Howie Bedell, interview with author, Pottstown, Pa., April 30, 2002.

47. Ibid.

48. Allen Lewis, "Phils End Drysdale Scoreless Inning Streak in 5–3 Loss," *Philadelphia Inquirer*, June 9, 1968.

49. Allen Lewis, "Plate Skid Adds to Allen's Philly Enigma," *The Sporting News*, September 28, 1968.

50. Allen Lewis, "Carpenter Planning Shakeup of Phillies," *The Sporting News*, October 19, 1968.

51. Carpenter, quoted in ibid.

52. Bob Skinner, quoted in Allen Lewis, "Phils Put Callison, Rojas, and Allen on Trading Block," *The Sporting News*, October 26, 1968.

53. Lewis, "Carpenter Planning Shakeup."

54. See Lewis, "Phils Put Callison, Rojas, and Allen on Trading Block"; and Russell Schneider, "Tribe Dickering for Allen, Shudders at Hefty Price," *The Sporting News*, November 30, 1968.

55. Allen, quoted in "Richie Allen Is Not All Bad Boy," *New York Times*, May 18, 1969.

56. Allen and Rojas, quoted in Wolf, "Let's Boo Allen," 53.

57. Dalrymple, interview with author.

58. Sandy Grady, "Allen's Latest Trip Might End in Trade," *Philadelphia Bulletin*, June 25, 1969; Stan Hochman, "Rich Allen's Latest Escapade May Be His Last," *Philadelphia Daily News*, June 25, 1969; and Wolf, "Let's Boo Allen," 54.

59. Richie Allen, quoted in Stan Hochman, "Rich Allen's Latest Vacation May Be His Last," *Philadelphia Daily News*, June 25, 1969.

60. Allen, quoted in Claude E. Harrison, "'I'll Play Somewhere, Maybe in Japan,' Richie Allen Asserts," *Philadelphia Tribune*, July 5, 1969.

61. Stan Hochman, "Time to Grow Up, Not Old," *Philadelphia Daily News*, June 26, 1969; and Bill Conlin, "Meeting the 'Reel' Rich Allen!" *Philadelphia Daily News*, June 6, 1969.

62. Conlin, "Richie Is Beautiful," 93–94; and Dick Young, "Allen Forgiving Philly Fans? Not Yet He Ain't," *New York Daily News*, April 16, 1969.

63. Willie Mays, quoted in Conlin, "Richie Is Beautiful," 88.

64. Ibid.; and author interview with Jackson.

65. Conlin, "Richie Is Beautiful," 94.

66. Allen, quoted in *Philadelphia Inquirer*, July 31, 1969.

67. Allen, *Crash*, 79.

68. Wolf, "Let's Boo Allen," 53. See also author interviews with Briggs and Jackson.

69. Bob Skinner, quoted in Bill Conlin, "Phillies' Ugliest Tug-of-War," *Philadelphia Daily News*, June 26, 1969.

70. Bob Carpenter, quoted in Sandy Grady, "Allen's Latest Trip Might End in Trade," *Philadelphia Bulletin*, June 25, 1969.

71. Skinner, quoted in Allen Lewis, "Skinner Quits—Had His Phil of Richie," *Philadelphia Inquirer*, August 8, 1969; and Claude E. Harrison, "Richie Allen Blamed as Skinner Quits as Manager of the Phillies," *Philadelphia Tribune*, August 9, 1969.

72. Conlin, "Richie Is Beautiful," 93.

73. Carpenter, quoted in "Skinner Quits"; and Carpenter, quoted in Allen Lewis, "No Quaker Meeting When Skinner Made His Exit," *The Sporting News*, August 23, 1969.

74. Allen, quoted in Allen Lewis, "'Skinner Pushed Panic Button ... So Did I,' Says Richie," *Philadelphia Inquirer*, August 9, 1969; Conlin, "Richie Is Beautiful," 93; and Allen, quoted in Wolf, "Let's Boo Allen," 53.

75. "Who's in Charge Around Here?" *The Sporting News*, August 23, 1969.

76. Myatt, quoted in Conlin, "Richie Is Beautiful," 93.

77. Allen, quoted in Wolf, "Let's Boo Allen," 53.

78. Ibid.

79. Conlin, "Richie Is Beautiful," 93.

80. Allen, *Crash*, 78; Wolf, "Let's Boo Allen," 51–53; and Conlin, "Richie Is Beautiful," 93. One of Allen's young fans, Chuck Brodsky, grew up to write a song about his hero's word-scrawling tendency titled "Letters in the Dirt." The song can be accessed on the web at: <oldballgame.freeservers.com/joeweb51.html>.

81. In 1969, Major League Baseball expanded from twenty teams to twenty-four and divided each league into eastern and western divisions. The Phillies were part of the National League's Eastern Division, which also included the Chicago Cubs, the Montreal Expos, the New York Mets, the Pittsburgh Pirates, and the St. Louis Cardinals.

82. "Phils Trade Allen to St. Louis, Phila. Gets Hoerner and Browne—Flood Plans to Retire as Player," *New York Times*, October 9, 1969.

83. Ibid.; and Allen, quoted in Mead, *Explosive Sixties*, 101.

84. Curt Flood to Baseball Commissioner Bowie Kuhn, December 24, 1969, quoted in Ward and Burns, *Baseball*, 411.

85. Bowie Kuhn, quoted in ibid., 411.

86. Curt Flood with Richard Carter, *The Way It Is* (New York: Trident Press, 1971), 188. Years later, Flood's wife insisted that her husband had "no special animus toward Philadelphia," but rather that he rejected the deal because it "violated his dignity as a man; he objected to being treated as chattel." (See Judy Pace-Flood, quoted in "He Opened the Floodgates," *Philadelphia Daily News*, August 30, 2002.)

87. Tim McCarver, interview with author.

88. See "Flood v. Kuhn," U.S. District Court of New York (1970); Curt Flood, "Why I Challenged Baseball," *Sport* 32 (March 1970): 10–13; Edmund P. Edmunds and William H. Manz, eds., *Baseball and Antitrust: The Legislative History of the Curt Flood Act of 1998, Public Law No., 105–297, 112 Stat. 2824* (Buffalo, N.Y.: William S. Hein, 2001); and William Gildea, "Curt Flood: Baseball's Angry Rebel," *Baseball Digest* 12 (February 1971): 55–61.

Conclusion

1. John G. Whittier, "Maude Mueller," in *The Poetry of John Greenleaf Whittier*, 7 vols. (Boston, 1888–89), 5:62.

2. See Frank Dolson, *The Philadelphia Story: A City of Losers Winners* (South Bend, Ind.: Icarus Press, 1981).

3. Bill James, *The Politics of Glory: How Baseball's Hall of Fame Really Works* (New York: Macmillan, 1994), 322–25.

4. David Wellman, *Portraits of White Racism* (Cambridge: Cambridge University Press, 1977), chap. 1; and George M. Fredrickson, *Racism: A Short History* (Princeton: Princeton University Press, 2002). Wellman argues that the motives and acts of individuals matter less than the systematic ways in which people of some races are disadvantaged in law and social life. Fredrickson takes this institutional definition of racism further, proposing that racism combines "an attitude or set of beliefs" with a set of "practices, institutions, and structures." While the "attitude" treats ethnic or cultural differences "as innate, indelible and unchangeable," the "practices" can range from "pervasive social discrimination to government-sanctioned segregation."

5. Kenneth L. Shropshire, *In Black and White: Race and Sports in America* (New York: New York University Press, 1996), 7–11.

6. Beverly D. Tatum, *"Why Are All the Black Kids Sitting Together in the Cafeteria?" And Other Conversations About Race* (New York: Basic Books, 1999), 7–12; and Glenn C. Loury, *Anatomy of Racial Inequality* (Cambridge, Mass.: Harvard University Press, 2002). Loury's argument that the lack of social capital puts blacks at a competitive disadvantage compliments Tatum's thesis that racism is systematic.

7. W. E. Cross Jr., *Shades of Black: Diversity in African-American Identity* (Philadelphia: Temple University Press, 1991). According to Cross, African Americans struggle to form an identity in a white mainstream society because of the racism inherent in it. The process of

resolving the dilemma is especially difficult during late adolescence and early adulthood when the individual is starting out on a career path and is forced to confront institutional policies that are racist. Cross maintains that there are various stages of racial identity development that unfold for an individual at this time. These stages include: *encountering* racism for the first time; *immersion* in a racist environment where the individual begins to grapple with what it means to be a member of a group targeted by racism; *internalizing* those cues, as well as stereotypes from a white world that reflects his blackness back to him; and *internalization-commitment*, in which the individual comes to terms with his or her own identity as a member of the African American race.

8. Chuck Tanner, quoted in Wright, "Another View of Allen," 9.

9. Mike Schmidt, interview with author, Jupiter, Fla., October 8, 1998.

10. Dick Allen, interview with author, Wampum, Pa., September 20, 2002.

SELECTED BIBLIOGRAPHY

Allen, Dick, and Tim Whitaker. *Crash: The Life and Times of Dick Allen*. New York: Ticknor & Fields, 1989.

Anderson, Dave. "1964: The Phillies Phlop." In *Pennant Races*, 255–88. New York: Doubleday, 1994.

Beck, Laurence. "The 10-Game Collapse." *Philly Sport* 2 (June 1989): 36–40.

Bunning, Jim. *The Jim Bunning Story*. Philadelphia: Chilton Books, 1965.

Callison, Johnny, with John Sletten. *The Johnny Callison Story*. New York: Vantage Press, 1991.

Clark, Joseph S., Jr. "Rally and Relapse, 1946–1968." In *Philadelphia: A 300-Year History*, ed. Russell F. Weigley. New York: W. W. Norton, 1981.

Conlin, Bill. *Batting Cleanup, Bill Conlin*, ed. by Kevin Kerrane. Philadelphia: Temple University Press, 1997.

———. "Richie Is Beautiful, He Don't Give a Damn for Nobody." *Jock* (January 1970): 88–94.

Cook, William A. *The Summer of '64: A Pennant Lost*. Jefferson, N.C.: McFarland, 2002.

Dolson, Frank. *Jim Bunning: Baseball and Beyond*. Philadelphia: Temple University Press, 1998.

Falkner, David. *Great Time Coming: The Life of Jackie Robinson from Baseball to Birmingham*. New York: Simon & Schuster, 1995.

Honig, Donald. *The Philadelphia Phillies: An Illustrated History*. New York: Simon & Schuster, 1992.

Jordan, David M. *Occasional Glory: A History of the Philadelphia Phillies*. Jefferson, N.C.: McFarland, 2002.

Kashatus, William C. "Dick Allen, the Phillies, and Racism." *Nine: A Journal of Baseball History and Culture* 9 (Spring 2001): 151–91.

Kelley, B. G. "The Boys of Bummer." *Inside Sports* 16 (October 1994): 76–81.

Kuklick, Bruce. *To Every Thing a Season: Shibe Park and Urban Philadelphia, 1909–1976*. Princeton: Princeton University Press, 1991.

Leggett, William. "The Rise and Fall of the Phillies." *Sports Illustrated*, March 1, 1965, 52–63.

Lewis, Allen. *The Philadelphia Phillies: A Pictorial History.* Virginia Beach, Va.: JCP Corporation, 1981.

Mead, William B. *The Explosive Sixties: Baseball's Decade of Expansion.* Alexandria, Va.: Redefinition, 1989.

McGrath, Tom. "Color Me Badd." *The Fan* 3 (September 1996): 36–42.

Nesfield, Carl. "New Team. New Town. New Richie?" *Black Sports* 16 (July 1971): 31, 62–63, 70.

Orodenker, Richard, ed. *The Phillies Reader.* Philadelphia: Temple University Press, 1996.

Paolantonio, S. A. *Frank Rizzo: The Last Big Man in Big City America.* Philadelphia: Camino Books, 1993.

Richter, Ed. *View from the Dugout: A Season with Baseball's Amazing Gene Mauch.* Philadelphia: Chilton Books, 1964.

Robinson, Jackie. *I Never Had It Made.* New York: Putnam, 1972.

Shatzkin, Michael, ed. *The Ballplayers: Baseball's Ultimate Biographical Reference.* New York: William Morrow, 1990.

Shropshire, Kenneth L. *In Black and White: Race and Sports in America.* New York: New York University Press, 1996.

Westcott, Rich. *Philadelphia's Old Ballparks.* Philadelphia: Temple University Press, 1996.

Westcott, Rich, and Frank Bilovsky. *The Phillies Encyclopedia.* Philadelphia: Temple University Press, 1993.

Wolf, David. "Let's Everybody Boo Rich Allen!" *Life* (August 1969): 50–53.

Wright, Craig R. "Another View of Dick Allen." *SABR Baseball Research Journal* 24 (1995): 2–14.

Wulf, Steve. "The Year of the Blue Snow." *Sports Illustrated,* September 25, 1989, 76–86.

INDEX

Pages with illustrations are indicated with *italics*.

St. Louis Cardinals, 1–2, 34, 37, 50,
57, 67, 75, 81, 82, 94, 98, 133–35,
137, 163–65, 170
Stallard, Tracy, 91–92
Stanky, Eddie, 27
Stargell, Willie, 76
Steevens, Morrie, 119–20, 125, 148
Stengel, Casey, 93, 98
Stephenson, John, 94
Stuart, Dick, 148
Sudol, Ed, 93
Sukeforth, Clyde, 23
Sullivan, Ed, 94
Sullivan, Frank, 58
Sullivan, Reverend Leon H., 78
Sutherland, Darrell, 72
Sutherland, Gary, 173
Swarthmore College, 56

Tabor, Jim, 28
Tanner, Chuck, 204
Tate, Mayor James H. J., 76, 78–79,
111, 121, 181–82
Taylor, Bob, 91, 93
Taylor, Tony, xi, 2, 4, 44, 49–50, 51,
52, 55, 70, 76, 80, 87, 104, 126,
131, 134–35, 144, 173, 175
biographical sketch, 214–15
quoted: on trade to Phillies, 50; on
saving Bunning's perfect game,
92; on team's decline, 176
Thomas, Frank, 72, 80, 110, 116, 128,
137–38, 150, 176, 204
biographical sketch, 215
fight with Allen, 149–54
released, 154–55
Torre, Joe, 98, 128, 131, 132
Triandos, Gus, 4, 67–68, 91–94,
124–25, 129, 133
biographical sketch, 215
quoted, 94, 141
Trice, Bob, 15
Tsitouris, John, 2, 103, 122

Uecker, Bob, 161, 167–68, 170
quoted, on Allen, 165–66

Vargo, Ed, 129
Veeck, Bill, Jr., 20, 224 n. 31
Veeck, William, Sr., 20
View from the Dugout by Ed Richter,
61–62

Waitkus, Eddie, 33, 194
Wake Forest, 52–53
Wakefield, Bill, 92
Wagner, Gary, 148, 167
Walker, Fred "Dixie," 27
Walker, Harry, 28, 30
Walls, Lee, 58
Wampum, Pa., 46, 125
Ward, John T., 94
Washington Senators, 110
White Bill, 37, 134, 161, 163–65, 164,
170, 183, 187, 191
White, Mike, 81
Whittier, John G. 201
Widmar, Al, 75
biographical sketch, 215
William Penn Charter School, 52
Williams, Billy, 98–99, 102
Williams, Marvin, xi, 22–23
Williams, Ted, 196
Williamsport, Pa. (Eastern League),
39, 45, 48
Wilson, Billy, 192
Wilson, Matt, 145
Wine, Bobby, 55, 60, 61, 64, 70, 80,
92, 93, 119, 144, 153, 173, 183
biographical sketch, 215
Wise, Rick, 4, 44, 72–73, 75, 91, 94,
106, 116, 139, 142, 175, 187, 190,
197
biographical sketch, 215–16
Woods, Goergie, 111
Wrigley Field, 89
Wulf, Steve, 145
Wynn, Jimmy, 81, 188

Yancey, Bill, 11, 35
Young, Dick, 176–77

William C. Kashatus, a professional historian and educator, holds a Ph.D. in history from the University of Pennsylvania. A regular contributor to the *Philadelphia Daily News*, he is also the author of several baseball books, including *Connie Mack's '29 Triumph: The Rise and Fall of the Philadelphia Athletics Dynasty* and *One-Armed Wonder: Pete Gray, Wartime Baseball, and the American Dream*. He lives in Chester County, Pennsylvania.